Generations and Globalization

TRACKING GLOBALIZATION

ROBERT J. FOSTER, EDITOR

Editorial advisory board:
Mohammed Bamyeh
Lisa Cartwright
Randall Halle

Generations and Globalization

Youth, Age, and Family in the New World Economy

Edited by Jennifer Cole & Deborah Durham

INDIANA UNIVERSITY PRESS
Bloomington & Indianapolis

This book is a publication of

Indiana University Press
601 North Morton Street
Bloomington, IN 47404-3797 USA

http://iupress.indiana.edu

Telephone orders   800-842-6796
Fax orders   812-855-7931
Orders by e-mail   iuporder@indiana.edu

© 2007 by Indiana University Press

The paper used in this publication meets the minimum require-
ments of American National Standard for Information Sciences—
Permanence of Paper for Printed Library Materials, ANSI
Z39.48-1984.

MANUFACTURED IN THE UNITED STATES OF AMERICA

Library of Congress Cataloging-in-Publication Data
Generations and globalization : youth, age, and family in the new world economy /
edited by Jennifer Cole and Deborah Durham.
    p. cm. — (Tracking globalization)
    Includes bibliographical references and index.
    ISBN 0-253-34803-X (cloth : alk. paper) — ISBN 0-253-21870-5 (pbk. : alk. paper) 1. Intergenera-
tional relations. 2. Age groups. 3. Globalization—Social aspects. I. Cole, Jennifer, date
II. Durham, Deborah Lynn, date III. Series.
    HM726.G45 2007
    305.209'0511—dc22
                                                                                    2006009629

1 2 3 4 5   12   11   10   09   08   07

Contents

ACKNOWLEDGMENTS

The final shape of this book is due to the critical input and support of many friends and colleagues. We would like to thank Jean Comaroff for her comments on the panel entitled "Global Ages: Childhood, Youth, and Old Age in a Time of Global Flows" that we put together for the annual meeting of the American Anthropological Association in 2001. Smita Lahiri, Anne-Marie Leshkowich, Karen Strassler, Ajantha Subramanian, and Christine Walley, members of the Cambridge Writing Circle in 2003–2004, gave important feedback on an early draft of the introduction. T. E. Woronov and Julie Livingston each gave helpful comments on the introduction as well. The anonymous reviewers for Indiana University Press, our series editor Robert Foster, and our editor Rebecca Tolen all provided insightful comments on all of the essays individually and as a whole. Above all we want to thank the contributors to the volume for their work, their patience, and their faith that this project would, one day, come to fruition.

Generations and Globalization

Introduction

Age, Regeneration, and the Intimate Politics of Globalization

JENNIFER COLE AND DEBORAH DURHAM

Consider three examples taken from chapters in this book:

In Europe, demographics, immigration, and changing economic realities have provoked a European Union–wide discussion about the relationship of older members of the population to society, and a questioning of what kind of social contract should be written between the younger, working population and those who have retired from the workforce, often under state-mandated age guidelines and with the aid of state pensions. The institutionalized practice of retiring from jobs and withdrawing from the public sphere has been challenged by energetic elderly activists and countered by "universities for the third age." No longer depicted as poor and physically failing, nor as occupying jobs needed by a now decreasing number of young people, the elderly are being asked to regenerate Europe by drawing on their lifetime accumulation of cultural wisdom and skills to build a new knowledge-based, flexible economy. But in 2003, as these policies were being developed, thousands of elderly across Europe died in a heat wave. Media stories about France asked why aging parents were left behind in cities by families on summer holidays, and failed by the state health network and hospitals.

An increasing number of South Asian seniors are immigrating to the United States in order to spend their last years with adult children who have moved there. While South Asians have traditionally seen caring for aged parents in a family home as an important part of a reciprocal intergenerational cycle, many today have difficulty reproducing this model of aging and family life. Since working children in the United States have little time to take care of their parents, some elders have begun to take advantage of services provided by the state, developing a new independence of their own. With no one at home to "make them tea," even though there is plentiful tea to be made, immigrant seniors are exploring new ways of aging. As one senior commented, "Why, we can even call 911 if something goes wrong. We tried it once. Why would we have to live with our children?" And for those who remain in South Asia, where both 911 and other public services are unavailable, there are now, in India, "children for hire" who will perform the intimate work of caring, ease the way into death, and arrange funerals, taking on these responsibilities in the place of adult children living overseas.

In China, middle- and working-class parents have become obsessed with American education. In response to the liberalization of markets and a growing sense that the spatial horizons of social mobility have moved beyond China's borders, parents are energetically seeking new ways to raise their children. Eager to bring up children who will take advantage of rapidly shifting economic opportunities, and to raise the "quality" of Chinese children, they hungrily purchase child-rearing manuals that promise to get their children into Harvard. But the extreme discipline some manuals require, and the independence and creative risk taking that others promote for children, make parents worry that they will destroy the interdependence and love that they perceive as constitutive of Chinese family life.

Age is a particularly fruitful lens through which to examine the kinds of social processes and social changes that lie behind these situations. Age and intergenerational relations are shaped by, but also shape, political and economic processes, and are centrally implicated in economic and political restructuring. Age is important, as well, because of its centrality in social reproduction. Not only are intergenerational relations important for passing on or modifying traditions, but intergenerational links are among the most intimate and powerful in social life. Social reproduction has been analyzed through a variety of frameworks, including race, class, and gender. To these we add age and generation. Age mediates relationships in the family and household, social cohorts across space, and history and change. In the course of these mediations, age links world-historical economic and social change with the intimate spaces of caring and obligation within the family. Using age as an analytic opens up new perspectives on contemporary social processes by highlighting the ways in which people experience the broader social and economic changes associated with globalization in their intimate lives.

It has become clear that shifts in the global economy, the transnational dissemination of ideas, and new forms of biopolitics are reconfiguring the nature of childhood, youth, and old age. But children, youth, and the elderly do not reconceptualize themselves or conform to new social patterns as isolated individuals or age groups. Rather, it is in the relationships between age groups that changes take shape, as people negotiate pragmatically and emotionally to manage the present and to reproduce desirable and livable futures. The chapters in this book look not at childhood, youth, adulthood, and old age as separate categories. Rather, we examine the intergenerational relationships in and through which age is constituted, and relationships across space and time are enabled. Focusing on how age and generation mediate processes of globalization and restructure social relations, the case studies gathered here describe the regeneration of the social world.

Globalization and Intimate Relations

In many ways the stories in the vignettes above conform to aspects of both popular and more scholarly accounts of globalization. Such accounts generally describe the global restructuring of capital and labor, a process that privileges knowledge and flexibility; a movement of people around the world in search of opportunity and jobs; increased flows of information and idea-laden commodities; and the emergence of a global economic and cultural landscape in which to envision possible life courses. According to a popular version, the free market enables goods, services, ideas, and people to circulate in new ways: Chinese girls go off to Harvard, retirees find meaning and fulfillment in flexible part-time jobs, and the American economy is stoked by knowledgeable workers from India and inexpensive goods produced by less skilled and cheaper labor around the world. In the process, peoples, goods, services, and ideas become deterritorialized, part of a new global reality, as they transcend older cultural and national boundaries (Friedman 2000). It is an image of the demolishing of old structures and a heady liberation by the market.

This popular view of liberatory globalization is simultaneously refuted and sustained by recent writing on the subject. Many scholars have argued against simple or optimistic models of increased mobility of capital, goods, or people. Instead, they note the highly unequal ways in which global economic processes operate, carving up the world in new ways instead of evening it out (Appadurai 1996; Friedman 2002; Hoogvelt 1997; Sassen 1998). Take, for example, structural adjustment, a process imposed by the International Monetary Fund and the World Bank to liberalize markets and facilitate the movement of capital across national borders. Originally designed to address the debt crisis in Latin America and Africa in the late 1980s, structural adjustment programs (SAPs) sought to spur economic growth in the private sector, bring in foreign investment, and diminish the dominance of local economies by state-owned enterprises and state policies. To reach these goals, SAPs limited government spending, dramatically devalued local currencies, put an end to state food subsidies and price supports, and reduced social services. They also demanded the privatization of industry and many state-run services such as power, transportation, and even water. These reforms led to both a loss of jobs for many local people and a more costly, and often less effective, delivery of services to the wider population. However, while such measures were aimed at luring capital investment, the investment they did attract proved more un-stable and less directed toward improving the living conditions of the strug-gling populations than the proponents of SAPs had hoped (see, for example, Hart 2002). By 1990, the average African income had plummeted to below its 1960s levels, while between 1960 and 1991 the share of global income going to the world's richest 20 percent rose from 70 percent to 85 percent. Meanwhile, the share going to the poorest dropped from 2.3 to 1.4 percent (Taylor, Watts, and Johnston 2002, 10–11, citing figures from the UNDP). When the Ameri-can company Bechtel took over the water utilities in Bolivia, local small businesses and middle-class homes were shocked by water bills that consumed a quarter of their monthly income.[1] The French company Suez first failed to meet targets in water and sewage provision in Argentina and then abandoned its contract when it failed to meet profit goals.[2]

While we often still look at the global economy in broad regional terms—international economic discussion holds that the South is notably poorer than the North, and treats places like Africa and Latin America as a unit—scholars of globalization note a new geography of wealth and poverty. Relations of wealth and poverty are now distributed across the globe, both within countries and between them. Capital and wealth link elites around the world, while the masses of those excluded and marginalized are found everywhere (Hoogvelt 1997). The rapidly increasing volume of consumer goods also contributes to this new geography of wealth by creating consumer-driven enclaves sur-rounded by people for whom these goods and the lifestyles they represent are increasingly hard to obtain (Comaroff and Comaroff 1999; Liechty 2003). Structural adjustment and the liberalization of economies contribute to this process: shrinking state bureaucracies and institutions, which fostered the growth of a middle class around the world in the mid-twentieth century, have given way to sharper class divisions. The movement of commodities and cul-tural products, and the rapid increase of circulating media and images, en-courage the "work of the imagination" through which people envision al-ternative possible lives (Appadurai 1996; Larkin 1997). But it also sharpens the sense of exclusion and marginality among people who cannot acquire those goods.

Studies of globalization have also emphasized the increased movement of people across national borders. Though reliable figures are notoriously hard to obtain, and although migration is a long-standing feature of the world system, it has increased remarkably since the end of World War II.[3] Some scholars estimate that there are over 100 million migrants globally, a number which appears to be increasing. When the numbers of immigrants are combined with statistics on the movement of refugees, as many as 150 million or more people have left their homes, 2.5 percent of the world's population (Chapin 1999–2000). Moreover, migration patterns are shifting. From 1920 to 1960, migra-tion occurred primarily from one European country to another or from Euro-pean countries to the United States. By contrast, since 1960 there has been a rapid growth of movement from developing countries and former colonies to Europe and North America, and to neighboring countries that provide economic opportunity or refuge from war. Such migration is fed by demographic shifts and age imbalances: while the population of Europe and America is aging, as birth rates plummet and life expectancies increase (Neilson 2003), in Africa nearly 50 percent of the population is under sixteen (Durham 2000).

These critical visions of globalization are reflected in the debates within the European Union about what to do with an aging population, debates that take place in the context of the demise of the welfare state and concerns about the relative merits of inviting in more immigrant labor or extracting new forms of labor from local populations. The story of Chinese parents who are obsessed with American education similarly responds to the demise of Chinese socialism and the sense that an increasingly uncertain economy requires children who are suited to its exigencies. And the story about aging South Asians who move to the U.S. reflects not only the ability to pursue opportunities beyond national borders, but increasing economic disparities that make some parts of the world more desirable to live in than others.

Whether they view the effects of globalization positively or negatively, most studies of globalization analyze it in terms of large-scale economic and cultural processes. Writing on globalization consistently focuses on state and market mechanisms as well as new technologies. For example, sociologists, economists, and geographers examine the ways in which a combination of new information technologies and laws regulating the movement of capital around the world have contributed to the decline of Fordist models of production, localized and under centralized control, and the emergence of flexibility, dispersal, and shifting sites (Harvey 1989; Johnston, Taylor, and Watts 2002; Sassen 1998). Perhaps as a consequence of focusing on large-scale processes, anthropological studies of globalization have often polarized "the global" and "the local." They have also tended to portray the contemporary drama as agonistically played out between these two reified forces (Kearney 1995).[4]

This book takes a very different approach to globalization. In particular, we examine how intergenerational relations between parents and children, youth and elders, are pivotal in shaping how broad-scale processes of economic globalization and state restructuring play out. We focus on the way in which widespread social and economic changes, particularly the rise of market-based liberalized economies and their entanglement with state policies and international rhetorics, provide new contexts for the life course and processes of social reproduction. Reciprocally, we examine how practices associated with intergenerational relations mediate large-scale processes of globalization. Each of the stories we began with takes place in the context of what we have come to call globalization, and in each case broad historical processes are being worked out and remade in terms of intergenerational negotiations. In different ways, each of the stories indicates that the processes of globalization do not take place "out there," but in decisions about specific relationships and specific social locations. What is more, the drama is often not between an outside global reality and the ties of a local set of beliefs, but is figured in the negotiations of people's everyday obligations and relationships as they struggle to shape livable presents and futures. A decision to move to a new country raises questions about relationships with those left behind and new arrangements for those relationships. The changing world economy presses parents to seek new ways of preparing their children or of drafting their own parents into new forms of flexible labor. Decisions regarding who will find money for water or other daily needs or who will work, when, and where are made in negotiations between members of households. As feminists have long argued, it is as much in the home as in financial markets and international agreements that the reproduction—and regeneration—of society takes place. In highlighting the intimate aspects of globalization, we are following the lead of those scholars who have pointed to the pivotal role of intimate social relations and kinship in shaping the dynamics of the colonial encounter, the emergence of modernity, and the development of capitalism more broadly (Stoler 2002; Stephens 1995b; Ong 1996, 1999; Ortner 2003; Yanagisako 2002).

Historical Process and Intergenerational Relations: States, Economies, and Age

Frederick Cooper asked, in an article title, "What Is the Concept of Globalization Good For?" (2001). He went on to note that many of the features of globalization, including increasing connections between diverse parts of the world, the spread of capital, increased mobility, and the development of linked cosmopolitan centers around the world, have marked much of the modern period, especially the colonial one. While the current moment is characterized by distinctive features, it is also true that by analyzing past processes we can better highlight the specific changes taking place today.

Social reproduction takes place by means of a combination of familial, economic, state, and local community structures; changes in these structures shape how, where, and with whom children are raised or the end of life is negotiated. But specific institutional arrangements vary both historically and cross-culturally. Periods of pronounced social change have often seen an increased concern with age. Examining the various social processes which have shaped age relations in different historical periods draws our attention to important patterns of social change and to important features of these processes, such as the symbolic force of age and the role of the economy, class, and state formation. By juxtaposing a range of historical examples, we can better illuminate the variety of ways in which broad-scale processes and intimate matters have historically intertwined.

Concerns with age—both with the nature and fate of specific age groups and with intergenerational relations—have marked many periods of economic, political, and social transition. In early modern Europe, for example, there was an efflorescence of child-rearing manuals to help redraw rapidly shifting class lines and class structures (Elias 1978). In early New England, where new models of authority were being tested against new forms of capital, a concern with fathers and sons erupted in Puritan sermonizing (Wallach 1997). Arguments about intergenerational responsibility also marked the early twentieth-century West in the wake of World War I, as new patterns of production and consumption, the nature of the nation-state, family size, and class were reorganized (Wohl 1979; Chudacoff 1989; Fass 1977). As Europeans colonized new parts of the world, they foregrounded ideas about childhood, youth, aging, and intimate familial ties as part of their efforts to build new social and economic systems.

Both cross-culturally and historically, age and intergenerational relations have provided important symbolism for structuring social relations. In East Africa, for example, age can be the object and means of much creative play, as elderly men of one age set enjoy being youth to an even older set by deploying a complex mixture of respect and joking (Baxter and Almagor 1978). Being "good to think" (Levi-Strauss 1963), and imbued with ideas about rights and obligations, generational relations are often mobilized to work with or against other sets of relationships: an opposition of elderhood (seen as internal and domesticated) and youth (associated with the wild, or with foreign elements) is a motif that is found in many times and places.[5] While studies of emotional discourse often focus on issues of gender (e.g., Lutz and Abu-Lughod 1990), it is clear that such discourses are also about age. Lack of emotional control is often associated with immaturity, effective and righteous anger with seniority, selfless nurturance with maturity, and jealousy with coevalness.

These associations mean that age and generational symbolism has often been used to naturalize situations of conquest and rule. During the sixteenth century, for example, Spanish theologians and historians referred to Indians in the Americas as "like children," a metaphor used to justify paternalistic imperialism by Spain, and one that gave shape to colonization (Vitoria 1991, cited in Hecht 2002, 10).[6] Similarly, eighteenth- and nineteenth-century images of Africans portrayed them as alternately childlike or robbed of their innocent youth and parental care by the slave trade. These images supported ideas of heroic masculine rescues by Europeans and of a patriarchal mission to educate and care for ill-guided primitives (Comaroff and Comaroff 1991). But such images were used not only in colonial situations. Constructions of age that emerged in nineteenth-century Europe and North America were shaped in a dialectical relationship with transformations taking place in colonial contexts, much as Stoler and Cooper (1997) have argued for ideas about class-based modernity. G. Stanley Hall's (1904) famous formulation of adolescence as a biopsychological condition directly linked children and youth with non-Western primitives through an evolutionary model. Age-based relationships continue today to be centrally connected with the racial/ethnic hierarchies developed under colonialism and imperialism, linking race, gender, and age with far-flung global relationships within the intimate economy of the home. Sherry Ortner (1991) has described how race and class are used to encode and enact generational (and gendered) divisions in the American household, organizing work, money, and decision making. Unsurprisingly, younger members are associated with lower-class and ethnically marked elements.

The symbolic deployment of age imagery and the use of evolutionary models justified practical interventions, both in the colonies and at home. For example, Hecht notes that in Latin America "children were a sort of ground zero for the colonial encounter, a point of entry through which Europeans not only interpreted the nature of the indigenous societies but also gained access to and sought to change them" (Hecht 2002, 11). Since most of the colonizers were men, Spanish conquerors in the seventeenth century sought to create new colonial families by marrying the daughters of indigenous lords. As children became the site of invention of a landed colonial society in Latin America, they also became, as in Europe and North America, the site for inventing and inscribing class divisions. While the offspring of the Spanish and a local elite Hispanicized through colonial schools were "adopted" into the ruling class, fears of abandoned, illegitimate, and unruly children prompted "save the children" campaigns and others designed as much to separate and protect the elite from the wayward population as anything else (Premo 2002; Rizzini 2002).[7] And similar concerns about age and class in the colonial context of the Dutch East Indies in the later nineteenth and early twentieth centuries have been described by Ann Stoler (2002). There, colonial authorities used children to police the boundaries of loyal colonial subjects through the creation of nurseries and the control of social space.

In the West, the use of evolutionary, developmental models justified adult intervention into children's lives to raise them up from a stage of savagery. These ideas also prompted the stronger delineation of age-graded spaces to protect and nurture both younger and older generations. The turn-of-the-century playground movement in the United States was one such response; complexly related was the development of age-grading in schooling and recreation (see Alaimo 1994, on France). The increasing management of childhood and youth by professionalized adults articulated with class agendas, so that prolonged periods of protected and guided schooling became necessary for access to desirable white-collar jobs in the new economy. By contrast, working-class youth were more likely to leave school and assume adult roles earlier, in less prestigious spheres. Schools, of course, have consistently been a tool with which colonizers and state institutions reorient the desires and aspirations of the young (Rogoff 2003). They are one of the primary sites where states and economies intertwine to not only re-create the child-subject, but also bring domestic relations and institutions under bureaucratic supervision and routines (LeVine, LeVine, and Schnell 2001; Richman, Miller, and LeVine 1992).

What is crucial to emphasize in the tensions and transformations surrounding intergenerational relations is the complexity with which state, economic, cultural, and social phenomena intertwine there. Writing in response to the outpouring of literature on "children in crisis," Sharon Stephens (1995b) argued that we are witnessing dislocations in what has provisionally structured children's place in modernity. Shifts in the industrial arrangements of labor, production, and consumption, the breakdown of modernist borders between "the private sphere" and public ones, and the changing role of the state in "policing the family" (Donzelot 1979) have made problematic not only childhood, but the entire set of age-based relationships. In order to understand these shifts, we need to look briefly at the set of arrangements that emerged in the context of the industrial revolution in Europe and North America. This period also provides one of the most dramatic examples of how biopolitics combined with economics to radically restructure the meaning of age and processes of social reproduction.

The move toward industrialization meant that more and more economic activity took place outside the household. At the same time, the number of children born to a typical family diminished, especially in urban areas (Kett 1977, 216; Chudacoff 1989, 93–95). Particularly among the urban middle classes, a feminine cult of domesticity emerged in which women were elevated as moral, spiritual, and emotional beings whose work it was to care for the home, which was now imagined as a "haven in a heartless world" (Lasch 1979). Whereas before children had been valued primarily for their labor, and had been integrated into the family through labor practices, by the mid-nineteenth century the urban middle classes valued their children for their sentimental worth (Zelizer 1985). Intimacy and sentiment, and the transfer of caring, became the center of intergenerational reproduction. Connected with this, middle-class children, along with the women who cared for them, became primary consumers (Veblen 1899), whose consumption habits drove new industries and were also produced by increasingly age-targeted production and marketing (Fass 1977; Schrum 2004). As the "good childhood" came to be one characterized by a prolonged period of protective and consuming nurture, these ideas became embodied in laws and institutions at home and abroad. Children outside the home were increasingly perceived as dangerous. As Sue Ruddick notes, "Modern adolescence—a particular form of youth characterized by a state of prolonged emotional, psychological and economic dependency—can be seen, then, to have birthed its doppelganger—juvenile delinquency" (2003, 336). Along with other parts of the population, juvenile delinquents become the object of attention of rapidly expanding state power, particularly in schools but also through tax, health and welfare, and economic policy.

At the same time that industrialization reshaped debates about children and adolescence, it reformulated the meanings of aging as well. Pensions and retirement were introduced for civil servants by European states in the late eighteenth century as part of the professionalization of public service and the undermining of sinecures occupied by the untalented and the unproductive old (Raphael 1964). But most people labored until unable to. In the mid-nineteenth century, "no provisions for mandatory or pensioned retirement existed that would detach old age from productive adulthood" (Chudacoff 1989, 19), and men and women on farms and in industrial workshops labored until incapacitated. A popular tract on the human body made no distinction, when discussing joints and walking abilities, between the physical capabilities of a man of twenty and a man of seventy (Chudacoff 1989, 24), although aches and rheumatism were recognized accompaniments to getting older. As Hareven explains, by the beginning of the twentieth century a variety of "medical and psychological studies by industrial efficiency experts focused on the physical and mental limitations of old age" (1995, 124). By 1954, one expert described how "different parts of the body age at different" rates (Chudacoff 1989, 165), neatly wedding the techniques of industrial efficiency analyses with medical science, and with the interests of various manufacturers of specific cures for specific points of aging. Insurance companies and body-care marketers offered diagnostic guides to the populace, prompting ongoing self-scrutiny for various signs of age and aging. Efforts by certain adult men to control access to industrial jobs resulted in limits on who could work at both ends of the lifespan: younger people were forced out of the workforce on one end, older people on the other. After the American Civil War, many businesses implemented "rewards" and pensions to remove older people from their workforce, but the rewards were small. A new life course emerged. The young were increasingly assigned (ideally) to a domestic space of care, consumption, and nurtured growth. The productive power and reproductive authority of mature adulthood were celebrated. And the retired elderly struggled between independence and dependency, a situation addressed if not resolved in the United States by the national Social Security Act of 1935.

This period culminated in a more organized and targeted production of sociological and biological knowledge about national populations, enabling more effective management, as well as promoting new forms of self-knowledge and self-monitoring among citizens, much as Foucault has argued (Foucault 1979; Burchell, Gordon, and Miller 1991). Along with shaping new subjectivities —many age-based—states also mobilized the new knowledge in techniques of government. Often they did so in response to demands by labor activists and other reformers who argued that the state was supposed to ensure the welfare of its citizens, and hence owed certain kinds of social benefits to families as part of a broader social contract.

This ideal of state responsibility for processes of social regeneration was differentially put into practice across the Soviet and Eastern bloc countries, in Western Europe, and in the United States. By the 1930s, however, a set of institutions was in place to regulate and ensure the reproduction of national populations. These institutions included schools to produce citizens for the new nationalist societies, and literate, moral workers for state bureaucracies and industrial enterprises. They also included various policies and subsidies to allow families to establish independent households based upon companionate marriage and fewer children. Finally, the state provided forms of welfare for those caught out by the market economy, or pushed out by new retirement practices. By the 1950s, in the United States and much of Western and Eastern Europe, the state was the dominant force shaping social reproduction. From direct policy legitimating where and how children could be raised, to subsidies like low-interest mortgages for young couples and tax breaks for parents of young children, to direct support of elderly retirees who no longer had a place in the new homes built by their children, states shaped the nature of the life course and processes of social reproduction (Coontz 1992; Donzelot 1979; Kligman 1998). While many, especially in impoverished urban and rural communities, were unable to attain the model of the nuclear family or independent elderhood toward which state efforts were directed, most felt the impact of state programs that reshaped the ways in which families were thought about, and how they educated and cared for their members.

Over the course of the 1980s, the role of the state as the dominant force in managing the social and economic lives of its citizens was challenged, variously, by the ideology embodied by Ronald Reagan in the United States, Margaret Thatcher in Britain, and Helmut Kohl in Germany, by the collapse of socialism in Eastern Europe, and by economic liberalization in China and Vietnam. In both the former socialist countries and the West, states began to decrease the amount of social support they provided, often turning the management of health, education, or housing over to private fee-for-service providers. They also pressured third-world countries to do the same in the name of fiscal responsibility, or compelled them by reducing economic subsidies that had been in place since the Cold War.

As laws were created around the world to allow capital to move more easily in and out of countries, corporations were increasingly able to take advantage of different costs of labor and investment in social reproduction across space (Katz 2002). At the same time, corporations benefited from new technologies and services for moving products and information across vast distances, allowing production to be widely dispersed. These much-discussed global capital flows are very mobile: they can be quickly withdrawn in times of stress, precipitating local financial collapses, as in Asia in the 1990s and Argentina in 2001–2002. The fluidity of capital, its rapid shifts, and its lack of investment in local social reproduction give it a "millenarian" and "occult" aspect to many people in developing countries. The uncertainties of where prospects come from and how they enter into community relations exacerbate tensions between generations, with the young questioning how their elders acquire money or opportunities, and vice versa (Comaroff and Comaroff 1999, 2000).

In their book *Empire*, Michael Hardt and Antonio Negri (2000) argue that states are no longer the dominant force in social reproduction, and therefore no longer the primary context for families and people seeking to regenerate their lives. Foucault (1978, 1979, 1980) has argued that in the late nineteenth and early twentieth centuries forms of statecraft were characterized more by the management of life than control over death—including the generation of knowledge about, and management of, specific practices around family and sexuality, medicine, and madness. By contrast, Hardt and Negri provocatively suggest that today older metropolitan institutions like the clinic and the education system, which are associated with the biopolitical power of the modern nation-state, are in decline, as are older mechanisms of nationalist citizenship. In their place, they argue, we are witnessing the emergence of new forms of "empire" characterized by horizontal, interlocking, and networking institutions that enter into people's lives and manage populations outside state agendas.

Since the 1970s, there has been an explosion of transnational, international, and grassroots organizations working to manage populations around the world, either bypassing, linking with, or opposing state programs. The Union of International Associations counted 280 intergovernmental organizations in 1972, and 2,795 international nongovernmental organizations. In 1984, the respective numbers rose dramatically to 1,530 and 12,686; counting local branches, there were 79,786 international and nongovernmental organizations in 1984 (Iriye 2002, 129). The early development of international nongovernmental associations seems to coincide with the development of global capitalism in the nineteenth century, but as Iriye points out, their projects had contradictory relationships to the interests of global capital (as well as to the nation building going on at that period). They were often at odds with the effects of capital in the developing world, yet promoted the liberal subject most suited to serve the interests of capital (Iriye 2002, 12–13).

As emergent forms of capital and the growing dominance of the "service economy" give new prominence to symbolic or affective labor, we find arrangements in which young women in South Asia, using names like "Megan" to ease the relationship, advise aging Americans about state services (Waldman 2003). Similarly, Christian child-sponsorship programs in the United States remake family and transnational interdependencies in Zimbabwe as they participate in a new global economy of care (Bornstein 2001). In Botswana, Westerners working with children orphaned by AIDS try to build intergenerational models of indulgent love and hugging care, to the frustration of their Tswana colleagues, who feel obligated to build relations of respect and mutual exchange of support and labor (Dahl 2005). Meanwhile, in the U.S., the work of caring is increasingly being taken up by third-world women who leave their own families behind in order to provide care and domesticity to families or to the elderly isolated in nursing homes, in Europe and the United States, where middle-class women increasingly seek to have both a career and a family (Ehrenreich and Hochschild 2002). Hardt and Negri are easily criticized for their lack of attention to a located, social subject embedded in relations of kinship (see Rofel 2002), which is precisely our focus here. Nevertheless, their analysis is useful for pointing out the intersection of new forms of labor with new ways of managing populations.

Taken together, these various forces offer a new language for the reproduction of domestic lives and community relations. Many of these policies and practices assume the production of a particular kind of subject, one freed from domestic ties and intergenerational relations to make choices in a global economy, even while in many places the withdrawal of state support, or increased financial insecurity, demand that people rely on family or other domestic ties for the material and moral support that enables social reproduction. For example, as T. E. Woronov's chapter on child rearing in China implies, parents can no longer rely on the government to provide jobs for their children in the new market-based economy, so they look for new educational models that will foster the characteristics that they believe will best prepare their children for the future and ensure their success. Similarly, both the elderly South Asians and the elderly Europeans written about by Sarah Lamb and by Jessica Greenberg and Andrea Muehlebach, respectively, have found that the structures once available to ensure their support are no longer in place, forcing them—and the families and societies of which they are a part—to create new models of both personhood and intergenerational care. Read together—and in conjunction with the other chapters of this book, which present examples ranging from Mexico to Madagascar and Botswana—these stories hint at how intimate relations of social regeneration play a central role in emerging state and economic formations. Kin work, caring, and domestic labor have always been integral to the organization of capital and the regulation and management of populations, but they are being stretched and used in new ways.

From Age to Regeneration

As Cooper noted in his article, in studying globalization, we must study how it takes place through "the struggle over the meaning of ideas as much as their transmission across space" and in "the specificity of the structures necessary to make [global] connections work" (Cooper 2001, 199, 189). The essays in this volume argue that a focus on age and intergenerational relationships provides new perspectives on globalization because it captures simultaneously the micro-scale of the body, family, and household relations and the larger scale of political and economic transformations. The approach developed here both builds on and diverges from earlier discussions of age and regeneration as analytical categories.

Age mediates the biological and the social, providing a powerful symbolic and practical terrain for marking and naturalizing relations of hierarchy and dependency, difference and sameness, as well as patterns of temporality. Age is centrally implicated in divisions of labor within and beyond households. The reorganization of production and consumption that has occurred at various historical junctures has profoundly shaped and reshaped the nature of intergenerational relations. This reorganization is visible in who can work and how, who can consume and what. These relations are both part of economic production and central to the reproduction of aging persons. Age is also constitutive of subject formation and subjectivity, as studies ranging from psychology and psychological anthropology (Briggs 1998; Rogoff 2003), to the work of the Centre for Contemporary Cultural Studies (Lave et al. 1992), to the work of Michel Foucault (1979) indicate in different ways. Further, age is a part of pragmatic and situational social practice, put to work by people in social and political settings in order to recognize, manipulate, and manage relationships (Durham 2004). In the United States today one sees the confluence of the simultaneously historical and pragmatic aspects of age in the broad puzzlement about youth and adulthood. While one recent book (Robbins and Wilner 2001) claims that twenty-somethings are undergoing something akin to a mid-life crisis, another study (Smith 2003) finds that Americans don't think of themselves as grown-up until age twenty-seven or more, and yet another newspaper article (Jefferson and Hey 2003) reports that the forty-fifth birthday is the "new 30th."[8] In 1997, the *New York Times* devoted its Sunday magazine for March 9 to America's "Age Boom" and the discovery of "a new stage of life" after middle age.[9] But this new stage is perplexing to those contemplating changes in state support of the elderly, some crippled and worn out from work in their late fifties, others bored with leisure in their late seventies. These stories index changing experiences of age—some of which have been documented since at least 1970 (Keniston 1972). They also reflect efforts by marketers and various other kinds of specialists to create new markets and publics based on new kinds of age categories.

While age has figured in historical studies of the West since at least the 1960s, when Philippe Ariès's *Centuries of Childhood* appeared, in anthropology there has been a persistent sense that age has not been given sufficient attention, despite periodic calls to recognize it as a basic principle in social relations and anthropological theory (La Fontaine 1978; Kertzer and Keith 1984; Cohen 1994). In recent years, that call seems to have been heard, as several studies have singled out age groups—such as children, youth, or the aged—in order to analyze social processes associated with modernity and globalization (Ruddick 2003; Scheper-Hughes and Sargent 1998; Stephens 1995a; Amit-Talai and Wulff 1995; Cohen 1998; Honwana and De Boeck 2005; Maira and Soep 2005).

The essays in this volume build upon this work. However, they also argue that studies of age must move beyond focusing on particular age groups (the recent trend), and take age itself as an analytic. To do so is to understand age as essentially relational, and fundamentally tied to processes of social reproduction. One is a child with respect to parents or older people; one is old with respect to a retirement system, expectations of continuous lifetime labor, or a new generation of mature leaders; one is a youth with respect to children and adults, or to the future and past, or to chronological standards circulated by social scientists and the United Nations. Childhood, youth, the "third age," and other categories are parts of unfolding lives, as well. People's experience, as they take up and occupy these different categories, is situated in relation to expectations regarding who they want to become and what kinds of lives they want to lead. Modifying and incorporating new sets of relationships through the life course is a means to achieve those transformations. Uncertainties about contemporary American adulthood, for example, have to do with uncertainty about whether shifting relations of independence from parents or support for dependent children are key to the transition from youth to adulthood. Age cannot be analytically separated from, or given priority over, other interpretive frames through which scholars have analyzed reproductive processes, including race, class, and gender. Nevertheless, by highlighting the relational issues associated with globalization as they are mobilized by people in their intimate lives and proximate relationships, age as a primary analytic opens up new perspectives into contemporary processes.

In making the argument that studies of age must go beyond a focus on single age groups to examine the complex nature of intergenerational relations, the case studies presented here also recuperate an earlier tradition of anthropological and sociological studies of the relationship between age, generation, and social reproduction (Baxter and Almagor 1978; Eisenstadt 1956; Fortes 1984; Goody 1962; La Fontaine 1978; Mannheim 1972; Wilson 1951). Early sociological and anthropological accounts approached age and generation from within a functionalist framework which assumed the stability of social systems made up of interlocking parts. Sociologists, concerned with the transition from traditional to modern society, saw generations as a key to understanding the relationship between continuity and rupture. According to one highly influential version of this model, the social roles and allegiances that one developed in the family were inappropriate to modern society, where allegiances were supposed to be diffuse and impersonal. Age groups, or peer groups, arose outside the family and satisfied the need for a kind of subject who would fulfill social roles based more on achieved criteria than on personalistic ones (Eisenstadt 1956): generations of peers, or cohorts, mediated between the family and broader social configurations. According to this view, peer groups, and youth groups in particular, provide a critical socializing mechanism, facilitating a transition from the private to the public domain by moving youth outside of the family and into a wider sphere of interaction.

Early anthropological studies similarly perceived age groups as crucial to cultural continuity. In these studies, generations figure as structurally opposed parts of kinship systems, persistent in their form and function even as the people in them live and die. Such structural generations are anchored in the distinction between parent and child, building upon that distinction to bind together groups of people as members of a generation structurally opposed to antecedent and descendant generational groups. The Ndembu villages described by Victor Turner (1957) revealed such generational oppositions in their ground plans: on one side of the circle of houses making up a village were the residences of people of one generation, on the other the residences of their children's generation and of their parents' generation, to both of whom they were "opposed." Particularly in the context of lineage systems, generations like these organized political leadership, inheritance, and marriage. Such generational relationships exist regardless of actual age, and people from "parent" and "child" and even "grandchild" generations may be of the same age, while two people in the same genealogical generation may be sixty years apart in age (Kertzer and Keith 1984).

These older accounts do remind us that generations are fundamentally about processes of social replacement. However, they remain problematic on several counts. First, like any functionalist interpretation, they elide the question of the relations of power in the process of reproduction, except insofar as a reified notion of "society" demands the reproduction of particular social forms. Second, they privilege continuity to such a degree, even in so-called modern society, that change is perceived as pathological, the breakdown of the system. While Marxist-inspired studies reintroduced notions of power as an aspect of social reproduction, and sometimes situated them in specific historical contexts, many remained functionalist in emphasizing the ways power worked against change and toward reproducing fixed social relations. For example, Pierre Bourdieu (1973) used the concept of reproduction to examine the perpetuation of class-based inequalities in Europe through the education system. Similarly, Paul Willis (1981) showed how the reproduction of a class society was perpetuated in part by the rebellion of working-class youth, who, in rebelling and rejecting the class-stratified behavior norms associated with the education system, ensured that they, like their fathers, would be qualified only for working-class jobs.[10]

By contrast, another view of generations highlights their role in historical change. In a piece entitled "The Problem of Generations," the sociologist Karl Mannheim (1972) defined generations as groups of youth who came of age at roughly the same time and who, because of their unique historical positioning, mediated processes of cultural change.

Mannheim argued against a demographic concept of generations as biologically, regularly spaced groups of people. He also felt that the romantic idea that generations uniformly embodied a "spirit of an age" was insufficient and argued strongly for recognizing the specific historical and sociological processes that gave an age cohort the sensibility of being different from their predecessors. Mannheim paid particular attention to the social "locations" and political relations which enabled generational consciousness, pointing out that "town youths" tended to dominate its propagation, because they had greater access to the forms of public culture through which it is forged.

Taking up Mannheim's point, and situating Mannheim himself politically and historically, Robert Wohl (1979) has explored how fin-de-siècle politics in Europe, and then later the experience of World War I and postwar economy and society, produced a variety of sharp claims for generational distinction across Europe, each different, and each socially located. In late nineteenth-century France, for example, claims to a new youth generation were made within intellectual and literary society; in postwar England similar claims were situated against the rapid breakdown of social class barriers and hostility toward politicians held responsible for the war. Across the Atlantic, in America, Paula Fass (1977) has described different but parallel processes. She argues that the expansion of the college-going population and the growth of state universities, the rise of a consumer culture that emphasized people's ability to make their own identities through marketed goods and lifestyles, and new small-family demographics in which a small number of closely spaced children were distinguished from older parents all contributed to an emergent youth culture distinct from the culture of parents.

Drawing these approaches together, we propose the apt term "regeneration" to highlight the mutually constitutive interplay between intergenerational relations and wider historical and social processes. The term invokes many of the issues associated with the phrase "social reproduction," which has long been used to discuss both the relationship between households and economies and the process through which societies re-create the social structures that enable continuity across time. In using the term "regeneration," however, we highlight the fact that generations, and the age-based relationships that they imply, are a key site through which to understand processes of social change.[11] While "(social) reproduction" has been used more to suggest the re-creation of particular social forms over time, we use "regeneration" to signal a more dynamic approach, one that is attentive to process.

Like the term "reproduction," with its nod to women's fertility, productive labor, and the mechanical duplication of a well-designed product, the root of our term, "generation," covers a wide range of conceptual territory. Though some have argued that the multiple meanings of "generation" only "sow confusion" (Kertzer 1983, 142), for our purposes the polysemy of the term is useful. Combining an emphasis on birth, growth, and kin relations with ideas about both shared histories and breaks in historical experience (Lamb 2001), "regeneration" captures the multiple ways in which age figures centrally in how families, communities, and social relationships regenerate in the contemporary moment. It is only by attending to both descent relations within the family and the ways in which historical experience, government programs, and economic processes configure age that we can adequately account for how intimate social relations figure in processes of globalization.

In many ways the concept of regeneration, which emphasizes the crucial role of generational relations in mediating processes of historical change, is similar to Mannheim's concept of "fresh contact." According to Mannheim, fresh contact takes place as young people, reaching adulthood, "come into contact anew" with their accumulated sociocultural heritage (1972, 368) and develop a novel perspective upon it, an observation made by Marx as well. While he notes that every individual undergoes "fresh contact" throughout his life, when changing residences or statuses, Mannheim suggests that there is a special historical force to the fresh contact of groups of people who come of age at the same time. That he speaks of "social rejuvenation" points to his emphasis upon youth in this process: he believed that the experimentation of seventeen-year-olds who are just learning patterns of behavior is poten-tially more radical than the experiments of the mid-life adult who has already formed a series of social entanglements and well-established patterns.[12]

The idea that young people are more open to ideas, more susceptible to "fresh contact" with inherited traditions as well as to the reorientating effects of historical events, is appealing because of its ability to link personal, bio-graphical time with wider historical contingencies, suggesting one possible mechanism of social change (Elder 1999). And it is true that youth—more than any other age group—often figure in how social change is imagined. Youth bear this burden insofar as they often represent the future of a nation or community, a phenomenon that was visible both in Mannheim's time and throughout the 1960s. This may be one reason that youth, more than other age groups, have been the subject of recent studies addressing the relationship between age, modernity, and processes of globalization (Arnett 2002; Hon-wana and DeBoeck 2005).

But given the relational nature of youth, one cannot analyze their role in social change without taking account of the complex generational rela-tions within which they are embedded (Cole 2004; this volume). New ideas about youth, and new experiences had by youth, take shape through chang-ing relationships, and not simply as young people (individually or in peer groups) contemplate new images, new economic opportunities, and new gov-ernment policies. If young people become more independent in Botswana, they can only establish this independence vis-à-vis their relationships with seniors and juniors (Durham, this volume). Similarly, changes in Chinese childhood are mediated and enacted by the children's parents (Woronov, this volume); among South Asians aging becomes a site of regeneration not be-cause the elderly confront new circumstances on their own, but because they must negotiate them through relationships with children and grandchildren (Lamb, this volume). The relational nature of age and generation, and the fact that transformations in the practices associated with one generation neces-sarily affect either the ascending or descending generation, mean that each of the papers gathered here suggests that "fresh contact" is part of a broader process of intergenerational transformation.

Regeneration in the Contemporary Moment: The Intimate Politics of Globalization

So how does all of this add up to an intimate politics of globalization? What do we mean by the phrase? It is worth recalling that in addition to indicating matters pertaining to sex and the family, the word "intimate" also indicates one's essential or innermost part. Intimacy is the space of both relationality and selfhood; this space is not, however, a "private sphere" held apart from wider political and public practice (Durham and Klaits 2002; Durham n.d.). By focusing on intergenerational relations, the papers in this volume suggest that if we want to understand the contemporary moment, then we must focus not only on broad questions of labor, capital, the management of populations, or the movement of commodities. In addition, we must take seriously the fact that these phenomena take place in the context of familial and generational relations. Instead of describing the chapters in their order of appearance, we use this final section to highlight some of the processes that our analytical perspective brings out.

First, all of the papers emphasize the importance of cycles of intergenerational exchange, and how the dynamics of this process are shaped by, but also mediate, broader global processes. Such exchanges are critical to the movement of people through their life cycles, and to the regeneration of households that can themselves engage in productive activity in a changing environment. Often, these exchanges take place over very long periods of time—obligations established in infancy may be recalled in old age or even after death by ancestors, or their descendants. In some of the chapters we see how intergenerational cycles of exchange can produce stability out of change. The chapter by Magazine and Sánchez, for example, makes precisely this point by exploring how the practice of *ayuda*, or a child's reciprocation of the nurture received since childhood, continues to structure transnational cycles of exchange. The reciprocation begins as soon as a child is able to toss feed out to chickens or perform other small household tasks, and continues as the child takes jobs and remits earnings; later, parents fund the establishment of their offspring's own marital households. This mode of exchange is also a way of constructing particular kinds of subjects who respond to others' demands. As a result, children who migrate abroad continue to give back to their natal families. Magazine and Sánchez note that in Tlalcuapan, the structure of childhood is quite stable, and that young people both sustain relationships with their parents and form new generative households of their own, despite the increasing importance of transnational labor migration to California.

By contrast, in Lamb's chapter, we see South Asian seniors migrate to the U.S., expecting a reciprocation of the care they gave their children who now live there. They find, however, that their sons and daughters work long hours, and cannot give their parents the bodily attentions that they expect. In response, older South Asian immigrants take advantage of state services, and use these services to forge new models of independent aging. In Botswana, too, new forms of work and programs devised by NGOs and the government intervene in the reciprocal exchanges that knit households and enable life-course transitions. There, young people find their contributions being reevaluated and the mode of maturing changing (Durham), as is also happening in Madagascar (Cole). Meanwhile, older people find it more difficult to attain an elderhood that is recognized through the care given by children (Livingston). In Europe, by contrast, the intergenerational contract devised by the welfare state, according to which the elderly withdrew from formal-sector work in order to make way for the young who would support them, is breaking down. The paper by Greenberg and Muehlebach discusses how changing attitudes toward the state, an increase in the elderly section of the population pyramid, and nationalism in the face of poor third-world immigrants have caused some policy makers to suggest rewriting the intergenerational contract and asking the elderly to come back to work.

Second, the papers demonstrate the tension between these models of personhood, based on care and intergenerational reciprocity, and the possessive, liberal individual promoted by neoliberal economic and state policies. In Madagascar, as Cole describes, economic liberalization has meant that consumer goods have flooded the country, fostering new forms of self-development among young urbanites. While transactional sex has long been a feature of attaining adulthood, establishing new households, and linking generations across time and space, changes in the economy mean that it has potentially destabilizing implications. Young women now mobilize sex to gain access both to goods and to the better life of the West that they represent; in doing so a few lucky women gain more status and power within their families than they would have had earlier. At the same time, they forge new self-directed means of achieving adulthood, measured more in terms of access to commodities than productive labor. In Woronov's chapter, we see consumerist logic extending into the means of child rearing; parents eagerly purchase a variety of advice manuals, hoping to raise independent children capable of adapting to expanding economic horizons.

In other chapters, the state and other agencies foster the creation of a liberal, possessive individual. Lamb's aging immigrants to the U.S. are one example, achieving new forms of self-reliance with the aid of state programs for the elderly. In Botswana, meanwhile, ideas of the independent subject, the undifferentiated citizen of a proudly liberal state, are promoted by government, NGOs, and by the shifting economies of care and belonging in households. Both the elderly and young people, discussed by Livingston and Durham respectively, negotiate the tensions between the hierarchical interdependencies that have structured kin relations and the promise of "developing oneself."

A key site where people work these tensions out is the struggle over the nature of intergenerational care. Earlier we noted that the growing dominance of the service economy gives new prominence to affective forms of labor; we also noted the rise of global consumerism. The chapters in this book demonstrate the conflicts that take place as people struggle to redefine both the nature of care and who should care for whom. In some cases, care is recognized in work performed for others (Durham; Magazine and Sánchez). Other cases more sharply register the effects of consumerism, as when people conceive of care as a daughter's willingness to buy a parent coveted commodities (Cole), or parents' ability to instill "quality" in their children by offering them new kinds of educational opportunities (Woronov).

In many of the chapters, new models of care coexist uneasily with older ones. For example, in Livingston's chapter, the model of care held by disabled elderly in Botswana comes into direct conflict with the model propounded by international NGOs. The NGOs try to foster the disabled elderly's independence by teaching them to take care of their own bodily needs. By contrast, some elderly people reject the NGO workers' efforts, invoking instead local models according to which elders have a right to rely on, and be coddled by, their children. And in Lamb's chapter, we see the contested process through which one kind of care—time—is substituted for another—money. In these chapters, as indeed in all the chapters of the book, we find that the core elements of intimacy that we noted above—relationality and selfhood—are a key site for the negotiation of new subjects and actors in today's circumstances.

Margaret Mead provided an image, once, of grandparents holding their grandchildren in their arms, unable to "conceive of any other future for their children than their own past lives" (Mead 1970, 1). While such an image inappropriately divides a perfectly cyclical past from a linear and uncertain present, it does draw attention to the central role of intergenerational relations in managing social reproduction. As we have argued, age is a key facet of this process, and an important point from which to understand social and cultural regeneration because of its relational nature and the way in which it mediates among the intimate domain of personhood, household hierarchies, and broader biopolitical and economic processes. As a result, practices which shape age and intergenerational relations are not secondary factors to be added on to discussions of globalization after the work of analyzing economic or cultural processes has been done. Rather, because the changing demands of culture and economy reshape the ways in which people forge intimate relations, intimate practices work to form new social hierarchies that constitute globalization in various sites around the world. The demands of intimate social relations also shape the movement of people, goods, programs, and cultures into the broader patterns of globalization. Focusing on intergenerational relations illuminates struggles over the meaning and effects of new kinds of social and economic conditions as well as newly emergent social patterns. It also reminds us that how we think about and treat children, youth, or the aged is central to how we create possible futures, whatever they may be.

NOTES

1. Exceptionally from a global perspective, Bechtel was forced to withdraw by civil unrest; see Finnegan 2002.

2. "Water Firm Suez in Argentine Row," January 24, 2005, http://news.bbc.co.uk/1/hi/business/4201461.stm.

3. Migration statistics are notoriously unreliable in part because definitions of what constitutes a migrant vary across national boundaries and because of illegal migration.

4. Mediating them are concepts like "hybridity" and "glocalization," which continue to be framed in terms of the polarity; cf. Werbner and Modood 1997.

5. For example, mythic heroes frequently experience youth "outside" social boundaries by gathering extra-social resources and powers, bringing these home both to transform their societies and to redomesticate their own generational experience through marriage, reconnecting with parents, or the like. The Sunjata epic of the Mali Empire, in which the founder of an empire leaves his community to confront and gather forms of power from other societies and to grow up, is a well-studied example (Austen 1999). One might also look at ancient Rome, where *adolescentia* extended to age thirty and *juventus* to forty-five, under the authority of the *patria potestas*. There, in the ritual known as Lupercalia, young men wearing nothing but goatskins ran "naked" around the city: they dispensed fertility with their goathide, their dangerous *celeritas* contrasting with the *gravitas* of the *seniores* (Fraschetti 1997). Reenacting the founding of Rome by Romulus and Remus, they mediated the relationship of the "wild" to the "city."

6. See Mannoni 1990 on the use of the parent-child metaphor in colonial domination.

7. Similar dynamics are visible today in discourses about, and violent treatment of, street children throughout Latin America (Hecht 1998; Scheper-Hughes and Hoffman 1998; Marquez 1999). Age is still used to shape international relationships with Africa today when, for example, the African population is described as 50 percent below the age of sixteen, or the number of AIDS orphans on the continent is enumerated, or conflicts there (or in other parts of the world) are described in terms of "child soldiers."

8. These stories are part of a much broader phenomenon, for over the last ten years there has been an explosion of stories about youth, children, and the elderly. To give but one example, between 1980 and 1990 the *New York Times* indexed 464 articles on childhood and children; in the next decade it indexed 772. Though these stories surely track changing conceptions, they also help to constitute new audiences, markets, and publics based on age.

9. See also Robbins and Wilner 2001.

10. Yet it is important to emphasize that Marxist insights into the interrelationship between age, generation, and social reproduction need not entail a static model. Claude Meillassoux, for example, analyzed how the management of women as laborers and wives was linked to the negotiation of (male) juniority to ensure control over resources in agricultural communities of West Africa, a control disrupted by labor migration as well as the new resources that people and polities used to construct social relationships under later colonial regimes (Meillassoux 1981).

11. In using the term "regeneration" we reverse the polarity established by Weiner (1980) in her argument that "reproduction" was a more dynamic analytical term than "reciprocity," which she found atemporal and mechanical. "Although the meanings of

reproduction and regeneration have areas of overlap, I try to emphasize two distinctions. In using 'reproduction' I am concerned with the cultural attention and meaning given to acts of forming, producing, or creating something new. 'Regeneration' refers to the cultural attention and meaning given to the renewal, revival, rebirth, or re-creation of entities previously reproduced" (71).

12. Mannheim implies that older groups, past the demands of mid-life adulthood, loosen up a bit and become more open to novelty and change. But his emphasis remains on youth.

WORKS CITED

Alaimo, Kathleen. 1994. "Adolescence, Gender, and Class in Education Reform in France: The Development of 'Enseignement Primaire Superieur,' 1880–1910." *French Historical Studies* 18 (4): 1025–1056.

Amit-Talai, Vered, and Helena Wulff, eds. 1995. *Youth Cultures: A Cross-Cultural Perspective*. London: Routledge.

Ariès, Philippe. 1962. *Centuries of Childhood: A Social History of Family Life*. Trans. R. Baldick. New York: Vintage Press.

Appadurai, Arjun. 1996. *Modernity at Large: Cultural Dimensions of Globalization*. Minneapolis: University of Minnesota Press.

Arnett, Jeffrey Jensen. 2002. "The Psychology of Globalization." *American Psychologist* 57 (10): 774–783.

Austen, Ralph, ed. 1999. *In Search of Sunjata: The Mande Oral Epic as History, Literature, and Performance*. Bloomington: Indiana University Press.

Baxter, P. T. W., and Uri Almagor, eds. 1978. *Age, Generation, and Time: Some Features of East African Age Organizations*. New York: St. Martin's Press.

Bornstein, Erica. 2001. "Child Sponsorship, Evangelism, and Belonging in the Work of World Vision Zimbabwe." *American Ethnologist* 28 (3): 595–622.

Bourdieu, Pierre. 1973. "Cultural Reproduction and Social Reproduction." In Richard Brown, ed., *Knowledge, Education, and Cultural Change*. Pp. 71–112. London: Tavistock.

Briggs, Jean L. 1998. *Inuit Morality Play: The Emotional Education of a Three-Year-Old*. New Haven, Conn.: Yale University Press.

Burchell, Graham, Colin Gordon, and Peter Miller, eds. 1991. *The Foucault Effect: Studies in Governmentality*. Chicago: University of Chicago Press.

Chapin, Wesley D. 1999–2000. "Immigration and Security: A Review of *The Global Migration Crisis: Challenge to States and to Human Rights* by Myron Weiner." *Journal for the Study of Peace and Conflict*. http://jspc.library.wisc.edu/issues/1999-2000/article3.html.

Chudacoff, Howard P. 1989. *How Old Are You? Age Consciousness in American Culture*. Princeton, N.J.: Princeton University Press.

Cohen, Lawrence. 1994. "Old Age: Cultural and Critical Perspectives." *Annual Review of Anthropology* 23: 137–158.

———. 1998. *No Aging in India: Alzheimer's, the Bad Family, and Other Modern Things*. Berkeley: University of California Press.

Cole, Jennifer. 2004. "Fresh Contact in Tamatave, Madagascar: Sex, Money, and Intergenerational Transformation." *American Ethnologist* 31 (4): 573–588.

Comaroff, Jean, and John L. Comaroff. 1991. *Of Revelation and Revolution: Chris-*

tianity, Colonialism, and Consciousness in South Africa. Chicago: University of Chicago Press.

———. 1999. "Occult Economies and the Violence of Abstraction: Notes from the South African Postcolony." *American Ethnologist* 26 (2): 279–303.

———. 2000. "Millenial Capitalism: First Thoughts on a Second Coming." *Public Culture* 12 (2): 291–343.

Coontz, Stephanie. 1992. *The Way We Never Were: American Families and the Nostalgia Trap.* New York: Basic Books.

Cooper, Frederick. 2001. "What Is the Concept of Globalization Good For? An African Historian's Perspective." *African Affairs* 100: 189–213.

Dahl, Bianca. 2005. "Transforming Children: The Contested Socialization of Orphaned Youth in Contemporary Botswana." M.A. thesis, Department of Comparative Human Development, University of Chicago.

De Boeck, Filip, and Alcinda Honwana. 2005. "Introduction: Children and Youth in Africa." In Alcinda Honwana and Filip De Boeck, eds., *Makers and Breakers: Children and Youth in Postcolonial Africa.* Pp. 1–18. London: James Currey.

Donzelot, Jacques. 1979. *The Policing of Families.* New York: Pantheon Books.

Durham, Deborah. 2000. "Introduction: Youth and the Social Imagination in Africa." *Anthropological Quarterly* 73 (3): 113–120.

———. 2004. "Disappearing Youth: Youth as a Social Shifter in Botswana." *American Ethnologist* 31 (4): 589–605.

Durham, Deborah. N.d. "Apathy and Agency: The Romance of Youth." In Jennifer Cole and Deborah Durham, eds., *Children, Youth, and Social Theory in Global Context.* Ms.

Durham, Deborah, and Frederick Klaits. 2002. "Funerals and the Public Space of Mutuality in Botswana." *Journal of Southern African Studies* 28 (4): 777–795.

Ehrenreich, Barbara, and Arlie Russell Hochschild. 2002. *Global Woman: Nannies, Maids, and Sex Workers in the New Economy.* New York: Metropolitan Books.

Eisenstadt, S. N. 1956. *From Generation to Generation: Age Groups and Social Structure.* Glencoe, Ill.: Free Press.

Elder, Glen. 1999 [1974]. *Children of the Great Depression: Social Change in Life Experience.* Boulder, Colo.: Westview Press.

Elias, Norbert. 1978. *The Civilizing Process: The Development of Manners.* New York: Urizen Books.

Fass, Paula S. 1977. *The Damned and the Beautiful: American Youth in the 1920s.* New York: Oxford University Press.

Finnegan, William. 2002. "Letter from Bolivia: Leasing the Rain." *New Yorker Magazine,* April 8.

Fortes, Meyer. 1984. "Age, Generation, and Social Structure." In David I. Kertzer and Jennie Keith, eds., *Age and Anthropological Theory.* Pp. 99–122. Ithaca, N.Y.: Cornell University Press.

Foucault, Michel. 1978. *The History of Sexuality.* Trans. Robert Hurley. New York: Pantheon Books.

———. 1979. *Discipline and Punish: The Birth of the Prison.* Trans. Alan Sheridan. New York: Vintage Books.

———. 1980. *Power/Knowledge: Selected Interviews and Other Writings, 1972–1977.* Ed. and trans. Colin Gordon. New York: Pantheon Books.

Fraschetti, Augusto. 1997. "Roman Youth." In Giovanni Levi and Jean-Claude Schmitt, eds., *A History of Young People*, vol. 1, *Ancient and Medieval Rites of Passage*. Pp. 51–82. Cambridge, Mass.: Harvard University Press.

Friedman, Jonathan. 2002. "Champagne Liberals and the New 'Dangerous Classes': Reconfigurations of Class, Identity, and Cultural Reproduction in the Contemporary Global System." *Social Analysis* 46 (2): 33–55.

Friedman, Thomas L. 2000. *The Lexus and the Olive Tree*. New York: Anchor Books.

Goody, Jack. 1962. *The Developmental Cycle in Domestic Groups*. Cambridge: Cambridge University Press.

Hall, G. Stanley. 1904. *Adolescence: Its Psychology and Its Relations to Physiology, Anthropology, Sociology, Sex, Crime, Religion, and Education*. New York: D. Appleton.

Hardt, Michael, and Antonio Negri. 2000. *Empire*. Cambridge, Mass.: Harvard University Press.

Hareven, Tamara K. 1995. "Changing Images of Aging and the Social Construction of the Life Course." In Michael Featherstone and Andrew Wernick, eds., *Images of Aging: Cultural Representations of Later Life*. Pp. 119–134. London: Routledge.

Hart, Gillian. 2002. *Disabling Globalization: Places of Power in Post-apartheid South Africa*. Berkeley: University of California Press.

Harvey, David. 1989. *The Condition of Postmodernity: An Enquiry into the Origins of Cultural Change*. Oxford: Blackwell.

Hecht, Tobias. 1998. *At Home in the Street: Street Children of Northeast Brazil*. Cambridge: Cambridge University Press.

———. 2002. Introduction to Tobias Hecht, ed., *Minor Omissions: Children in Latin American History and Society*. Pp. 3–20. Madison: University of Wisconsin Press.

Honwana, Alcinda, and Filip De Boeck, eds. 2005. *Makers and Breakers: Children and Youth in Postcolonial Africa*. Oxford: James Currey.

Hoogvelt, Ankie. 1997. *Globalization and the Postcolonial World: The New Political Economy of Development*. Baltimore, Md.: Johns Hopkins University Press.

Iriye, Akira. 2002. *Global Community: The Role of International Organizations in the Making of the Contemporary World*. Berkeley: University of California Press.

Jefferson, Elana Ashanti, and Barbara Hey. 2003. "45 Is the New 30; Fortysomethings Are the New Babes." *Miami Herald*, July 15. http://www.miami.com/mld/miami herald/.

Johnston, R. J., Peter J. Taylor, and Michael Watts, eds. 2002. *Geographies of Global Change: Remapping the World*. 2nd edition. Malden, Mass.: Blackwell.

Katz, Cindi. 2002. "Stuck in Place: Children and the Globalization of Social Reproduction." In R. J. Johnston, Peter J. Taylor, and Michael Watts, eds., *Geographies of Global Change: Remapping the World*, 2nd edition. Pp. 248–259. Malden, Mass.: Blackwell.

Kearney, Michael. 1995. "The Local and the Global: The Anthropology of Globalization and Transnationalism." *Annual Review of Anthropology* 24: 547–565.

Keniston, Kenneth. 1972. "Youth: A 'New' Stage of Life." In Thomas J. Cottle, ed., *The Prospect of Youth*. Pp. 631–654. Boston, Mass.: Little, Brown.

Kertzer, David I. 1983. "Generation as a Sociological Problem." *Annual Review of Sociology* 9: 125–149.

Kertzer, David I., and Jennie Keith, eds. 1984. *Age and Anthropological Theory*. Ithaca, N.Y.: Cornell University Press.

Kett, Joseph F. 1977. *Rites of Passage: Adolescence in America, 1790 to the Present*. New York: Basic Books.

Kligman, Gail. 1998. *The Politics of Duplicity: Controlling Reproduction in Ceausescu's Romania*. Berkeley: University of California Press.

La Fontaine, Jean S., ed. 1978. *Sex and Age as Principles of Social Differentiation*. A.S.A. Monograph 17. London: Academic Press.

Lamb, Sarah. 2001. "Generation in Anthropology." In N. J. Smelser and Paul B. Baltes, eds., *International Encyclopedia of the Social and Behavioral Sciences*. Pp. 6043–6046. New York: Elsevier.

Larkin, Brian. 1997. "Indian Films and Nigerian Lovers: Media and the Creation of Parallel Modernities." *Africa* 67 (3): 406–440.

Lasch, Christopher. 1979. *Haven in a Heartless World: The Family Besieged*. New York: Basic Books.

Lave, Jean, Paul Duguid, Nadine Fernandez, and Erik Axel. 1992. "Coming of Age in Birmingham: Cultural Studies and Conceptions of Subjectivity." *Annual Review of Anthropology* 21: 257–282.

LeVine, Robert A., Sarah E. LeVine, and Beatrice Schnell. 2001. "'Improve the Women': Mass Schooling, Female Literacy, and Worldwide Social Change." *Harvard Educational Review* 71 (1): 1–50.

Lévi-Strauss, Claude. 1963. *Totemism*. Trans. Rodney Needham. Boston: Beacon Press.

Liechty, Mark. 2003. *Suitably Modern: Making Middle-Class Culture in a New Consumer Society*. Princeton, N.J.: Princeton University Press.

Lutz, Catherine A., and Lila Abu-Lughod, eds. 1990. *Language and the Politics of Emotion*. Cambridge: Cambridge University Press.

Maira, Sunaina, and Elisabeth Soep. 2005. *Youthscapes: The Popular, the National, the Global*. Philadelphia: University of Pennsylvania Press.

Mannheim, Karl. 1972 [1952]. "The Problem of Generations." In *Essays on the Sociology of Knowledge*. Pp. 276–320. London: Routledge and Kegan Paul.

Mannoni, Octave. 1990 [1956]. *Prospero and Caliban: The Psychology of Colonization*. Trans. Pamela Powesland. Ann Arbor: University of Michigan Press. Originally published as *Psychologie de la Colonisation* (Paris: Seuil, 1950).

Marquez, Patricia C. 1999. *The Street Is My Home: Youth and Violence in Caracas*. Stanford, Calif.: Stanford University Press.

Mead, Margaret. 1970. *Culture and Commitment: A Study of the Generation Gap*. Garden City, N.Y.: Natural History Press.

Meillassoux, Claude. 1981. *Maidens, Meal, and Money: Capitalism and Domestic Community*. Cambridge: Cambridge University Press.

Neilson, Brett. 2003. "Globalization and the Biopolitics of Aging." *CR: The New Centennial Review* 3 (2): 161–186.

Ong, Aihwa. 1996. "Cultural Citizenship as Subject Making: Immigrants Negotiate Racial and Cultural Boundaries in the United States." *Cultural Anthropology* 37 (5): 737–762.

———. 1999. *Flexible Citizenship: The Cultural Logics of Transnationality*. Durham, N.C.: Duke University Press.

Ortner, Sherry. 1991. "Reading America: Preliminary Notes on Class and Culture." In Richard G. Fox, ed., *Recapturing Anthropology: Working in the Present*. Pp. 163–189. Santa Fe, N.M.: School of American Research Press.

———. 2003. *New Jersey Dreaming: Capital, Culture, and the Class of '58*. Durham, N.C.: Duke University Press.

Premo, Bianca. 2002. "Minor Offenses: Youth, Crime, and Law in Eighteenth-Century Lima." In Tobias Hecht, ed., *Minor Omissions: Children in Latin American History and Society*. Pp. 114–138. Madison: University of Wisconsin Press.

Raphael, Marios. 1964. *Pensions and Public Servants: A Study of the Origins of the British System*. Paris: Mouton.

Richman, Amy L., Patrice M. Miller, and Robert A. LeVine. 1992. "Cultural and Educational Variations in Maternal Responsiveness." *Developmental Psychology* 28 (4): 614–621.

Rizzini, Irene. 2002. "The Child-Saving Movement in Brazil: Ideology in the Late Nineteenth and Early Twentieth Centuries." In Tobias Hecht, ed., *Minor Omissions: Children in Latin American History and Society*. Pp. 165–180. Madison: University of Wisconsin Press.

Robbins, Alexandra, and Abbey Wilner. 2001. *Quarterlife Crisis: The Unique Challenges of Life in Your Twenties*. New York: Penguin Putnam.

Rofel, Lisa. 2002. "Modernity's Masculine Fantasies." In Bruce M. Knauft, ed., *Critically Modern: Alternatives, Alterities, Anthropologies*. Pp. 175–193. Bloomington: Indiana University Press.

Rogoff, Barbara. 2003. *The Cultural Nature of Human Development*. Oxford: Oxford University Press.

Ruddick, Sue. 2003. "The Politics of Aging: Globalization and the Restructuring of Youth and Childhood." *Antipode* 35 (2): 334–363.

Sassen, Saskia. 1998. *Globalization and Its Discontents*. New York: Free Press.

Scheper-Hughes, Nancy, and Carolyn Sargent, eds. 1998. *Small Wars: The Cultural Politics of Childhood*. Berkeley: University of California Press.

Scheper-Hughes, Nancy, and Daniel Hoffman. 1998. "Brazilian Apartheid: Street Kids and the Struggle for Urban Space." In Nancy Scheper-Hughes and Carolyn Sargent, eds., *Small Wars: The Cultural Politics of Childhood*. Pp. 352–388. Berkeley: University of California Press.

Schrum, Kelly. 2004. *Some Wore Bobby Sox: The Emergence of Teenage Girls' Culture, 1920–1945*. New York: Palgrave Macmillan.

Smith, Tom W. 2003. "Coming of Age in 21st Century America: Public Attitudes towards the Importance and Timing of Transitions to Adulthood." Chicago: National Opinion Research Center (NORC), University of Chicago.

Stephens, Sharon, ed. 1995a. *Children and the Politics of Culture*. Princeton, N.J.: Princeton University Press.

——. 1995b. "Children and the Politics of Culture in 'Late Capitalism.'" Introduction to Sharon Stephens, ed. *Children and the Politics of Culture*. Pp. 3–48. Princeton, N.J.: Princeton University Press.

Stoler, Ann Laura. 2002. *Carnal Knowledge and Imperial Power: Race and the Intimate in Colonial Rule*. Berkeley: University of California Press.

Stoler, Ann Laura, and Frederick Cooper. 1997. "Between Metropole and Colony: Rethinking a Research Agenda." In Frederick Cooper and Ann Laura Stoler, eds., *Tensions of Empire: Colonial Cultures in a Bourgeois World*. Pp. 1–56. Berkeley: University of California Press.

Taylor, Peter J., Michael J. Watts, and R. J. Johnston. 2002. "Geography/Globalization." In R. J. Johnston, Peter J. Taylor, and Michael J. Watts, eds., *Geographies of Global Change: Remapping the World*, 2nd edition. Pp. 1–17. Malden, Mass.: Blackwell.

Turner, Victor. 1957. *Schism and Continuity in an African Society: A Study of Ndembu Village Life.* Manchester: Manchester University Press.

Veblen, Thorstein. 1899. *The Theory of the Leisure Class: An Economic Study of Institutions.* New York: Macmillan.

Vitoria, Francisco de. 1991. "On the American Indians." In Anthony Pagden and Jeremy Lawrance, eds., *Vitoria: Political Writings.* Pp. 231–292. Cambridge: Cambridge University Press.

Waldman, Amy. 2003. "More 'Can I Help You?' Jobs Migrate from U.S. to India." *New York Times,* May 11. http://www.nytimes.com/.

Wallach, Glenn. 1997. *Obedient Sons: The Discourse of Youth and Generations in American Culture, 1630–1860.* Amherst: University of Massachusetts Press.

Weiner, Annette. 1980. "Reproduction: A Replacement for Reciprocity." *American Ethnologist* 7 (1): 71–85.

Werbner, Pnina, and Tariq Modood, eds. 1997. *Debating Cultural Hybridity: Multicultural Identities and the Politics of Anti-racism.* London: Zed Books.

Willis, Paul E. 1981 [1977]. *Learning to Labor: How Working Class Kids Get Working Class Jobs.* New York: Columbia University Press.

Wilson, Monica. 1951. *Good Company: A Study of Nyakyusa Age-Villages.* Oxford: Oxford University Press.

Wohl, Robert. 1979. *The Generation of 1914.* Cambridge, Mass.: Harvard University Press.

Yanagisako, Sylvia. 2002. *Producing Culture and Capital: Family Firms in Italy.* Princeton, N.J.: Princeton University Press.

Zelizer, Viviana. 1985. *Pricing the Priceless Child: The Changing Social Value of Children.* Princeton, N.J.: Princeton University Press.

1

Chinese Children, American Education

Globalizing Child Rearing in Contemporary China

T. E. WORONOV

Around the turn of the millennium, visitors to Beijing's largest bookstore, the six-story, state-owned Xinhua store at Xidan, might have noticed a new genre of books for sale. Among the rows and rows of books in the education section devoted to various aspects of child rearing were dozens of displays showing books with titles such as *How Americans Raise Their Daughters*, or *How to Raise Your Child to Get into Yale*, or *Sports and Art Classes in American Schools*. Clearly, there was something about American educational practices that Chinese authors were eager to write about, and that Chinese parents were eager to buy.[1]

As I learned during two years of fieldwork in elementary schools and among families in Beijing, American educational practices are the object of tremendous curiosity in the capital, so much so that I regularly struggled to extract information from various informants who were equally intent upon interviewing me. "Is it true," I was asked, "that American classrooms only have fifteen students? Do teachers and students actually sit on the floor? Do parents really throw their children out of the house at age sixteen so that they'll learn to be independent?" I fielded these kinds of questions not only from the Chinese parents and professional educators whom I was attempting to interview, but from all manner of people I spoke with in Beijing: taxi drivers and bus conductors, neighbors in my housing complex, and tofu vendors at the local outdoor market—all of whose first questions to me, upon learning that I am American, were about children in the U.S.

Why is American education of such interest to Chinese parents and educators? And what do their particular questions tell us about the highly contested issue of social reproduction—specifically, the question of how to prepare the next generation to meet the challenges of the future—in contemporary China? This chapter examines American educational practices as an ideological and marketing phenomenon in urban China today. I will focus on data gathered during my fieldwork and on two of the most popular volumes published in this deluge of information, both of which were huge sellers in the Beijing publishing market. *Harvard Girl Liu Yiting* and *Quality Education in the U.S.* were both ubiquitously available on the streets of the capital in 2001, selling over a million copies each and spawning follow-up volumes by the authors as well as countless imitators. Based on these materials, this chapter is a discussion of some of the global child-rearing tactics parents in different social classes are considering as possible ways to prepare their children for a transnational future. I argue that ongoing debates about how best to raise the next generation of Chinese children are linked both to the contingencies of China's national development and to the country's growing links to global capitalism. In their rapidly changing economy, urban Chinese parents are facing many contradictory pressures as they try to raise children who are simultaneously patriotically Chinese and globally cosmopolitan, and whose morals are both collectivist and capitalist. These tensions are condensed in the concept of children's "quality," which links the ideology of national development to children's development, and displaces concerns about the nation's future development into crises over child rearing at the level of individual Chinese families.

In China, social reproduction is understood to take place at the intersection of three pedagogical sectors: school-based education (*xuexiao jiaoyu*), family-based education (*jiating jiaoyu*), and the broad category of "societal" education (*shehui jiaoyu*), which refers to the wider social context in which education takes place. Because none of these sectors is seen to operate independently of the others, much of the child-rearing literature in China combines advice on practices that Americans would separate into "formal" and "informal" education, or into "education" (in schools) and "child rearing" (in homes). Within this context, I suggest that the recent fascination with American education indicates a growing change in how these sectors divide up the responsibility for raising China's children. The state is reducing or eliminating socialist-era welfare provisions, devolving responsibilities for employment and welfare onto individuals. At the same time, social reproduction is increasingly seen as the responsibility of individual families. American education, as it is defined in the best-selling genre of child-rearing manuals, provides both the model of how this can be accomplished and the goal of producing children who can attain American-style economic success. As Cole (this volume) notes, in the transformation from state socialism to global capitalism, value is increasingly derived from outside the nation's borders.

As Bourdieu and Passeron (1977) point out, all social reproduction is linked to class reproduction; in Beijing, parents are reacting to these transnational child-rearing models differently depending on their social class. Just as the state is ending the paternalism that was the hallmark of the socialist era, the middle and lower classes in China's capital are increasingly responsible for purchasing newly commodified welfare provisions that were formerly the purview of the socialist state. The question of who will care for these people in the future is now a central issue to these families, raising the serious question of children's changing responsibilities to their parents in the face of the breakdown of state-sponsored health, welfare, and retirement benefits. As I argue below, parents assess transnational child-rearing practices both practically and affectively, as they try to raise children who are simultaneously global subjects and recognizably Chinese.

Quality Children, Quality Nation

The spate of books, articles, and general discourse about American child rearing appeared in the context of serious reflection in China about whether or not local educational practices were adequate and appropriate for preparing a new generation of Chinese children for the future. There is tremendous social consensus in China that the nation's future goal is wealth, power, and respect within the international community, and that the only way to achieve this goal is through economic development. In the past twenty years, changing policies linked to national development have entirely reconfigured urban China's social and economic landscape; the question for parents is how to prepare children for these new and shifting conditions.

In the late 1970s, Chinese leader Deng Xiaoping initiated the first in a series of "opening and reform" policies with the "Four Modernizations" program, designed to rapidly modernize China's agricultural, industrial, defense, and science and technology sectors by importing foreign technology and management methods. In the early 1990s, these reforms accelerated extremely quickly, as the Chinese government began to dismantle the formerly centralized, planned economy, with the goal of replacing the radical egalitarianism of the Mao era with Western-style rational management techniques (Meisner 1996). Since then, foreign investment and an export-oriented economy have led to explosive economic growth and exponential rises in urban standards of living (White 1993).

During the past decade, this economic growth has been accompanied by large-scale state withdrawal from previously all-encompassing urban social welfare programs. The Chinese state is systematically smashing what had been known as "the iron rice bowl," which had guaranteed life-long employment, housing, and health care for many urban residents. Thus, new forms of wealth and economic opportunity that were unimaginable only ten years ago have also led to increasing insecurities about families' abilities to provide for themselves the basic services that until very recently had been the purview of the state. This new wealth, therefore, has also meant rising income disparities, as well as a rapidly widening income gap between China's urban and rural areas, and between the developed eastern seaboard and the impoverished western inland regions.

This move from Maoist egalitarianism to economic development through linking China with circuits of global capital has been predicated on wide-ranging ideological changes. Socialist-era values of collectivism, frugal self-denial for the national good, and devotion to building the communist future have given way to competition, economism, and a new, Western-style consumerism. At the same time, ideological and economic restructuring have been matched by a radical demographic shift resulting from the state's one-child-only policy. Since they were first implemented in the early 1980s, the state's birth control policies have been so successful in urban areas that virtually no children born in China's cities today have siblings.[2] In this context of the extremely rapid rate of socioeconomic, ideological, and demographic change, it is no wonder that Chinese parents, educators, and officials are concerned about social reproduction and how to prepare children for the nation's future.

During the past decade, these concerns have largely been framed as the problem of children's "quality" (*suzhi*). *Suzhi* is a common, everyday term in China, although its meaning is as fuzzy in Chinese as it is in English; at various times "quality" can refer to a child's educational level, bodily strength, height, patriotism, or morality.[3] Because of this, the word "quality" acts as a floating signifier in contemporary China, a term that is deployed in different ways in different contexts for different sociopolitical ends. In spite of the word's lack of a concrete referent, however, absolutely everyone I ever spoke with in Beijing believed strongly that *suzhi* is far too low in China, and that the quality of the population—particularly children—urgently needs to be raised to enable the nation to meet the challenges of the future.

Key to China's transformation from poverty, backwardness, and Maoist-era revolutionary excess is thus a new regime of biopolitics that posits lowering the size, but raising the quality, of the population. Economic development is predicated on linking China's formerly isolated economy with the global system, and the concept of *suzhi* is a way of defining the kind of high-quality subjects who could construct this new economy, bringing wealth and power to the Chinese nation (Anagnost 1997). Processes designed to raise children's quality are metonymic of those applied to the national economy. Just as national development is predicated on rational management, capital investment (particularly in high technology), and producing high-quality commodities for export, so does the goal of raising children's quality stipulate that parents should raise their children using methods proven by scientific experts, invest in capital equipment such as computers, and orient their children's developmental goals to the foreign market.

The Chinese central government's concern that national development will not be possible without appropriately developed children led to a set of education reform policies announced in the summer of 1999. Called "Education for Quality" (*Suzhi Jiaoyu*), this reform program has the specific goal of raising the quality of the nation's children in order to meet the economic needs of the new millennium. Although the actual policies that have been and will be implemented to achieve these goals are somewhat underelaborated, in its policy statements on the "Education for Quality" reform the Chinese government has been exceptionally clear about what it sees as the challenges facing the nation. In a 1999 speech to the Chinese State Council discussing the urgent need for education reform, Premier Zhu Rongji stated,

> Education is the essential foundation for economic development and social progress, and is the most important route to raising the quality [*suzhi*] of our people and their creative abilities. It is also the most reliable guarantee of how to increase our nation's strength in the global community, and our competitiveness in the twenty-first century. . . . In order to rapidly carry out our nation's modernization, radically strengthen our ability to compete internationally, greet the new century's opportunities and challenges, we have to put great effort into education . . . to foster high-quality workers and all kinds of professionals who are well suited to meet the requirements of the modernizing economy. (Ministry of Education 1999, 24)

The ability to study hard and learn facts, the education reformers further claim, will not be enough in the future; children instead need to be "well-rounded" (*quanmian fazhan*) so that they will have the physical and moral fitness to inherit China's new globalizing economy. Teachers, parents, and the state will have to work to foster children's creativity, independence, nationalism, and physical fitness, all factors identified as essential to producing a new generation of high-quality patriots who will be suited to the exigencies of the new economy. According to the official *Suzhi Jiaoyu* materials, all aspects of children's education, including curriculum, pedagogy, assessment, family-based child rearing, extracurricular activities, homework, sports, and even their eating habits, will need to be reformed in order to produce the high-quality children necessary for the future.

Although an in-depth discussion of the Education for Quality movement is beyond the scope of this paper, it is important to note a contradiction at the heart of this call for reform which did not escape the notice of the parents and teachers I spoke with in Beijing. All parents, teachers, and children in Beijing were painfully aware that in spite of the government's calls for "creativity" and an end to reliance on rote memorization, higher education is still rationed in China through an exam system based precisely on students' ability to memorize. Coveted slots in universities, seen as the absolutely essential prerequisite for future economic success, are allocated through a grueling system of local and national exams which culminate in the standardized university entrance exam administered to graduating high school seniors. Although officials of the Education Ministry are slowly introducing revisions to this test, entering college still depends almost entirely on a student's ability to memorize huge amounts of factual information.

Yet in spite of real structural constraints, parents and teachers all agreed: times are changing at an alarming rate, and education must change as well. And, although people rarely agreed on the exact definition of "quality," everyone I spoke with in China agreed that Chinese children have low quality, and that this quality must be raised for the good of the children, their families, and the nation as a whole. How, then, should children be prepared for the future? What kinds of children will be successful in China's new economy? It was in this context that everyone began talking about American child rearing, and the rash of materials on American education hit the market in Beijing.

Imagining America: Children and the
Cultural Politics of Transnationalism

The ideology of Education for Quality posits children as the link between China's present and its future, and between the nation as a collective and the individual families of which it is composed. But why are specifically American practices so intriguing? The answer is two-fold, connected to what the U.S. represents both as a model of capitalism and as the imagined representative of transnational space.

First, since Chinese parents wonder how best to prepare children to enter the economic system defined by global capitalism, they look to the nation that educates the best capitalists: the United States. The syllogism is simple: according to Chinese understandings, the U.S. must have achieved its status as the wealthiest and most powerful nation in the world by properly educating its youth. Therefore, the U.S. provides an appropriate model for education in China. As several people in Beijing told me directly, "We have to learn from you Americans how to educate our children. After all, you have a lot more practice than we do in raising capitalists." It is important to note, however, that in this scheme Chinese parents and educators do not intend to (re)produce their children as Americans. Instead, their goal is to identify and distill only the practices that make Americans good capitalists, and implement those. Nor are "capitalism" and "Americanization" simply conflated. In the view of Chinese educators, the U.S. is not entirely isomorphic with "global capitalism"; instead, America merely exemplifies successful national development in the global economy, and therefore provides the best possible model for parents and teachers to follow.[5]

At the same time, these best-selling child-rearing manuals on American education are only one segment of a much larger (and highly profitable) literary genre in contemporary China that describes life as an émigré in the English-speaking world. In China, national development and increasing links between the local and the global economies have not only led to a new search for appropriate models, but have also radically changed the concept of upward mobility, via new sociospatial hierarchies. Thus, parents and educators who are seeking the best ways to make their children upwardly mobile must attend carefully to changing opportunities afforded through the global system. These opportunities are transnational, connected with movements across borders.

Throughout Chinese history, but especially during the Maoist era, upward *social* mobility has always also been *spatial* mobility. During Imperial times, upward mobility into the ranks of the scholar-officials who administered the empire often meant moving to larger towns or provincial centers.[6] In this century, during the Mao era the state fixed all Chinese citizens in a spatial hierarchy through a system of residential permits. Even today, every Chinese person holds a residence permit or *hukou*, which classifies him or her as a rural resident or an urbanite. Each person's *hukou* classification is assigned at birth, inherited from the mother, and, until the past few years, was extremely difficult to change. In addition, the *hukou* system was not a simple binary between urban and rural; instead in the Mao era it was based on a spatial hierarchy that ranked every location in China. The centrally administered cities of Beijing, Shanghai, and Tianjin were at the top of the urban hierarchy, followed by provincial capitals, then smaller cities, and then towns. Below this were all of China's rural areas, where more than 60 percent of the population hold their *hukous*. Movement down the hierarchy was always possible: urban *hukou* holders could easily change their classification to rural, or could move from a large city to a smaller one; lateral movements were also possible. But movement up the scale, such as from a rural *hukou* area to an urban one, or from a small town to a larger city, was extremely difficult. The state controlled all upward spatial movement by a series of quotas, one of which was allocated through education. University students could move to a large city to attend college, and all university graduates were assigned state-sector jobs that carried urban *hukous*; in this way, educational achievement was directly linked to upward mobility, indexed by movement in space.

In the past decade, however, as the Chinese economy has become connected to the world economy, the Chinese sociospatial hierarchy has expanded to encompass the entire globe. As Ong (1997) points out, one effect of globalization in contemporary China is that the nation-state is no longer the only container for imagined communities (Anderson 1983). At the turn of the millennium, people's horizons of desire for their lives and their children's have expanded beyond China's territory out into the world (cf. Stephens 1995). Upward mobility for children is increasingly defined as movement outside of China's borders and into places associated with global wealth and power (Liu 1997).

Problems of child rearing thus revolve around these two concepts of the West, both of which are represented by the U.S. Just as the model of capitalist development is defined as lying outside the Chinese nation-state, so upward mobility is defined spatially as movement to the economic core. The growing media genre that describes life as a Chinese émigré in the Anglophone world serves as a form of "mediascape," or a set of scripts that present "narratives of possible lives" (Appadurai 1990, 299; see also Yang 1997; Chen 1995; Ong 1999). Parents who only a decade ago imagined their children moving to the high-status cities of Beijing or Shanghai can now envision for them possible lives in New York, Sydney, or Toronto.

Chinese books on American educational methods present contrasting technologies to show how to prepare children for the capitalist economy and achieve this spatially defined upward mobility. The following section explores the specifics of the two best-selling volumes in this genre. They are very similar in that both are linked to the trajectories of the global economy. In one, children are the ultimate exportable commodity, high enough quality to be acceptable at the ultimate arbiter of quality, Harvard. In the other, child rearing has moved from local to global production, as a father describes his son's education in an American elementary school. Yet the methods they propound for achieving this mobility are extremely different, reflecting both class differences between the two authors and how concepts of children's development have changed over the decade that separates the children at the center of each book. And, although these books were huge best-sellers and widely discussed and debated, Chinese parents had problems actually implementing both books' recommendations. I argue that these problems reflect class differences in contemporary Beijing, as members of different classes have differing access to transnational space, both as a literal destination and as an imagined future for their children.

Raising a Harvard Girl

Child Rearing and Rational Management

In the spring of 1999, eighteen-year-old high school senior Liu Yiting, from Chengdu, the capital of Sichuan Province, became the first Chinese student to be accepted as a full-fellowship undergraduate at Harvard.[7] She immediately became the object of tremendous media attention in China, and her family was besieged with requests for information as to how they educated their child to reach this level of educational success. In response to these requests, this young woman's mother, Liu Weihua, compiled a description of all the child-rearing methods she used with her daughter that produced such exalted results. Published in summer 2000 as *Harvard Girl Liu Yiting* (Liu and Zhang 2000), this child-rearing manual was reprinted at least thirteen times; by the time I purchased it in 2001, Liu Yiting was a household name in Beijing, and her mother's book was available at every bookstore and newsstand in the capital.[8]

As *Harvard Girl* makes clear from the first page, Liu Yiting's achievement was not a fluke, but was instead the outcome of her mother's detailed educational plans, which she began to implement even before the child was born. Upon conceiving her daughter, mother Liu Weihua was determined, in her words, to raise her child "scientifically." To do so, she put into effect a long-term plan to raise the child's *suzhi* (quality), with the assistance of several foreign child-rearing manuals that had been translated into Chinese in the early 1980s. The advice she then passes on to other Chinese parents is liberally sprinkled with quotes on child rearing attributed to such people as Thomas Edison, Pavlov, and former Sony Corporation chairman Akio Morita.

Liu Weihua kept a diary throughout her daughter's youth in order to scientifically document her child-rearing efforts and the results she achieved. Excerpts from this diary illustrate the many pointers she offers her readers. For example, when the baby was only two weeks old, Liu began training her daughter's attention span by using her fingers and stuffed toys to track the child's vision. By the age of nine months, Liu was deliberately putting objects out of Yiting's reach, requiring the baby to work ever harder to grasp what she wanted, in order to teach her persistence and to overcome difficulties. Liu Weihua took every moment with her child as a pedagogic opportunity; all daily practices were justified as a way of potentially teaching something useful. For example, when Liu or her mother took the baby for a stroll through their neighborhood after dinner—a virtually universal practice in urban China—she used this time to teach Yiting socialization skills and to encourage her to engage with others. At the same time, Liu Weihua used the strolling time to teach her daughter the names of all the objects they saw along the way, a practice which she identified in the book as enabling the child to talk, read, and write at a precociously early age.

This precociousness is repeated throughout the book, as the author makes clear that speed is of the utmost importance. Liu Weihua devoted much energy to comparing her daughter with other children in the neighborhood, noting how much faster Yiting acquired speech, fine motor coordination, and basic math and literacy skills. Upon reading this book, a parent of a child above the age of twelve to eighteen months could easily despair that it was already too late to begin the rigorous training that high-*suzhi* children require.

On her fourth birthday, Yiting began to read under her mother's tutelage. At the same time, Liu Weihua actively investigated the possibility of turning her daughter into a prodigy by beginning home tutoring of the first-grade curriculum, usually taught to children two or three years older. At that acceler-ated speed, she calculated that Yiting could finish high school and enter university by age twelve. However, Liu Weihua eventually rejected this plan for financial reasons: she would not have been able to pay for the tutors required to teach Yiting the higher-level math and science classes necessary to pass the university entrance exam. Philosophically, Weihua notes that it was probably for the best; after all, by continuing her education with her age cohort, Yiting developed better social skills, and was eventually able to enter Harvard, an option not available through the "prodigy" route.

Yiting's life is described as one of discipline, diligence, and time manage-ment. The mother praises her child for her precocious demonstrations of self-control and self-denial, and notes how with proper training she was able to focus her concentration for long periods without distraction and could tolerate all manner of hardships in order to reach her goals. In this respect, the book is resolutely not a manual of child psychology. Yiting's happiness is largely beside the point, and the things she does enjoy are generally instrumental to her mother's training plan. Thus, treats of ice cream and fresh fruit, the child's favorites, are doled out parsimoniously so as to teach the values of frugality and selflessness. Her mother uses activities Yiting enjoys, such as jumping rope, as vehicles for training discipline and perseverance; for example, she required the child to jump rope for an increasing number of minutes every day until she was able to win a rope-skipping contest at her elementary school. Yiting's own feelings are, literally, an open book: in *Harvard Girl* Liu Weihua quotes freely from her daughter's own diary to illustrate how Yiting's thoughts and emotions were developing along approved lines in conjunction with her behavior.

For Chinese readers, this book documents the rapidly changing social situation in China during the early reform era. Liu Yiting was born in 1981; her life has been virtually contemporaneous both with the start of the one-child-only policy (widely implemented in 1980) and with Deng Xiaoping's wide-ranging economic reforms (first initiated in late 1978). Liu Weihua's child-rearing strategies very clearly reflect the politics and the constraints of the times. As was (and still is) extremely common in urban China, for several years Liu Weihua had to turn over care of Yiting to the child's grandparents, who lived in a distant province; her employment did not allow her the time to care for her child, nor did she have enough money to hire caregivers. Weihua conscientiously provided her mother and Yiting's other caregivers with copies of the manuals she used to implement early child education, requesting that they read these materials, carry out their directions on a daily basis, and write frequent reports to her on the child's development. Intermixed with these stories of devoted family care are casual references to the politics and eco-nomics of the time: disruption in the household with the return of a relative who had been sent to a labor reform camp fifteen years earlier during the Cultural Revolution; the lack of access to telephones and other convenient methods of communication; the time constraints placed on parents by their employers in a planned economy with no labor mobility.

Liu Weihua is an outstanding example of the first generation of mothers who responded to the state's call to lower the quantity and raise the quality of the new generation. She exemplifies how to inculcate new forms of quality in a child, forms defined not by revolutionary praxis, selfless devotion to the na-tional good, or joining the laboring masses but by technocratic skills measured by educational achievement. To do so, Liu Weihua became the technocratic manager of her daughter's life, monitoring and controlling not only her time and activities, but those of all the other caregivers in Yiting's life. In this she was a model of a new kind of parenting for China's new era of globalization: the family as factory, and the parent as manager, rationally producing high-quality children. Following Emily Martin's (1987) work on the symbolic links between reproduction and the discourse of capitalist production, I suggest that in Liu's model, child rearing became tantamount to a rationalized industrial process, in which appropriate inputs are allocated and controlled in order to produce a high-quality output. In China's reform era, this model posits child rearing as a form of labor that has to be planned, managed, rationalized, and performed according to the appropriate models, so as to achieve the desired high-quality results (Veloso 2002; Martin 1987; Taylor 1999).

Harvard and the Space of Global Capital

In China, prodigies are made, not born; the premise of the entire *Harvard Girl* book is that any child, if raised the right way, can enter Harvard. This fetishization of Harvard in Liu's book (the cover of which shows Yiting holding her admission letter from the university) makes sense in the context of the dual functions the U.S. serves in the Chinese child-rearing literature. Harvard serves as both the best possible arbiter of children's quality and the ultimate destination for upwardly mobile movement.

Throughout the 1980s, one definition of "quality" was extremely clear: a university education. As soon as the national university entrance exam was reinstated in the late 1970s, after having been abolished during the Cultural Revolution (ca. 1966–1976), university degrees marked China's elite. College graduates were widely seen as the people who could best develop the nation, and who increasingly formed China's most privileged social group. It is clear in her text that Liu Weihua began grooming her daughter for admission into a prestigious university before the child could even walk. For example, Yiting was sent to her first day of school in first grade with the admonition that she would have to be among the top three students in her school when she finished sixth grade. Only then, she was warned, would she be able to enter a highly ranked junior high school, the first step toward eventual successful completion of the college entrance exams. And, beginning in first grade, Liu Weihua scheduled and monitored Yiting's study time to the minute, in order to prepare her for the rigors of the university exams twelve years in her future.

But the social context changed radically as Yiting reached junior high school. Beginning in 1992, Communist Party leader Deng Xiaoping greatly accelerated China's economic reform and opening to global investment. This had a tremendous and almost instantaneous effect on urban Chinese people's daily lives: the creation of a labor market, new housing opportunities, possibilities for capital investment, and domestic and international travel. As discussed above, this freeing up of Chinese bodies—to move to new jobs, new homes, new localities—also meant that the spatial hierarchies which had been in place since the 1949 revolution expanded greatly: now the imaginary of social mobility included the entire world. The pinnacle of a child's success was no longer admission into Beijing University, China's top-ranked university; upward mobility was increasingly measured by linking to the wider global system (Liu 1997).

If, as discussed above, Americans achieve their economic successes and global status through their education system, then, logically, the highest-quality Chinese child must be linked to the most famous—and, therefore, highest-quality—American educational institution: Harvard. In this respect, within China Harvard is a sign that condenses the educational processes that produce America's global strength and power. A symbol simultaneously both global and local, Harvard is seen as the epitome of the production of global value, and is deployed within China as the symbolic pinnacle of sociospatial success (cf. Sahlins 1988). Access to this source of foreign power and wealth has the potential to transform the future; admission to Harvard becomes the ultimate proof of ability and the greatest method to increase social status.

For Liu Weihua and her readers, China's reforms are thus not merely a set of economic policies, nor does the shift to global capitalism mean only the increasing availability of ideas, media, and products from other parts of the world (Appadurai 1990). For Chinese parents, just as for families in Botswana (Durham, this volume), China's links to the global economy also mean new family strategies, ways of using child rearing to link their families with global sources of value. As parents muster the different kinds of educational processes and resources available, child-rearing methods must change in order to produce an upwardly mobile child who can move upward into transnational space.

Ethnography in the U.S.

Like Liu Yiting, Huang Quanyu is also a household name in Beijing. Currently an educational consultant in the U.S. and China, he is the author of *Suzhi Jiaoyu zai Meiguo* (Education for Quality in the U.S., 2001). This book, an ethnographic study of American educational practices, was reprinted eighteen times, and was the best-selling nonfiction book in China that year. Since then he has published two follow-up volumes (*Play: The Cradle of Education for Quality in the U.S.*, and *Family-Based Education in the U.S.*). His high school–aged son, Huang Kuangyan, has also written a volume in Chinese about his experiences growing up in the U.S. All have sold well.

Although he holds a Ph.D. in education from an American university, Huang's books are written from his perspective as a parent raising a son in the U.S. rather than from that of an expert in educational theory. His "quality" book thus follows the model of a classic ethnography of socialization in the manner of Margaret Mead: it is based on participant observation in the target culture, and focuses on a category of practice ("education for quality") that holds meaning for his (Chinese) readers, not his (American) informants. In this case, he is interested in locating those practices in the U.S. that raise the "quality" (*suzhi*) of children such that Americans are able to achieve their astonishing success, defined by Huang as their enormous wealth and their ability to garner Nobel prizes. All of his ethnographic insights are comparative, and serve to illustrate his recommendations for improving the Chinese education system.

Huang's upper-middle-class suburban America is a land of bake sales, soccer leagues, and ballet classes, where his son's educational problems consist of conflicts with art teachers over how to teach drawing, and with his soccer coaches over how to get more time on the playing field. By fifth grade, Kuangyan had been admitted into a special class for the gifted and talented; in the text Huang claims that every American elementary school has an equivalent program, and treats the pedagogy and curriculum of this program as normative for all education in the U.S. Later, Kuangyan entered an elite private high school; this, too, is unmarked in the text. No Chinese person reading this book would ever know of the many problems Americans believe to be plaguing their education system, such as violence, school failure, and funding crises.

By erasing class, race, and region, Huang is able to use the schools and families in his suburban field site as representatives of American culture, not a particular class position. On this ground, American educational successes are a result of "American culture," while in comparison, failures of the Chinese education system are equally a result of cultural flaws. This, too, has historical antecedents: China has a long history of assessing its national poverty and weakness in relation to the world's imperial powers as stemming from flaws in Chinese "culture," and of attempting to eradicate those aspects of its culture which are seen as a brake on national development.[9]

In Huang's view, American "culture" is radical methodological individualism, mediated through a healthy dose of the Protestant ethic. Citing Abraham Maslow and G. H. Mead, Huang says that unlike Chinese, Americans value the real, inner person, rather than the superficial social roles each person has to play in life. Because the American education system encourages individual development and nurtures each student's genuine self, American children are self-actualized while their Chinese counterparts are not. Americans also teach their children to recognize and express their own needs and desires, while Chinese wait for others to recognize their abilities and needs. This gives American children the confidence to take risks and develop entrepreneurial skills. Huang further says that education is egalitarian and not hierarchical, which he claims stems from Americans' beliefs that all people are equal in the eyes of God. Parents and teachers in the U.S. are friends with children, who feel free to question and challenge their teachers and other adults, and in the process learn to create their own knowledge. In China, however, children are expected to be obedient and respectful, which translates pedagogically into students' having to memorize teachers' words by rote. In sum, American individualism, respect for children's inner selves, and egalitarianism are precisely what enable Americans' high levels of economic achievement.

Huang's guide through the thicket of American culture is his son, Kuangyan, who comes across in the text as a bright young man who is constantly surprising his parents with his Americanisms. Kuangyan's needs—to write a book report for school, prepare for an eighth-grade science fair, or just have his opinions heard and taken seriously by adults—are mined as cross-cultural data. Kuangyan's experiences with his teachers, coaches, classmates, and principals are described, analyzed, and presented to readers as indexes of how American educational and child-rearing practices are superior to Chinese in producing "high-quality" children who know more than facts and can do more intellectual tasks than memorize. For example, when their eight-year-old son arrived home and announced that he had to complete a research project for his second-grade class, his doctoral-candidate parents laughed at him: how could a child conduct research? In the end Huang lavishes astonished praise on the American assumption that even eight-year-olds can research a topic, and details his young son's growing ability to identify, research, and solve problems.

In particular, Huang portrays himself as constantly taken aback—but eventually delighted—with an education system that enabled his son to completely recast the expected relationship between a Chinese parent and child. To Huang's astonishment, Kuangyan challenged some of his father's criticisms with the comment "when you say that it hurts my feelings." He claims that in Chinese tradition such a comment would be unthinkable; Huang uses it as evidence of his child's growing ability to think and stand up for himself. In China, the traditional cultural value that "children respect teachers while teachers love students" prevents educators from recognizing the abilities of even very young children, who are instead expected to obey and respect their elders, and reproduce only what they're taught.

The focus on culture as the source of Chinese educational weaknesses and American strengths has another, more politicized dimension that does not escape Chinese readers. As mentioned above, *Quality Education in the U.S.* is only one of the most recent in a ten-year-old best-selling genre in China that describes life in America from the perspective of Chinese émigrés. As Chen (1995) and Yang (1997) point out, texts in this genre are read domestically as an elliptical critique of Chinese politics. For example, Huang includes a long disquisition on what he understands as American notions of meritocracy in education, which he defines as policies intended to develop children's "natural talent" and allow those with the "highest abilities" to rise to the top of the education system. To Chinese readers, this is a thinly veiled critique of China's radical egalitarian educational policies during the Cultural Revolution. In the same vein, debates in Kuangyan's gifted and talented class on contemporary events are presented as an implicit contrast to Chinese education, where political opinions are mandated and tested.

Beyond the question of politics, however, this book and its accompanying photos of the lush playing fields outside Kuangyan's private high school open to Huang's Chinese readers an entirely new imaginary: elite Western education. The level of detail he provides in describing the odd practices of the hugely admired Other—upper-middle-class Americans—demystifies the ways Americans produce value in their children and paints a vivid picture of the kind of lives led at the upper reaches of global capital. Huang devotes most of one chapter to describing the rites and rituals associated with the junior high school science fair; he documents in exceptional detail the arcana of intramural sports; he even translates into Chinese the entire pamphlet of rules and regulations that his son's school provides for parents.

This is one way to see ethnographically how global imaginaries are produced at the local level. Through Huang's ethnography, American educational practice becomes imaginable; Chinese parents who read his descriptions have opened to them new ways of thinking about the production of children. Huang's book describes a culture that produces value in children in very different ways, and provides a detailed guide to how this is being done. At the same time, this description gives Chinese parents a new horizon of desire for themselves and their children, a way to imagine new possibilities for lives lived in the space of global capital, as embodied by the Cincinnati suburbs.

Class and Technologies of the Family

In spite of the many differences between these two best-selling volumes, there are some interesting similarities.[10] Both Liu Weihua and Huang Quanyu identify new kinds of educational strategies, ways to prepare children for the future that they predict China's youth will face. The authors' proposed methods differ, but their goal is the same: a high-quality child, produced through appropriate educational practices. "Quality" is understood as a set of skills and abilities which enable a child both to produce value in a newly globalized economy and to eventually become upwardly mobile, defined as moving out of the Chinese territory and into global space. Liu Weihua's readers can imagine their own child at Harvard; Huang's readers can compare the details of their own child's education with that offered at the center of global wealth and power. Thus, for both authors (and their readers in China), national economic policies that link the Chinese economy with global capital have produced not only new imaginaries and opportunities, but child-rearing methodologies which may allow a family to achieve transnational upward mobility.

The differences between the two books are also telling. Liu Weihua's family strategy is managerial and high-modernist. She is the model mother who manages the raw material of her child, forming the next generation as a high-quality product which receives the imprimatur of the most highly valued global institution.

I talked to many parents in Beijing about *Harvard Girl*. Several of my wealthier informants admitted that they had purchased and read the book, but that they really did not like it very much. "She didn't give Yiting a lot of freedom," said one friend, the owner of an exclusive private preschool in Beijing. "My friends and I all agree: there wasn't a lot of concern for what the child herself ever wanted. We didn't like that."

Like these upper-class Chinese parents, I read *Harvard Girl* with a slowly mounting sense of horror. Yiting was made to study in the noisiest part of the house to learn concentration; required to jump rope every day to learn the discipline to train for competitions. Her study time was scheduled to the fraction of a minute; as she got older she was required to sit perfectly still with her homework and review books, with no distractions allowed. Study breaks were also timed to the second; she worked off the accumulated stress and energy of long periods of sitting still by running up and down the stairs of the apartment building in which she lived.

In this respect, the biggest problem with this book is, perhaps, its age. Liu Weihua, raising her child in the 1980s, was still deeply concerned with inculcating in her daughter particularly Chinese values: determination, perseverance, an ability to tolerate hardships, a willingness to forego immediate satisfaction for the delayed gratification of future achievement. These moral values are not only a remnant of "traditional Chinese culture"; they were also the basis for moral action during the Mao era (Yang 1994). But by the year 2000, these values read as decidedly old-fashioned to many well-off urban Chinese parents, who are increasingly drenched in the values of the bourgeois West: self-actualization, creative self-expression, and instant gratification through consumption. Liu Weihua wrote about how to use Chinese technologies of the family to produce an upwardly mobile child; among young, upper-middle-class Chinese parents the concern now is how to use Western technologies to accomplish the same thing.

In contrast, *Quality Education in the U.S.*, written about a child born in the early 1990s, reads like a training manual for embourgeoisement. Rather than managing his child's education, Huang presents a model of *laissez-faire* parenting. The American model he describes strongly resembles neoliberal economic theories which posit a hands-off regulatory approach to the economy, in order to allow the invisible hand to guide the market to optimum performance. In Huang's view, parenting must similarly allow children to identify and cultivate their true, inner selves. In this model, the child himself contains innate value, and Huang praises American educators for recognizing innate differences within children. This elitism, disguised as meritocracy, is what he claims produces success in the global economy. This is in direct contrast to Liu Weihua's assumption that any child can be made into a prodigy if the right kinds of parental efforts are applied; her readers are encouraged to believe that any of their children can also be accepted to Harvard.

For Huang, children must be released from their social roles—particularly the rigid, hierarchical parent-child relationship of Chinese tradition—in order to realize their innate abilities and to become independent and creative risk-takers. This is in many ways a definition of technologies of the self in the classic liberal model described by Foucault (1978, 1988, 1991) and Rose (1999): children are taught the "conduct of conduct" through an education system predicated on locating, nurturing, and extending the "true self" within each child. Foucault and subsequent writers argue persuasively that this concept is at the heart of the bourgeois liberal subject.[11] Huang's description of American education is propounding not only a different kind of education system, but an entirely new concept of the child as cultural and political subject: from the socialist subject of China's revolution, to the self-propelled bourgeois subject of American liberalism.

As I discussed family strategies and differing child-rearing practices with informants across Beijing, it became clear that their interpretations of the messages encapsulated in these two best-selling books depended at least partially on social class. Parents with high levels of education, international connections, and healthy savings accounts saw Liu Weihua's book as hopelessly inappropriate. Liu Yiting may have been admitted to Harvard, but she does not display the independent self-actualization so evident in the American children Huang Quanyu describes. These parents can aspire—and afford—to send their child to American high schools and then to elite universities, so that the next generation can begin the motion across space that indexes and produces social value. They are interested in the best ways to produce self-actualized children, and the most up-to-date American methods are relevant and tempting to them.

Many Beijing residents, however, are not getting wealthy in China's new economy. Instead, they are hanging on as best they can amidst extremely rapid change and insecurity. They are terribly concerned to prepare their single children for the future by teaching them the necessary skills to enter the new economy and to have access to upward mobility by moving through transnational space. However, to these parents, too, Liu Weihua's recommendations seem inappropriate—not just because when implemented they may produce the wrong kind of child-subject, but because these parents have been unable to inculcate Liu Yiting–style discipline in their children.

For example, when I visited the home of some friends in Beijing, the mother of the family was sighing in annoyance at her gangly teenage son, who was stretched out in front of the television, intently updating his statistical notes on his favorite NBA players. "If he spent as much time on his homework as he does watching basketball, he'd be at the top of his class," she told me. Having read *Harvard Girl* and other books in that genre, both she and her son were quite anxious to be connected with the wider world beyond China, to have access to global knowledge, practices, and ideas. For the mother this meant her son's admission into an elite American university, while the young man imagined center-court seats at a Lakers game. "I can't imagine how many American parents are saying the exact same thing about their kids right now," I replied, hoping to assuage some of her concern. Her response, however, was incredulity: having also read Huang's book, she believed that no American teenager would waste so much time watching television.

Another, more distressing, example occurred in a small working-class elementary school in Beijing where I was conducting fieldwork. At the school's open house for parents, the principal tapped me on the shoulder to ask if I could talk with one of the parents, who had asked to meet with me. When I entered the school's conference room I found a woman in her early thirties, anxiously wringing her hands.

"I wanted to ask your advice because you're American," she told me. "My daughter isn't disciplined. She has no interests at all except playing. I've tried to get her to take art and music classes, and enrolled her in extracurricular math and English classes, but she didn't want to do any of them and refused to do any work. She just plays. Tell me what I should do to get her to stop playing so much."

"How old is your daughter?" I asked, expecting a frustrated mother of a recalcitrant sixth-grader.

"She's six," she replied. "She just started first grade."

I paused for a moment, then gave the only answer I could think of. "Don't you think it's normal for a six-year-old to want to play?" I asked. "Maybe she'll get more disciplined as she gets a little older."

The woman's eyes filled with tears. "If that's all you can say, then I guess I'll just leave now," she told me, and left the room, sniffling. My heart sank at my inability to help her and with pity for her child; at the same time, I was fascinated by her assumption that as an American—from the belly of the capitalist beast—I would have expert advice ready on how to instill in her child the discipline necessary for the capitalist economy.

"But We Love Our Children"

If Liu Weihua's methods for getting a child into Harvard are causing much frustration among middle- and working-class parents in Beijing, Huang Quanyu's Americanized methods are even less accessible. "I don't know how you Americans do it," sighed one of my friends in Beijing, the father of a sixth-grade son. "It's a real problem for us Chinese." The problem, in his eyes, is the difference between parent-child relations in China and those which they believe characterize American families.

Everyone I spoke with in Beijing, agreeing with (and perhaps quoting) Huang Quanyu, believed that Americans raise capitalists by fostering two specific skills: independence and creative risk taking. It was common knowledge in Beijing among the people I spoke with that American parents begin fostering independence in their children very early. I was told, for example, that American parents do not feed their babies after they are weaned. Instead, food is placed in front of the child, who will, upon getting hungry and desperate enough, teach himself how to eat. To Chinese parents, who demonstrate love and concern by following even middle school–aged children around the house with special morsels of food, this is an inconceivable cruelty. This is what makes the American model difficult for middle-class Chinese parents to implement, for inculcating independence requires harder hearts than they are capable of.

Other examples abound. When an American child falls down, her parents will not help her up and comfort her, for she must learn to take risks and help herself if she fails. Most difficult of all is the American practice of severing all ties between parents and their offspring as soon as the child graduates from high school as a way to force children into living independently. Chinese parents I knew would sigh in frustration over this practice, reminding me that families are still very important in Chinese culture, and bemoaning their inability to ever raise sufficiently independent children. "We want our children to be independent and creative like you Americans," my friends would tell me, "but we love our children too much. We could never be so coldhearted to them."

All of my efforts to counter these Chinese urban legends about American education were in vain; I was never sure that my interlocutors believed me. Several were visibly surprised when I mentioned that even as an adult I was still in close contact with my family in the U.S. Huang Quanyu does not help this situation much, for his ethnography of middle-class American life does little to dispel these stereotypes of American child rearing. He notes in passing how, during holiday celebrations, his American friends put all the children at a separate dining table, allowing them to "feed themselves"; in another section he marvels at how an American couple he befriends ignore their tantrum-throwing toddler, waiting for him "to cry himself out." While he uses both of these examples to praise Americans for allowing children to "be themselves," the implication Chinese readers derive is of emotional distance and lack of human warmth among family members. Nothing was able to shake parents' conviction that the love Chinese parents feel for their children formed an obstacle which prevented them from ever attaining American-style independence and its concomitant economic success. The independence of American children seems to come at a very high cost.

I never learned the origin of any of these "facts" about American child rearing; but the truthfulness of these practices is largely beside the point. Chinese parents' misunderstandings of American child rearing are "not [derived from] the reality of what the West offers, but, like Occidentalism in general, [are] a self-contained, self-referential reality, the terms of which are determined in local standards" (Besnier 2002, 554; see also Chen 1995).

What is this "love" that's at risk? It is, of course, a structure of feeling: a collective, social, and private space beyond semantic availability, an emergent force that is not yet ideology (Stoler 2002). As both Lamb (this volume) and Durham (this volume) point out, the question of familial love and care—which seems so vulnerable at the moment—is related to the new economy. I believe that in China, as the social welfare system breaks down, all that's left for most families are affective bonds. How can their relations with their own children resemble cold, heartless, capitalist social relations, the way they do in the U.S.? And if their children don't love them back, who or what will support them in their old age? I also suggest that it is around these kinds of affective relations within the family that a particularly *Chinese* child is being developed. As children and child rearing are increasingly influenced by global economic, political, and cultural forces and flows, and as Chinese parents attempt to distill American child-rearing practices that produce good global capitalists, (some) family relationships are becoming privileged as the way that Chinese-ness is assured in the next generation. As Huang himself argues, a reductionist notion of "Chinese culture" is seen as the source of inadequate child-rearing skills, and as preventing Chinese children from achieving American-style economic success. Some analysts have described this way of imagining the nation as increasingly rooted in the family, rather than the collective, as a newly resurgent form of Confucianism (Tu 1994); the data I'm presenting, however, argues that these moves are mirrored in neoliberal forms of the family and political participation globally (see Greenhalgh 1994b; also Ong 1997; Comaroff and Comaroff 2005; Magazine and Sánchez, this volume). In other words, in a marvelous irony, the reductionist notion of "Chinese culture"—here coded as "familial love"—that these families see as inhibiting their children's participation in global capitalism is in many ways the same reductionist culture—coded as "Confucianism"—that many Chinese people in Southeast Asia claim forms the basis of their capitalist successes (Ong 1999).

Epilogue: The Backlash

Most likely in response to the significant frustration many Chinese parents felt with carrying out the suggestions of Huang's and Liu's volumes, at the end of 2001 and into 2002 yet another wave of child-rearing manuals hit Beijing's booksellers. With titles such as *Relax, and Still Send Your Child to Harvard* and *Don't Worry So Much about Your Children*, these books promised to reduce pressure on parents and children, yet still produce high-quality, globalized youth. As one book cover proclaimed, "Every parent can do it!"

Yet the contents of these books belied the advertising; while the *Relax* book claimed that the model child at the center of the book's child-rearing regime was "just a regular girl," closer examination shows that she was China's youngest software engineer, a student leader at top-ranked Beijing University, and at the book's publication was a doctoral candidate in physics at Harvard. The author of the *Don't Worry* volume graduated at age twenty-eight from Harvard Business School.

This indicates that even though the specific methods may be contested, there is still tremendous concern over how to raise a high-quality child who is prepared to succeed in the new economy and to move beyond China's borders into global spaces defined by institutions such as Harvard. It remains to be seen whether or not this new round of books will provide better child-rearing techniques for parents across a range of social classes in Beijing, or if yet another crop of manuals will be required to keep addressing this problem. What is clear is that the question of how to prepare children for the uncertain future is still a central issue in China, and that the answer will, at least for now, be couched in terms that refer to America.

NOTES

I would like to thank the Committee on Scholarly Communication with China and the American Council of Learned Societies for funding my research in Beijing from 1999 to 2001. Writing this chapter was made possible by the Spencer Foundation and the Lichstern Fund of the Department of Anthropology at the University of Chicago. I have benefited tremendously from the generous comments and assistance of the editors and of Mary Ann O'Donnell, Lourdes Gutierriez, Wang Gan, Alex Dent, Jeffrey Jurgens, Jennifer Gaynor, and Helen Faller. All translations from Chinese are my own.

1. "China" in this chapter is an admittedly inaccurate shorthand for urban China. Although 60 percent of China's population live in rural areas, the practices and discourses described below are largely confined to the nation's larger and more prosperous urban centers.

2. China's birth policies have changed over time. For a history, see White 1994; Greenhalgh 1994a.

3. The problem of population quality is not confined to children; tremendous discursive effort is also put into identifying and ameliorating low quality among various groups of Chinese adults as well. See Anagnost 1997; Jeffery 2001.

4. According to the Chinese State Council, approximately 9 percent of China's eighteen- and nineteen-year-olds are able to enter universities (Ministry of Education 1999, 5).

5. China has a century-long history of identifying and following foreign models in education. These models have largely, although not exclusively, been American. See, e.g., Pepper 1996.

6. There is an extensive literature on upward mobility during various segments of China's long Imperial past; Chaffee (1995) includes a synopsis of the arguments that link success in the Imperial examination system with social mobility.

7. All Chinese names in this text are in Chinese order, family names first.

8. The *New York Times* (April 14, 2002) places sales of this volume at 1.1 million; the Harvard University alumni magazine says sales exceeded 1.43 million (Levenson 2002, 88).

9. A large literature discusses the role of "tradition" and "culture" in China's modernization efforts at the turn of the century. See Huters 1993 for a synopsis.

10. I thank Mary Ann O'Donnell for her assistance with this section.

11. See also the collections Barry, Osborne, and Rose 1996; and Burchell, Gordon, and Miller 1991.

WORKS CITED

Anagnost, Ann. 1997. *National Past-Times: Narrative, Representation, and Power in Modern China*. Durham, N.C.: Duke University Press.

Anderson, Benedict. 1983. *Imagined Communities*. New York: Verso.

Appadurai, Arjun. 1990. "Disjuncture and Difference in the Global Cultural Economy." *Theory, Culture, and Society* 7: 295–310.

Barry, Andrew, Thomas Osborne, and Nikolas Rose, eds. 1996. *Foucault and Political Reason: Liberalism, Neo-liberalism, and Rationalities of Government*. London: UCL Press.

Besnier, Niko. 2002. "Transgenderism, Locality, and the Miss Galaxy Beauty Pageant in Tonga." *American Ethnologist* 29 (3): 534–566.

Bourdieu, Pierre, and Jean-Claude Passeron. 1977. *Reproduction in Education, Society, and Culture*. Trans. Richard Nice. London: Sage Publications.

Burchell, Graham, Colin Gordon, and Peter Miller, eds. 1991. *The Foucault Effect: Studies in Governmentality*. Chicago: University of Chicago Press.

Chaffee, John W. 1995. *The Thorny Gates of Learning in Sung China*. Albany: State University of New York Press.

Chen, Xiaomei. 1995. *Occidentalism: A Theory of Counter-Discourse in Post-Mao China*. Oxford: Oxford University Press.

Comaroff, Jean, and John Comaroff. 2005. "Reflections on Youth, from the Past to the Postcolony." In *Makers and Breakers: Children and Youth in Postcolonial Africa*. Alcinda Honwana and Filip De Boeck, eds. Pp. 19–30. London: James Currey.

Foucault, Michel. 1978. *The History of Sexuality*. Trans. Robert Hurley. New York: Vintage.

——. 1988. "The Ethic of Care for the Self as a Practice of Freedom." In *The Final Foucault*. James Bernauer and David Rasmussen, eds. Pp. 1–20. Cambridge, Mass: MIT Press.

——. 1991. "Governmentality." In *The Foucault Effect: Studies in Governmentality*. Graham Burchell, Colin Gordon, and Peter Miller, eds. Pp. 87–104. Chicago: University of Chicago Press.

Greenhalgh, Susan. 1994a. "Controlling Births and Bodies in Village China." *American Ethnologist* 21 (1): 3–30.

——. 1994b. "De-Orientalizing the Chinese Family Firm." *American Ethnologist* 21 (4): 746–775.

Huang Quanyu. 2001. *Suzhi Jiaoyu zai Meiguo* [Education for Quality in the U.S.]. Guangzhou: Guangdong Educational Press.

Huters, Theodore. 1993. "Ideologies of Realism in Modern China: The Hard Imperatives of Imported Theory." In *Politics, Ideology, and Literary Discourse in Modern China: Theoretical Interventions and Cultural Critique*. Liu Kang and Xiaobing Tang, eds. Pp. 147–173. Durham, N.C.: Duke University Press.

Jeffery, Lyn. 2001. "Placing Practices: Transnational Network Marketing in Mainland China." In *China Urban: Ethnographies of Contemporary Culture*. Nancy Chen, C. Clark, S. Gottschang, and L. Jeffery, eds. Pp. 23–42. Durham, N.C.: Duke University Press.

Levenson, Eugenia V. 2002. "Harvard Girl." *Harvard Magazine*, July–August 2002. http://www.harvardmagazine.com/on-line/0702109.html.

Liu Weihua and Zhang Xinwu. 2000. *Hafo nuhai Liu Yiting* [Harvard Girl Liu Yiting]. Beijing: Zuojia Chubanshe.

Liu, Xin. 1997. "Space, Mobility, and Flexibility: Chinese Villagers and Scholars Negotiate Power at Home and Abroad." In *Ungrounded Empires: The Cultural Politics of Modern Chinese Transnationalism*. Aihwa Ong and Donald M. Nonini, eds. Pp. 91–114. New York: Routledge.

Martin, Emily. 1987. *The Woman in the Body: A Cultural Analysis of Reproduction.* Boston: Beacon Press.

Meisner, Maurice. 1996. *The Deng Xiaoping Era: An Inquiry into the Fate of Chinese Socialism.* New York: Hill and Wang.

Ministry of Education, People's Republic of China. 1999. *Shenhua jiaoyu gaige, quanmian tuijin suzhi jiaoyu* [Strengthen Educational Reform, Fully Implement Education for Quality]. Beijing: Gaodeng Jiaoyu Chubanshe.

Ong, Aihwa. 1997. "Chinese Modernities: Narratives of Nation and of Capitalism." In *Ungrounded Empires: The Cultural Politics of Modern Chinese Transnationalism.* Aihwa Ong and Donald M. Nonini, eds. Pp. 171–202. New York: Routledge.

——. 1999. *Flexible Citizenship: The Cultural Logics of Transnationality.* Durham, N.C.: Duke University Press.

Pepper, Suzanne. 1996. *Radicalism and Education Reform in 20th-Century China: The Search for an Ideal Development Model.* Cambridge: Cambridge University Press.

Rose, Nikolas. 1999. *Governing the Soul: The Shaping of the Private Self.* London: Free Association Books.

Sahlins, Marshall. 1988. *Cosmologies of Capitalism: The Trans-Pacific Sector of "The World System."* Proceedings of the British Academy 74.

Stephens, Sharon. 1995. "Children and the Politics of Culture in 'Late Capitalism.'" Introduction to *Children and the Politics of Culture.* Sharon Stephens, ed. Pp. 3–48. Princeton, N.J.: Princeton University Press.

Stoler, Ann. 2002. *Carnal Knowledge and Imperial Power: Race and the Intimate in Colonial Rule.* Berkeley: University of California Press.

Taylor, Janelle Sue. 1999. "Mediating Reproduction: An Ethnography of Obstetrical Ultrasound." Ph.D. diss., University of Chicago.

Tu, Wei-Ming. 1994. *The Living Tree: The Changing Meaning of Being Chinese Today.* Stanford: Stanford University Press.

Veloso, Leticia. 2002. "The Right-Bearing Baby: Childrearing Practices, 'Real Childhood,' and Stratified Reproduction in Brazil." Rio de Janeiro: Unpublished ms.

White, Gordon. 1993. *Riding the Tiger: The Politics of Economic Reform in Post-Mao China.* Stanford: Stanford University Press.

White, Tyrene. 1994. "The Origins of China's Birth Planning Policy." In *Engendering China: Women, Culture, and the State.* Christina K. Gilmartin, Gail Hershatter, Lisa Rofel, and Tyrene White, eds. Pp. 250–278. Cambridge, Mass.: Harvard University Press.

Yang, Mayfair Mei-hui. 1994. *Gifts, Favors, and Banquets: The Art of Social Relationships in China.* Ithaca, N.Y.: Cornell University Press.

——. 1997. "Mass Media and Transnational Subjectivity in Shanghai: Notes on (Re)Cosmopolitanism in a Chinese Metropolis." In *Ungrounded Empires: The Cultural Politics of Modern Chinese Transnationalism.* Aihwa Ong and Donald M. Nonini, eds. Pp. 287–322. New York: Routledge.

2

Continuity and Change in San Pedro Tlalcuapan, Mexico

Childhood, Social Reproduction, and Transnational Migration

ROGER MAGAZINE AND
MARTHA ARELI RAMÍREZ SÁNCHEZ

This chapter explores the effects of accelerated transnational migration on children's activities and on intergenerational relations in the Mexican village of San Pedro, Tlalcuapan, Tlaxcala. During the first three-quarters of the twentieth century, sons and daughters from ages eight to eighteen traveled to nearby cities to work as domestic servants, contributing most of their earnings to the family budget. With increasing opportunities for year-round employment in the U.S. service sector in the 1970s, however, this pattern soon changed. As older, but generally still unmarried, sons and daughters began to take advantage of these opportunities, the increased value of remittances sent to parents soon made it possible to keep younger siblings close to home, safe from the abuses of domestic service, and in school for longer. Yet it is important to add that these changes, while not inconsequential, are the foreground to significant continuities. Younger children have not stopped working despite the improved economic situation and pressure from schools. Rather, they contribute to the family economy in new ways in and around the home and continue to treat their relationship with parents as one of interdependence. Also, and in connection with the previous point, while the dynamics of social reproduction have shifted, their overall form has not: Tlalcualpeños, young and old, continue to propel the domestic development cycle by a series of long-term exchanges. We will suggest that these continuities may even contribute to U.S. employers' apparent preference for rural Mexican labor, which would imply that local processes of social regeneration are not simply products of or responses to broader political-economic processes—they may help to shape them as well, albeit in unintended ways.

These changes and continuities were clearly reflected in two aspects of village life that caught our notice during fieldwork.[1] First, we observed that children begin contributing to the household economy as early as the age of two and continue to do so until they marry and thereby attain the status of full adulthood. Ten- or eleven-year-olds, for example, often dedicate up to twelve hours a day to such activities, which include feeding domestic animals, cleaning and other domestic chores, working in the fields, and helping their parents in work outside the home. Tlalcualpeños rarely see these long hours as abusive or exploitative, and furthermore, they do not usually see this work solely as a means to teach children to be responsible, hard-working adults. Instead, they view these activities as one half of an exchange with parents in which the latter provide unmarried daughters and sons with nurture in the form of food, clothing, school expenses, and spending money and, eventually, with an inheritance. In other words, children do not work primarily out of necessity or for educational reasons, but rather because familial relations and the process of social reproduction are conceived of in terms of interdependence.

The second aspect of village life that initially caught us off guard was the number of houses constructed in a suburban California style, complete with automatic garage door openers. We soon learned that more than half the villagers work in California and maintain strong ties to village life as evidenced not only by the houses but also by the recent completion of several public works projects, including schools and roads, funded directly and indirectly by remittances. Further research revealed links between transnational migration and the presence of children working there in the village. The remittances from migrants make possible not only the automatic garage door openers, but also the obviation of children's work as domestic servants in nearby cities. And furthermore, most villagers describe migration in terms of participation in exchanges between sons and daughters and parents, so that unmarried sons' and daughters' motivations are the same as those of their younger siblings working close to home: they migrate and send remittances in reaction to the nurture their parents have already given them and in anticipation of the inheritance they will one day receive. Thus, while this recent phase of global capitalist expansion has clearly left its mark on sons' and daughters' activities and on intergenerational relations, villagers have incorporated the changes into the broader framework of earlier practices of social reproduction. Before proceeding with our discussion of these recent changes, we will describe this broader framework of local practices of social reproduction within which they occur. But first, a point of reference for comparative purposes is needed.

A Modern European Version of Childhood and Social Reproduction

The comparison we wish to draw is to a conception of childhood that emerged in Europe during the seventeenth and eighteenth centuries (Ariès 1987). It is important to note from the start that this comparison between childhood in Tlalcuapan and this version of childhood with European origins is not an abstract contrast between the so-called traditional and modern. Rather, each side of the comparison is based on empirical sources, and we treat them as two culturally and historically specific versions among many. Our aim is conceptual contrast within the confines of this chapter. We employ this European version as our point of reference not because we privilege its distinctiveness, but rather because it holds a privileged position in the social sciences. Further, instead of assuming that childhood in Tlalcuapan exists in a temporally separate, traditional world that "articulates" with the modern one, our intention is to show that it is just as much part of contemporary global capitalism as is the European version and just as open to influence, transformation, and adaptation.

According to Philippe Ariès, in this European version of childhood children are seen as a category of persons distinct from adults, characterized by their innocence and fragility (1987, 434). They therefore require special care and treatment from adults as parents and as educators to protect them from and prepare them for the adult world, including, in particular, the world of work (541). An education system emerges to fulfill these objectives of protection and preparation (434), as does a new family form dedicated to the promotion and well-being of sons and daughters (534).

Marilyn Strathern (1992), in her discussion of twentieth-century English kinship, puts it somewhat differently. To paraphrase, children are born into a state of nature. Their successful conversion into fully human social individuals (their socialization) requires the inculcation of cultural conventions through education. At the same time, the reproduction of society depends upon the successful transmission of its cultural conventions through individuals from one generation to the next. One of the cultural conventions children must learn for social reproduction to occur is how to act as independent individuals; that is, as agents capable of authoring their own acts and taking charge of the socialization of the next generation. Another is the importance of society itself and its reproduction through socialization. Once transmitted, each of these conventions constitutes one side of motivation, which is imagined as a combination of "will" coming from within individuals as agents and of social convention itself, as when people are said to act following social values. Thus, while for Ariès the relationship between independent adults and dependent children derives from and resolves the problem of children's innocence and fragility, for Strathern it derives from and resolves the broader problem of social reproduction—in the dual sense of reproducing socialized individuals and society itself—in the face of nature's reappearance in each new generation of children.

The issue of reproducing capitalist relations of production is often imagined in a similar manner: unless people are taught the social significance of work, a "stone-age economics" prevails in which they only work to fulfill natural basic necessities. But the problem is also more specific. Capitalism requires different kinds of persons/workers in different places and times: for example, disciplined in the context of Fordism (Harvey 1990, 126) and flexible in that of flexible accumulation (Martin 1994). Studies such as Paul Willis's *Learning to Labour* (1977) look specifically to childhood and the education system to explain how both particular types of workers and class relations more generally are reproduced with limited need of force. A similar perspective is present in migration studies. Roger Rouse, for example, argues that the Mexican migrants he studied in California don't simply adapt to life in the U.S. Rather, they are the objects of disciplinary "cultural pressures that work to make their daily habits and routines more consistent with the interests of capital" (1992, 31). One of the principal ways that these pressures work is by causing migrants to internalize "values and beliefs so that eventually they will regulate themselves" (31). He adds briefly that "similar but much less rigorous influences" have emerged in the migrants' hometown (31). Presumably, Rouse would explain decisions to migrate in the first place in terms of these influences and the values and beliefs they promote. Our findings suggest, however, that the difference between forms of motivation found by Rouse in the U.S. and those we found in Tlalcuapan is not one of degree or even content, but one of kind. That is, a key difference between Tlalcualpeños and the settled migrants Rouse describes is not that the former have experienced less cultural pressure to internalize values nor that they have internalized different values. Instead, we posit that the whole notion of the internalization of beliefs and values, which is inextricably linked to the modern European version of childhood and social reproduction described above, has limited utility for understanding why Tlalcualpeños do what they do. Following a brief description of the research setting, we will approach the question of what motivates Tlalcualpeños to work and to migrate through a look at local notions of childhood, social reproduction, and intergenerational relations.

San Pedro Tlalcuapan

Tlalcuapan is a village of approximately 2,700 residents located five kilometers from Santa Ana Chiautempan, the municipal seat; a half-hour drive from the city of Tlaxcala, the state capital; a forty-minute drive from Puebla, a regional industrial center; and a two-hour drive from Mexico City. The village lies at the foot of the volcano known as La Malinche, in a densely populated rural area including over fifteen other villages. Tlalcualpeños are Spanish-speakers, although members of the oldest generation also know Nahuatl, an indigenous language. While they are not classified as indigenous according to official, language-based definitions, they share many of the sociocultural features found in villages throughout the Mesoamerican region. These include community membership defined by descent and reinforced through participation in community projects, such as the celebration of fiestas for patron saints, and a development cycle of domestic groups characterized by virilocal postmarital residence and ultimogeniture of the dwelling site.

Up until the mid-nineteenth century the land currently occupied by the village formed part of a hacienda, El Rancho de San Juan. The villagers' predecessors were bound to the hacienda as peons until it closed down and the villagers received part of its land.[2] Currently, most residents own small plots dedicated to the cultivation of corn and beans. In addition, the village possesses communal land on the volcano's slope that residents use for pasture and for the collection of firewood and mushrooms for consumption and for sale. Up until forty years ago, these were the principal economic activities within the village. Tlalcualpeños did not work in the textile and other industries in Puebla and Mexico City that employed most of the residents of some of the other villages in the area over much of the twentieth century. Nor did they specialize in the artisanal production of a particular product such as blankets, bread, or pottery, as did residents of still other villages in the area. This lack of participation in local or regional economic activities meant that when the bracero program[3] became available to villagers in 1957, many families took advantage of the opportunity and sent fathers and sons to work as seasonal agricultural laborers in southern California.

In the late 1970s, the migration pattern among villagers began to change, principally in response to the increasing demand for Mexican workers in the U.S. service sector brought about by the "growing polarization of the [U.S.] labor market" (Rouse 1991, 13).[4] Fathers and sons started to stay in California year-round, settling principally in two cities, Oxnard and Costa Mesa.[5] Many of them left seasonal agricultural jobs to work in the service sector as cooks, dishwashers, waiters, cashiers, and gardeners. Their remittances became the chief source of income for their wives, children, mothers, and younger siblings at home. Some of these migrants obtained U.S. residency and brought family members to live with them. So many villagers now live in California that Tlalcualpeños often state that now there are two Tlalcuapans, one in California and one in Tlaxcala. They consider the communities in Oxnard and in Costa Mesa to constitute one Tlalcuapan because the two communities gather together to celebrate the fiesta of the village's patron saint and for other ritual purposes. It is important to note that villagers living abroad still consider themselves to be Tlalcualpeños in the original Tlaxcalan sense. This means that they build and maintain houses in the village, even if the houses remain unoccupied except for occasional return visits, and that they continue to contribute to community projects dedicated to public works and to the worship of the village's patron saints. While residents of other villages in the region have long described themselves collectively as bakers, weavers, potters or factory workers,[6] Tlalcualpeños now refer to themselves collectively as *mojados* ("wet-backs"). Of course, the people currently in the village are not, at least at the moment, *mojados*. Yet most of them take advantage of economic opportunities created by migrants' earnings. As migrants build houses and make monetary contributions to public works projects and fiestas in the village, those who remain have been able to earn a living as construction workers, electricians, plumbers, and musicians.

Childhood in Tlalcuapan

As we already noted, during the initial phases of fieldwork we were struck by the early age at which children begin contributing to the household economy and the amount of time they dedicate to doing so. While our argument here has more to do with the meaning of their economic activities than the simple fact that children in Tlalcuapan perform them, its significance would be reduced if we were talking about the meaning of washing a few dishes or walking the dog. A description of these activities is therefore necessary. Our description should be read as an attempt to provide a general idea of these activities, and not as negation of variation and conflict. Of course both the quality and quantity of children's activities vary depending on a number of factors, including stage in the domestic groups' development cycle (sibling order) and the specific means of generating income. Further, this description does not at all fit the children of a few families who place greater emphasis on education. These children's parents occupy positions in the government bureaucracy in the nearby state capital and aspire to similar futures for their children. It is important to note, however, that this variation is insignificant to most residents, who place hope for betterment in migration. Moreover, since migration is in fact usually more lucrative than a bureaucratic post, this variation does not constitute the basis for class formation.

By the age of two, boys and girls participate in simple domestic tasks, such as removing corn kernels from the cob. Over the next few years their participation increases to include feeding small domestic animals such as chickens and sweeping the floor. Until the age of five, children are still cared for and supervised in these activities by their mothers or older siblings. They also play during much of the day, and may attend preschool. Children from six to nine years of age perform more complicated domestic tasks such as caring for younger siblings, supervising younger siblings' work, feeding larger domestic animals, and washing dishes, dedicating from four to six hours daily to these activities. They also attend elementary school from 8:00 AM to 12:00 PM and play two to three hours a day.

By the age of ten, alongside their domestic chores, sons and daughters begin to perform tasks outside of the house and patio for the first time. They participate in the labor-intensive phases of the agricultural cycle, helping their

Figure 2.1. A three-year-old girl collecting dry corn stalks and leaves for animal feed. *Photo by Martha Areli Ramírez Sánchez.*

fathers and older siblings to sow and harvest corn on family plots. Further-more, many of the boys ten and eleven years of age assist their fathers in their work as plumbers, electricians, tailors, musicians, bakers, and construction workers, while girls of the same age assist their mothers when the latter earn money taking in laundry, cooking for fiestas, or cleaning others' houses. Be-tween these domestic and extra-domestic tasks children this age may be oc-cupied up to twelve hours a day. At the age of twelve, children begin to take larger animals such as cows out to pasture and to collect wood for sale and domestic use on the nearby mountain slopes. At fourteen, most children have begun middle school and nearly all of them assist their parents in the latter's money-making activities as well as helping out with domestic tasks and assist-ing in the fields. Beginning at age sixteen, when they finish middle school,[7] sons and daughters begin to spend more and more time performing wage-work independently of their parents' activities. The young women usually work in domestic service, in the textile industry, or in the service sector in nearby Santa Ana or the city of Tlaxcala, while the young men often find jobs in the automobile industry in Puebla. Yet, as long as they remain single, they con-tinue to donate all or nearly all of their earnings to the family budget.

Tlalcualpeños describe these activities as *ayuda* ("aid" or "help"), refer-ring to the fact that their efforts are oriented toward helping their families, reserving the term *trabajo* ("work," or in this case "labor") to refer to salaried employment. Yet the categories of *ayuda* and labor are not mutually exclusive, since most unmarried sons and daughters use money they receive from salaried employment as *ayuda*, passing all or most of their earnings on to their parents. Childhood in Tlalcuapan can be understood, at least in part, as a life stage in which unmarried sons and daughters provide *ayuda* to their parents (see Durham, this volume). It is also a life stage in which unmarried sons and daughters receive nurture from their parents in the form of food, clothing, school expenses, and spending money. Sometimes Tlalcualpeños consider these two acts—children's providing of *ayuda* and parents' providing of nurture —separately as independent donations. That is, children help their parents because that is what good, responsible sons and daughters do, and parents nurture their children because that is what good, loving parents do (see Good 1988, 172). However, Tlalcualpeños also observe that these apparently isolated donations are in fact related, constituting an exchange of *ayuda* and nurture on a daily basis. Thus, older sons and daughters, who are more productive and thus provide more *ayuda*, generally receive greater amounts of nurture in the form of larger quantities of food, costlier school supplies, and more spending money.

The fact that parents and children exchange *ayuda* and nurture carries two important implications for a comparison with notions of childhood and parent-child relations of modern European origin. First, parents and children are mutually dependent upon each other in a material sense, and thus there is no connection between adulthood and independence or between childhood and dependence. Instead, personhood, in general, is characterized by interdependence. Second, the fact that Tlalcualpeños do not see children as helpless and dependent does not mean that they view them as modern Western adults view themselves: as independent individuals capable of authoring their own acts. Rather, parents cause their children to contribute to the household economy by providing them with nurturance while children cause their parents to provide nurturance and, eventually, an inheritance by contributing to the household economy. Thus their interdependence is not just material, it is personal as well. That is, it is not simply that they need what the other has; they need the other to provide it for them.

In Tlalcuapan as in many other Mexican villages (see Good 2005), these exchanges, more than biological relatedness, constitute the parent-child relationship. Adoption, for example, is realized through these exchanges, and offspring who don't provide *ayuda*—a situation that seems only to occur when sons or daughters live far from the village, and even then rarely—may be disowned and disinherited. The issue of inheritance suggests that these exchanges go beyond daily provisions of *ayuda* and nurture. We now turn to this long-term dimension of these exchanges and their role in processes of social reproduction.

Long-Term Exchanges, the Domestic Development Cycle, and Social Reproduction

Studies of the development cycle of the domestic group are usually concerned with portraying the family in diachronic perspective and not with the problem of social reproduction per se. They are interested in the motion and not the motor. However, the development cycle and its stages can provide a framework for examining social reproduction. According to Robichaux (1997), the distinguishing features of the Mesoamerican development cycle of domestic groups are virilocal postmarital residence and ultimogeniture of the dwelling site. The former is a pattern in which newlyweds reside with the groom's parents while they are saving money to build their own dwelling. Robichaux explains that this coresidency is usually virilocal because of a patrilineal bias in Mesoamerican kinship, but the newlyweds may reside uxorically if the bride has few or no brothers and the groom many (156–157). As soon as the couple has saved enough money, they construct their own dwelling on a "nearby or adjacent plot donated by the parents of the husband, though in some cases construction may be on a house lot donated by the parents of the wife" (156). Ultimogeniture of the dwelling site refers to the fact that the youngest son (*el xocoyote*), along with his wife and children, remains in the parents' house, cares for his parents in their old age, and inherits the house when his father dies. While the *xocoyote* inherits the house, the inheritance of land is "equally divided among all males, with some female participation in the inheritance" (161). Thus, in Tlalcuapan, as in many other Mexican villages, one finds, broadly speaking, two kinds of residential units. One consists of a married couple, their unmarried children, and, in the case of the *xocoyote*, the husband's parents if they are still alive. The other consists of a married couple living together with their unmarried children and their married sons, along with the latter's wives and children. Here we will refer to the first residential unit as the nuclear stage and the second arrangement as the extended stage.

Moving toward an interest in social reproduction, Downing (1973) and González Montes (1992) suggest that inheritance in Mesoamerica can be understood as a series of long-term exchanges between parents and children that may begin when children marry and continue after the parents' deaths. Children care for their parents in old age and for their souls after their deaths, and in exchange they inherit land, often as soon as they marry and almost always while the parents are alive. In Tlalcuapan, we found that these long-term exchanges begin much earlier: as soon as a child is born. A look at three families, the Méndez family, the Castillo family, and the Jiménez family, in different stages of the domestic cycle, will help to illustrate the contemporary workings of these exchanges.

The Méndez family is in an early period of the nuclear stage. The parents, both age thirty-five, have six children between the ages of one and thirteen. The father earns money as a musician in a band, while the mother cultivates corn on the family plot with the help of her four sons between the ages of nine and thirteen. These sons also earn money working for other village residents during the harvest. A six-year-old daughter helps with domestic chores, while a one-year-old daughter has not yet begun to provide *ayuda*. It is notable that the family, whose sons and daughters are still too young to migrate to California, lacks many of the consumer goods, such as beds, warm clothing and shoes for the winter months, and store-bought food items beyond the basics (such as flour, sugar, oil, and coffee), that families in other stages of the domestic cycle possess.

In an interview, the father noted that his one-year-old daughter receives more in a relative sense than his other children, since she receives food and clothing but doesn't yet provide any *ayuda*. The same kind of imbalance in the exchange of *ayuda* for nurture exists in the case of the six-year-old daughter, but to a lesser extent. In this early stage, young children receive unreciprocated nurture from their parents, which explains the Méndez's lack of extra spending money for consumer goods. However, this nurture is only unreciprocated in the short term, as we will see in the example of the next family.

The Castillo family consists of a sixty-year-old father, a forty-eight-year-old mother, five single sons ages 29, 28, 25, 20, and 14, and four single daughters ages 21, 17, 12, and 7. The four eldest sons and the oldest daughter live and work in Costa Mesa, California. The sons work as cooks and dishwashers in one restaurant, and the daughter works as a cashier in another. All of them remit most of their earnings to their parents. The three youngest daughters live with their parents in the village and help out with domestic chores and with the raising of animals. The youngest son also lives with his parents and assists his father in his job as a construction worker and both his mother and father in the cultivation of corn on the family plot. The Castillo family can be considered to be in the same stage of the domestic cycle as the Méndez family, even though the children are much older and most of them live away from home, since none are married and they all continue to work in order to provide *ayuda*. Yet the Castillo family is distinct from the Méndez family in that none of the children receives unreciprocated nurture, and the older sons and daughters provide unreciprocated *ayuda* to their parents.

When we refer to unreciprocated *ayuda*, we do not mean to say that the older Castillo children receive no nurture at all from their parents. Their mother nurtures even her oldest children by putting away or investing part of their remittances for their future use. But there is definitely an imbalance between the large amounts of *ayuda* they provide and the smaller amounts of nurture they receive. This unreciprocated *ayuda* allows the parents and younger siblings to reduce their workload and has permitted the purchase of numerous luxury items including a sports car, various televisions and VCRs, a microwave oven, a vacuum cleaner, and an electric razor. Once again, however, this *ayuda* is only unreciprocated in the short term, as the example of the Jiménez family demonstrates.

The Jiménez family has entered the extended stage of the domestic cycle. The residential group includes a forty-two-year-old father, a forty-year-old mother, a nineteen-year-old son along with his seventeen-year-old wife and newborn child, a seventeen-year-old son, and a fourteen-year-old daughter. The family runs a bakery, a *tortillería*, and a small store out of their house. The father, the mother, and the two younger children dedicate much of their time to these businesses. The eldest son did as well until he married, at which time he found a job working as a mechanic in a nearby town. His wife occasionally helps out with the businesses when she is not too busy attending to her baby. The eldest son does not hand over any of his earnings to his parents. He uses them to buy clothing, diapers, furniture, and other necessities for himself, his wife, and their child and to save for the construction of a separate dwelling. His parents provide the young couple not only with shelter, water, and electricity, but with food as well.

Children in Tlalcuapan, as stated above, receive nurture in exchange for their *ayuda* on a daily basis. Imbalances in this daily exchange, seen in the cases of the Méndez and Castillo families, constitute the basis for long-term exchanges. When the parents of the Méndez family provide their one-year-old daughter with unreciprocated nurture, they do not do so only to fulfill her daily needs. Rather, Tlalcualpeños see this providing of nurture as an effort to place her in their debt and thus to cause her to act subsequently on their behalf as a provider of *ayuda* (see also Good 2005). Similarly, when the older sons and daughters of the Castillo family give their parents unreciprocated *ayuda*, their intention is to cause their parents to act in the future. Specifically, they provide unreciprocated *ayuda* to cause their parents to pay for their weddings, to house and feed them while they are saving money as newlyweds, and to bequeath land to them on which to build their own dwellings. This connection between sons' and daughters' providing of unreciprocated *ayuda* and their parents' financial support during and immediately after their marriage is reflected in the eldest Jiménez son's explanation of his current living arrangement: "It's because I already worked. Now I don't help because I'm married. My parents paid for my wedding and they pay for my food now because I already helped them. I gave them money when I worked."

In sum, these long-term exchanges fuel the development of the domestic cycle and constitute a process of social reproduction (see Lamb, this volume). It is important to note, however, that this is not the modern European version of social reproduction described above. Tlalcualpeños imagine that children are born into a state of indebtedness and not a state of nature. Therefore, they do not view social reproduction as the problem of converting natural beings into social ones through the transmission of society's values. Obviously, villagers realize that certain knowledge and skills must be passed from one

Figure 2.2. A fourteen-year-old girl working after school in the family business, a *tortillería. Photo by Martha Areli Ramírez Sánchez.*

generation to the next, but this body of knowledge is not equated to anything like society or culture and this transmission is not given the weight of social reproduction as it is in the modern European version. Or, in other words, they do not see the internalization of knowledge, beliefs, or values as an integral part of the process of social regeneration. Further, the motivating agents causing social reproduction are not independent adult willpower and social convention, but rather other persons: parents or their unmarried sons and daughters. Unlike the agency of independent individuals that causes those same individuals to act, Tlalcualpeños' agency causes others to act on their behalf. Thus, when unmarried sons and daughters work to provide *ayuda* they are acting in reaction to their parents' agency and on behalf of their parents, while at the same time they are being agents who will cause their parents to pay for their weddings and help them to establish independent households. It is important here to distinguish between working *for* one's children or aging parents and working *on their behalf.* In the context of the modern European version of childhood described above, people frequently see themselves as unselfishly working for their children or aging parents. The claim of unselfishness makes sense, because they motivated themselves to act in this way. Among Tlalcualpeños, such a claim to unselfishness would make little sense because their work is not just for others; it is motivated by them.

Formal Education and Conflicting Notions of Childhood

Now that we have laid out the broader framework of local practices of social reproduction and intergenerational relations, it is possible to examine certain shifts in these practices that have occurred as part of the most recent phase of capitalist globalization. In particular, two manifestations of this process of globalization have had noticeable effects on our focus of interest: the rising importance of formal education since the late 1970s and rapidly increasing levels of year-round migration to the U.S. during this same period.

The village's first primary school was established in 1928. According to the oldest villagers, however, practically no one studied more than a couple of years because they had to help their parents, by working either in the fields or for wages outside the village. Some add that they had no need to study, since their work did not demand education, and they saw school as an inappropriate place for sons and daughters to spend their time. This attitude toward formal education began to change in the late 1970s, as new kinds of jobs became available to villagers. As Tlalcualpeños began to switch from agricultural to service-sector jobs in California, potential migrants came to value skills such as reading and writing, arithmetic, and spoken English. Also, as young people remaining in the village moved from domestic service to industrial and service-sector jobs, their employers began to demand these skills as well as primary or middle school diplomas. This shift in employment opportunities at home and abroad coincided with an increase in remittances from villagers now permanently residing in California, making it unnecessary to send school-aged sons and daughters out of the village to work (see below). Two sizeable investments by villagers at home and abroad reflect this increasing interest in formal education. In 1974, Tlalcualpeños built a new primary school, only half of which was paid for by the government. Then, in 1980, they renovated and enlarged the school building, principally with remittances from migrants abroad.

It is interesting to note, however, that this increased involvement in formal education has not significantly decreased the time children dedicate to providing *ayuda*. The combination of regular school attendance and providing *ayuda* to parents means that a typical day for an eleven-year-old begins at 5:00 AM, when he or she wakes up, feeds the domestic animals, and helps to prepare younger siblings for school. He or she attends school from 8:00 AM to 12:00 PM and then spends up to ten of the next twelve hours assisting his or her parents in the fields or in their work. In other words, regular school attendance has added a set of activities to children's daily schedules, but it has not replaced any of the activities they describe as *ayuda*.

Besides adding activities to children's schedules, regular school attendance has also resulted in the gradual introduction of a new notion of childhood among village residents. This new notion is a variation of the modern European version of childhood described above and emphasizes that children need to be cared for and disciplined by adults and that they need to be taught to take care of and to discipline themselves. At the school, ideas about bodily hygiene are frequently used to stand for children's general delicate state, the care they require, and the discipline they must learn. Teachers scrupulously check students' bodily and oral hygiene. Those who come to school without bathing or brushing their teeth are exhibited as bad examples in front of their peers. The lesson is not just about children's current states of being, but about their future success in the world of work as well. Teachers portray the school as a key site in the process of social reproduction, or, better, of social "preproduction," since the social state being produced has never before existed in the village.

Teachers have in large part succeeded in their efforts, and most Tlalcualpeños currently see schooling not only as a means to obtain certain jobs, but also as an appropriate activity for children. Currently, only three families in the village refuse to send their children to school, and other parents speak badly of these families because of their refusal. Further, many Tlalcualpeños have adopted, at least partially, the notion of social reproduction promoted in schools. Some can now be heard voicing the notion that children are physically delicate and require special treatment. As a sixty-five-year-old man noted, "Before, our parents didn't know how to take care of us. Now anything happens to a child and they take him to a doctor." Others make reference to education and the bodily metonym of hygiene to talk about hopes for their children's futures. For example, one twenty-three-year-old factory worker, who recently became a father, told us, "I want my son to go to school. I want him to be well prepared and to have another type of job. I don't want him to be a dirty person [un mugroso] like me. I want him to be better than we were."

It is important to note, however, that these notions of childhood and social reproduction have become established in the village without wholly displacing local versions. As children's daily schedules suggest, Tlalcualpeños, both young and old, continue to see childhood as a time for providing ayuda, and, in most contexts, they continue to see their actions not as individual efforts to achieve success by following social convention, but rather as the causes and effects of others' actions. To explain how these new versions can be introduced without displacing the old, we posit that these two notions of childhood and social reproduction occupy different slots in a Tlalcualpeño symbolic order. They are not two different manners of understanding or resolving the same problem; they constitute two separate sets of problems and solutions altogether. Thus, our use of the same terms—"childhood" and "social reproduction"—to refer to these two sets of social ideas and practices should not be confused with local classifications. Villagers' statements to the effect that the new ideas introduced through formal education are replacing their former state of ignorance about childhood should not simply be dismissed as reproductions of what teachers have told them about themselves. Rather, such statements reflect the fact that what is being introduced through the schools is not simply a new set of values to replace an older set, but rather a whole idea of social reproduction whose emphasis on the transmission of values is completely novel.

Most of the time, these two sets of notions and practices coexist peacefully. On occasions, however, tensions arise. Parents, for example, may express their frustration with the school's financial demands. One thirty-nine-year-old mother of six stated,

> When I was in school, I went with my everyday clothing. There weren't any uniforms. We went just as we were when we got up and when we got back we went straight to the fields. Now, it's like a money vacuum. They ask them for toothbrushes, clothing for special events, and toilet paper for the bathroom. Yes, the times do change.

This tension between the two notions of childhood is most noticeable during the harvest, when families cannot do without their children's full-time *ayuda*. School attendance drops drastically during this time of year, and students miss enough classes to risk failing the year, according to national standards. Teachers, however, respond by covering for the students: they don't report the absences, and, working outside official school policy, they pardon three absences for each special assignment completed, for each instance of participation in extracurricular activities, or for each contribution, in cash or labor, to school improvement projects. This response by teachers reveals their ambiguous position as both representatives of the national education system and residents of nearby villages socially and culturally similar to Tlalcuapan. While teachers consider promoting a modern Western notion of childhood to be part of their job, most of them understand perfectly well the dilemma of the harvest, since they too cultivate corn and many of them could not do so without their own children's *ayuda*. Even families that seem to value education and the prospect of their children's individual achievement over *ayuda* and interdependence, preferring to hire laborers and keep their children in school during the harvest, for example, have not entirely abandoned these local practices involving intergenerational exchanges. These families, although somewhat exceptional in the village, confirm our suggestion that modern European notions of childhood and social reproduction have become established in the village without wholly displacing local versions, since, as we proposed above, these two sets of notions and practices are not two different manners of understanding or resolving the same problem, but rather two distinctive sets of problems and solutions altogether.

The Effects of and on Transnational Migration

From the middle of the nineteenth century up until the beginning of international migration in the late 1950s, most families in Tlalcuapan cultivated a subsistence crop, corn, on small family plots. In addition, they obtained cash from two resources: the sale of firewood collected on the slopes of the nearby volcano, La Malinche, and sons' and daughters' wages for work as domestic servants. At the age of eight or nine, children were taken by their parents to live with and work for a family in a nearby city. Tlalcualpeños now in their sixties and seventies remember that their fathers would come to collect their wages directly from their employers every month. In their late teens, they left their jobs and returned to the village to live and to marry. Tlalcualpeños explain that, at the time, it was necessary for sons and daughters to work away from home because there was nothing for them to do, and thus no way for them to provide *ayuda*, in the village. According to a seventy-seven-year-old villager,

> Before, there was no work here. None for the old people and none for the young. As a boy I went to the volcano to collect firewood and then I went to Santa Ana to sell it door to door. Later, my father placed me as a domestic servant in the city of Tlaxcala. I didn't even know how much I made because my father collected my pay. My employers gave me clothes and shoes. Not good ones, but they worked, and sometimes it was better than being at home.

Simply put, sons and daughters couldn't help their parents at home or in the village because there wasn't anything for them to do there. Their parents, without easy access to wage work, were left with enough time to easily perform the only tasks requiring attention in the home and the village: domestic chores and corn cultivation. Thus the only way for sons and daughters to provide *ayuda* was to work outside the village. Since they were unskilled laborers, the principal occupation open to them was domestic service, which provided the added benefit of a place to sleep and eat.

In the late 1970s, this age-based division of labor began to change. With the shift in the U.S. labor market that made year-round employment in the U.S. a possibility, a number of economic opportunities emerged for those who remained in the village. For example, migrants hire those who have stayed behind, extended family members in particular, to construct houses for them in the village. These building projects have permitted a number of villagers to establish themselves as contractors and construction workers. In addition, the need for plumbers, electricians, and glass-cutters has led still other villagers to establish themselves in these lines of work. Furthermore, migrants send substantial monetary contributions to village leaders[8] in charge of community projects. These projects include paving roads, building schools, constructing a water and drainage system, restoring the village church, and celebrating the annual fiestas of patron saints. Prior to migration, the few public works projects undertaken were completed through collective labor (*faenas*), organized by village leaders. Currently, village leaders in charge of public works projects use cash contributions from migrants and smaller amounts collected from those who stayed behind to hire construction workers, plumbers, and electricians from the village to complete these projects. The leaders in charge of fiestas (*mayordomos*) use these cash contributions to organize elaborate celebrations. They hire musicians to perform and cooks to prepare large quantities of food. Once again, residents have taken advantage of these new sources of income, establishing themselves as musicians in the case of men and cooks in the case of women.

While we do not wish to imply that these businesses constitute a long-term solution to the village's economic problems, they have, for the moment, significantly altered the economic activities of village residents including children. With their parents working as construction workers, electricians, musicians, and cooks, there is a lot for sons and daughters to do near to home. Their help is needed around the house, in the fields, and as assistants in their parents' work. Thus, due to the economic changes brought by migrants' remittances, it is no longer necessary to send children away to work as domestic servants; there are plenty of opportunities for them to provide *ayuda* at home. It can no longer be said that there is no work in the village.

For Tlalcualpeños this shift is both bitter and sweet. Recognizing that domestic laborers work hard, long hours, that they are poorly paid, and that they are frequently abused by employers, they claim that they are happy that their children do not have to suffer what many of them experienced. Also, they welcome the fact that their younger sons and daughters are at home and that they don't have to feel sad and suffer because they miss them as parents did in previous generations. However, they now miss their older sons and daughters and other relatives who live year-round in the U.S. It is important to note that Tlalcualpeños do not attribute these two forms of suffering previously caused by domestic labor to sons' and daughters' status as children. That is, they do not claim that sons and daughters working as domestic servants missed their parents because as children they were unilaterally emotionally dependent upon them. Rather, they state that as family members, both parents and children miss each other. Further, they do not claim that in the past sons and daughters suffered abuse as domestic servants because they were defenseless, vulnerable children. Instead, they posit that sons and daughters suffered abuse as workers, whose employers were aware of and took advantage of their lack of alternative sources of income.

The fact that Tlalcualpeños have not come to see sons and daughters as dependent, defenseless children is further evidenced by the fact that eleven- and twelve-year-olds, for example, continue to dedicate as many as twelve hours a day to helping their parents, despite the improvements in the community's economic situation. In other words, the remittances from migrants have brought about a shift in the location and content of children's activities, but not in the existence or the form of those activities: childhood in Tlalcuapan is still considered a time for providing *ayuda* to parents.

This local version of social reproduction can even help to explain what propels villagers' migration to California. Let us recall the Castillo family for a moment. The sons and daughters who are in the U.S. work in order to send their earnings home to their parents, who, in turn, save part of the money to return to their sons and daughters when they marry. Both the parents and the sons and daughters (on return visits) clearly stated to us that the latter migrate to provide *ayuda* for the former and for younger siblings. The logic of this transnational migratory work is no different than that of previous generations, who say they were placed in domestic service by their parents and never laid hands on their earnings. Parents are the instigators and immediate beneficiaries of their sons' and daughters' transnational migration. From the standpoint of motivation, migratory work, no less than other productive activities, is inextricable from local notions and practices of social reproduction and intergenerational relations.

We do not mean to suggest that attention to motivation alone is sufficient to explain Tlalcualpeños' migration. If they could earn the same amount in the village as in California, few would leave. Structural factors, such as the shift in the U.S. labor market mentioned above, must also be taken into account to explain migration. Yet, since most villagers could subsist without leaving the region even under these structural conditions, some attention to motivation beyond the survival strategies of stone-age subsistence economics is needed to explain their lengthy and often dangerous migration. We wish to suggest that this form of motivation, connected to specific modes of social reproduction and intergenerational relations, propels Tlalcualpeños north of the border and that, in addition, it has not seriously deterred employers in California from hiring them or others from culturally similar Mexican villages. Moreover, further attention to these local versions of social reproduction and intergenerational relations in future research might have much more to reveal about Mexicans' migration to the U.S. If we are to take seriously the notion that particular capitalisms require or at least benefit from specific kinds of persons/workers, then it is possible that employers in the U.S. are attracted to something about Mexican migrants, such as those from Tlalcuapan, for other reasons in addition to their vulnerability due to their illegal status. The Mexican countryside is by no means the only source of inexpensive, flexible labor for U.S. employers, and yet Mexican migrants seem to be displacing segments of an American-born underclass—African Americans in particular—as well as some migrants from other places, first in seasonal agricultural work and now more recently in low-paying service and industrial jobs.[9] Might this be at least partially attributable to U.S. employers' attraction to a person/worker who is motivated to work without having to internalize a work ethic? Could it be that a motivation to work that comes from other persons, other times, and another place (the nurture parents provided in the past and the inheritance parents will provide in the future) facilitates these migrants' exploitation (see Woronov, this volume)? Does the mode of social reproduction described here eliminate some of the contingencies of a modern European mode that depends on the actions of people who see themselves as independent individual subjects? We realize that this is a sensitive issue and would like to emphasize that our intention is not to blame migrants themselves, or even migration, for the displacement of native-born workers when and where this occurs, or to suggest that migrants offer no resistance to capitalist exploitation. Nor do we wish to imply that employers' turn away from native-born workers has anything to do with the latter's capabilities or skills. Rather, we are interested in how local processes of social regeneration—and in this case the fact that migrants are in the U.S. on behalf of others and not as individual subjects—may inadvertently feed into aspects of global capitalism, such as workers' exploitation and the pitting of members of different ethnic groups against one another as they compete for jobs not just as individuals but as members of these groups.

Conclusions

Tlalcuapan presents an interesting case for exploring how the latest phase of globalization shapes and is shaped by local versions of social reproduction and intergenerational relations. The emerging demand for year-round Mexican migrant labor in the U.S. has remade many aspects of life in the village. Relative to the past, the local economy is booming thanks to migrants' remittances, as evidenced by the accelerated construction of new houses and the completion of various public works projects. For residents, perhaps the most significant change is the fact that they no longer have to send their young sons and daughters to work as domestic servants in nearby cities. Now, remittances from older sons and daughters, as well as the improved local economy in general, have obviated the need to send children off to work in what were often abusive situations. The absence of older sons and daughters or, from another perspective, the existence of a whole other Tlalcuapan in California is another significant effect of this shift provoked by broader economic transformations. Meanwhile, the increased interest in, or at least tolerance of, formal education, made possible by the shift in the location of children's activities, has introduced an alternative version of childhood and social reproduction to the village. Residents can now be heard referring to children as delicate and to education and the inculcation of values, rather than participation in exchanges, as the key to a better future.

However, these shifts in intergenerational relations and the introduction of a new version of childhood and social reproduction, rather than constituting a complete reworking of life in the village, reflect the villagers' incorporation of new circumstances into an already existing framework of social regeneration (see Lamb, this volume; Cole, this volume). Villagers have integrated into their daily lives the new versions of childhood and social reproduction introduced through schools without displacing local versions, as evidenced by the fact that while young sons and daughters no longer have to labor as domestic servants and thus can attend school, they continue to work long hours in and around the home. With parents occupied in various jobs related to the booming local construction business, for example, young sons and daughters are expected to do housework, to care for domestic animals, and to assist their parents in other ways. Overall, childhood is still considered a time for contributing to the household economy by working, described in the local idiom as providing *ayuda*. Meanwhile, the older sons and daughters living in California, despite the distance and their year-round absence, continue to see their work in terms of providing *ayuda* to their parents. They send home most of their earnings in the form of remittances, just as a generation ago children working as domestic servants passed their whole salaries directly on to their parents.

In general, Tlalcuapeños today, whether in Mexico or California, tend to share with previous generations notions and practices of social reproduction. They continue to see their work in the context of a series of life-long exchanges between generations. Sons and daughters of all ages are motivated to work and provide *ayuda* to their parents by the latter's previous and current provision of nurture and future bestowal of inheritance. This continuity in the form of intergenerational relations, in fact, is what has made possible shifts within the village, rather than the creation of a wealthy Tlalcuapan in California and the persistence of a poor one in Mexico. We have even suggested that local versions of social reproduction motivate migration and work in ways that may make Tlalcualpeños attractive employees, since their motivation need not come from instilling a work ethic, but rather comes from a series of exchanges with others already begun. Thus, while the recent phase of globalization has reshaped intergenerational relations in the village, continuity in the local form of social reproduction has, if we are correct, helped shape certain labor demands in the U.S., skewing them toward a preference for rural Mexican migrants over migrants from other places and a U.S.-born underclass.

However, while Tlalcualpeños are still able to incorporate these changes into old forms and while the local economy seems to be doing better than ever before, it is unclear what the future holds. The effects of the changes wrought upon life in the village are still to be seen, leaving the future of a number of aspects of village life uncertain. For example, it is still too early to predict the range of possible effects—cultural, social, demographic—of having half the village population in the U.S. Further, it appears that inequalities are emerging in the village based on families' differing abilities to participate in transnational migration: as evidenced by our case studies, there is a widening gap between families in different stages of the domestic cycle and between families with more children who can migrate and those with fewer. And finally, more than ever before the local economy depends upon a distant demand for labor over which villagers have absolutely no control and which could disappear at any moment when capitalism's demands inevitably shift once again in reaction to new crises.

NOTES

The research for this chapter was funded by the Universidad Iberoamericana as part of the projects entitled "Education, Labor, and Poverty" and "Global Transformations and the Destiny of the Indigenous/Peasant Community." We are thankful for this generous support. We would also like to thank the volume editors, Jennifer Cole and Deborah Durham, as well as the anonymous reviewers for their comments and suggestions. The responsibility for all shortcomings, however, is ours alone.

1. The ethnographic data on which this chapter is based were collected during nine months of fieldwork in 2000, 2001, and 2002. The research included intensive participant observation among four families and casual participant observation among a number of others; twenty-eight interviews with villagers from different age groups; and a survey distributed to 120 middle school students about their activities and their attitudes toward those activities.

2. In 1930, Tlalcuapan was officially recognized as a village, which allowed it to receive a land grant from the government.

3. The bracero program was set up in 1942, in response to labor shortages caused by World War II, as an agreement between the Mexican and U.S. governments to bring Mexican workers to the U.S. on short-term contracts to perform seasonal agricultural labor. Obviously, when the program ended in 1964, Mexicans continued to cross the border, although now illegally, to do the same work.

4. Rouse also states that the acceleration of migration in recent years must be explained in the context of changes occurring within Mexico, specifically the "diversion of capital to industry and commercial agriculture . . . since the 1940's" (Rouse 1991, 13). However, since agricultural plots in Tlalcuapan were never large enough to constitute a significant source of income, the decline in support of small-scale agriculture did not have a serious impact on villagers. Rather, it could be said that the potential for migration was already there in Tlalcuapan, waiting for an opportunity to arise.

5. Oxnard is located about eighty miles north of Los Angeles, and Costa Mesa about forty miles south.

6. It is common for almost entire villages to become factory workers, artisans, or migrants, since villagers tend to help their family members and friends to get jobs with the same employer or to get established in the same business.

7. While in recent years most Tlalcualpeños have finished middle school, only a handful finish high school or attend university, since the occupational opportunities most of them consider—migration to the U.S., a small business in the pueblo, or wage labor in Santa Ana—do not demand more than a middle school education.

8. By "village leaders" we mean people who hold what are referred to locally as *cargos*.

9. There is debate over the extent to which this is true or even whether it is the case at all (see, for example, Cherry 2003). However, there seems to us to be sufficient evidence to suggest that it is at least true for segments of the workforce in certain regions, judging from the fact that in recent years illegal migration—of which Mexicans constitute a significant part—has increased while unemployment among American-born Latinos and African Americans has also increased.

WORKS CITED

Ariès, Philippe. 1987. *El niño y la vida familiar en el Antiguo Régimen.* Trans. Naty García Guadilla. Madrid: Taurus.

Cherry, Robert. 2003. "Immigration and Race: What We Think We Know." *Review of Black Political Economy* 31 (1–2): 157–184.

Downing, T. E. 1973. "Zapotec Inheritance." Ph.D. diss., Stanford University.

González Montes, S. 1992. "Familias campesinas en el siglo XX." Ph.D. diss., Universidad Complutense.

Good, Catharine. 1988. *Haciendo la lucha: Arte y comercio nahuas en Guerrero.* México, D.F.: Fondo de Cultura Económica.

———. 2005. " 'Trabajando juntos como uno': Conceptos nahuas del grupo doméstico y la persona." In *Familia y parentesco en Mesoamérica: Unas miradas antropológicas.* David Robichaux, ed. Pp. 275–294. México, D.F.: Universidad Iberoamericana.

Harvey, David. 1990. *The Condition of Postmodernity.* Cambridge, Mass.: Blackwell.

Martin, Emily. 1994. *Flexible Bodies: Tracking Immunity in American Culture from the Days of Polio to the Age of AIDS.* Boston: Beacon Press.

Robichaux, David. 1997. "Residence Rules and Ultimogeniture in Tlaxcala and Mesoamerica." *Ethnology* 36 (2): 149–171.

Rouse, Roger. 1991. "Mexican Migration and the Social Space of Postmodernism." *Diaspora* 1 (1): 8–25.

———. 1992. "Making Sense of Settlement: Class Transformation, Cultural Struggle, and Transnationalism among Mexican Migrants in the United States." In *Towards a Transnational Perspective on Migration: Race, Class, Ethnicity, and Nationalism Reconsidered.* Nina Glick Schiller, Linda Basch, and Cristina Blanc-Szanton, eds. Pp. 25–52. New York: New York Academy of Sciences.

Strathern, Marilyn. 1992. *After Nature: English Kinship in the Late Twentieth Century.* Cambridge: Cambridge University Press.

Willis, Paul. 1977. *Learning to Labour: How Working Class Kids Get Working Class Jobs.* Aldershot, England: Gower.

3
Fresh Contact in Tamatave, Madagascar
Sex, Money, and Intergenerational Transformation

JENNIFER COLE

The Rhythm of the Times

In Tamatave, a large port town on Madagascar's east coast, Sunday afternoon is the maid's time off. At that time, the thousands of young women who have come from the countryside to work as servants in the homes of wealthier families are released from the oppressive conditions in which they labor the rest of the week. The normally quiet beach fills up with groups of young women cruising the waterfront, arms clasped together. Young men tease them and follow at their heels. Vendors set up at the side of the road to sell peanuts, coconut candies, and shots of rum. The crush of bodies is so intense that people have to walk single file to force their way through the crowd. I am here to interview a group of high school youth, ages fifteen to eighteen.

The young people I am here to meet come from fairly modest backgrounds; their parents are generally employed at the port or involved in small-scale trade. However, they are enrolled in the lycée and feel themselves considerably more sophisticated and cosmopolitan than the young maids and rickshaw pullers who crowd the beach. They have chosen the location for our meeting to be well away from places frequented by their parents. Nevertheless, they distinguish themselves from their surroundings by lounging about with ostentatiously bored expressions, and comment to each other that it has been "just eons" since they have come down *au bord* (short for *au bord de la mer*, at the seaside), as the popular beachfront locale is called in local parlance. Given their nonchalant demeanor and the fact that they are facing an oldster like myself, I fear this interview is going to be a disaster. Then Farida, a girl of seventeen dressed in a body-hugging stretch knit dress and platform shoes, starts talking about her friend who earns money by having sex with *vazaha*, the Malagasy word for Europeans.

> My friend, she works as a prostitute [*manao makorely*]. She has a boyfriend who is still young. He is handsome and still in school. When she goes to the nightclub, the boy brings her there. She works [finding Europeans] and the boy, he just waits for her. And when she gets off work, they go home together and she keeps her money with that boy—so if there happens to be a *vazaha* who wants to sleep with her, then she says that that boy is her brother. And the *vazaha*, he thinks that he is his brother-in-law, but really it is his competition.

The group is instantly animated. Aurelie, dressed in a slinky flowered dress, takes up the theme.

> This couple I know, they were very poor. But the girl, she was very pretty! And she told her husband she wanted to work as a prostitute. She found a *vazaha*. She brought him home, and she said that her husband was really her brother! And the *vazaha*, he bought them many things. He gave them a boat [for fishing]. And then one day the *vazaha* came unannounced and surprised the couple [together] and he realized that this man was definitely *not* her brother. And now he has had that boy put in jail.[1]

At this point the boys in the group are starting to squirm. I ask the group if it is wrong for women to choose a richer European man but secretly support a Malagasy lover. Farida answers first.

> Well, if a *vazaha* who had a lot of money liked me, I'd go with him whether I liked him or not to get money, sure, and then I'd use that money to support my boyfriend.

The other girl nods assent, but Rodrigue, formerly lounging to the side with his baseball cap turned backward, suddenly loses his cool.

> In terms of what makes me a Malagasy, I could not accept that, even if she were just my girlfriend, I would break up with her immediately. And I wouldn't agree to such an arrangement no matter how poor I was. What they did, it is because of poverty and it signals the destruction of Malagasy culture [*la culture Malgache*; he used the French] and it will just make things worse if we do that. Even the girl who proposed that plan to her husband, you can see that she has lost what makes her Malagasy! [*Disgustedly*] And the man, he accepted! That is what is ruining our ancestral land. We love money just too much now. Our social life is a mess. And we won't get rid of our poverty even if we do things to get money quickly. It ruins our culture. And, didn't you see, their wealth didn't last long, did it? It was like water from a sieve, it all fell through [their hands] again.

Figure 3.1. Two young women who occasionally work as prostitutes. *Photo by Jennifer Cole.*

The girls, slightly chagrined, looked away, pretending to be absorbed in the flux of bodies around us.

These kinds of conversations about sex, money, gender, and morality occurred frequently throughout the course of my research in Tamatave. The phenomenon these youth referred to was part of a generally perceived increase in girls' use of sex to earn money, a complex economy among young people in which sex, consumption, and social status are intimately intertwined. Despite a long history of different kinds of transactional sexual relationships in this region, both youth and adults I spoke with claimed that the current commodification of sexual relationships and the kinds of social arrangements that they entail are new phenomena. They date the change to the early 1990s, the postsocialist period associated with economic liberalization during which Madagascar experienced an influx of consumer goods as well as new forms of media, and people began to carve out new domains of production and service. The rampant exchange of sex for money was part of the new Malagasy times, in which people do things however they can. As the popular singer Rossy put it in the song entitled "Bal Kabosy," "Everyone just does what they please; you go to the dance, and you follow the rhythm of the times" (Rossy 1994).

From Youth Culture to Intergenerational Transformation

In this chapter I use the phenomenon of transactional sex as a lens through which to theorize the relationship between youth and social change. My aim is to move the analysis of youth from a focus on youth culture to a consideration of intergenerational transformation.

Youth's participation in the informal sexual economy in Madagascar has much to contribute to an emergent anthropology of youth (Wulff 1995; Durham 2000; Liechty 2002; Sharp 2002; Stephens 1995; Weiss 2002). This recent writing about youth has moved away from assumptions guiding the older psychological anthropology of adolescence, the great strength of which was to demonstrate the cultural and historical variability in managing the transition to adulthood (Whiting, Burbank, and Ratner 1986; Mead 1928). What was problematic about this earlier approach was that it conceptualized youth as incomplete cultural actors and assumed that the transition to adulthood was profoundly shaped by species-wide biological factors.

In keeping with the current theoretical emphasis on relations of power and resistance, more contemporary studies of youth have recuperated an alternative sociological tradition that focuses on youth culture and the ways in which youth are social actors actively engaged in the construction and reconstruction of social and cultural forms (Amit-Talai and Wulff 1995; Hall and Jefferson 1993; Hebdige 1979; Bucholtz 2002; Sharp 2002). Most explicitly developed by the Birmingham school of cultural studies, this approach highlights the fact that people who are differently positioned with respect to both class and the life cycle may participate in and value different social and cultural practices. Drawing on structuralist conceptions which see culture as made of an ordered pattern of signs, scholars like Hebdige (1979) argue that youth express their agency by creatively reordering the signs and symbols of the dominant culture through their use of particular commodities. In the context of scholarship on Africa, similar assumptions are implicit in Friedman's (1990) study of *les sapeurs*, unemployed Congolese young men who engage in status competition by means of elegant, brand-name clothes. In so doing, they build up alternative forms of prestige and power that are viewed as a threat by state authorities. And in Madagascar, Walsh (2003) has examined how marginalized young men who seek their fortune in highly risky sapphire mining use forms of conspicuous consumption to assert their agency, rather than invest it in local networks in which they are almost certain to be subordinate.

In many ways it is tempting to draw on this kind of analysis to explain the phenomenon of sex for money in contemporary Tamatave. After all, there is a long-standing acceptance of youthful sexual experimentation among many groups in Madagascar (Astuti 1995; Bloch 1998; Feeley-Harnik 1991). Moreover, most of the girls I knew exercised considerable resourcefulness and skill in their pursuit of Europeans and older wealthy men, and in at least some cases these girls are actively flouting class hierarchies through their acquisition of desirable commodities. However, to analyze young women's participation in the sexual economy in this way is problematic on two counts. First, in emphasizing the concepts of both youth culture and youth agency, this position runs the risk of fetishizing and reifying the category of youth, separating youth off from the families and communities in which they live. It also risks fetishizing resistance and agency, a point that becomes acutely visible when one begins to explore the morally ambiguous contexts in which youth find themselves. Second, such an approach fails to conceptualize youthful consumption practice relationally with respect to the larger intergenerational matrix of which it is a part. In Friedman's analysis, for example, we learn nothing of the consequences of *les sapeurs*' actions for the families in which they are presumably embedded; in Walsh's analysis we get little sense of more encompassing social and economic dynamics. Nor do we get an adequate sense of the powerful economic constraints that shape youthful practice.

In contrast to these views, I argue for a diachronic approach that places youth in changing historical, political, and economic circumstances by focusing on the role of transactional sex in creating new patterns of marriage, kinship, and intergenerational relations. In order to move beyond a synchronic focus on youth culture and take seriously youth's participation in processes of social regeneration, this chapter proposes a framework inspired by the work of Karl Mannheim. In his classic essay "The Problem of Generations" (1972), Mannheim argues that because of the finite nature of the human lifespan, all societies are constantly faced with both the problems and the advantages of what he calls "fresh contact"—the fact that there is a certain distance in how each new generation approaches and assimilates shared cultural material. On the one hand, he acknowledges that the continuous emergence of new human beings means a loss of cultural material as each new generation discards some aspects of the past cultural heritage and reinvents or keeps others. On the other hand, he points out that "[generational change] alone makes a fresh selection possible when it becomes necessary: It facilitates re-evaluations of our inventory and teaches us both to forget that which is no longer useful and to covet that which has yet to be won" (1972, 294). Such an approach highlights the ways in which youth's structural liminality—the fact that they are less embedded than adults in older networks of patronage and exchange—makes them uniquely positioned to take advantage of new social and economic conditions.

Consistent with Mannheim's insights, scholars of the lifespan have shown how the particular political-economic context in which youth enter a labor market and start to form families shapes the ways in which people reproduce and transform households and communities (Elder 1987, 1999; Newman 1996). Moreover, and in contrast to the view that the experiments of youth are soon incorporated into normative structures, this literature demonstrates that

experiencing a particular set of events during youth can have lasting consequences on a person's adult identifications and orientations to the world. For
example, Weisner and Bernheimer (1998) have shown that many people who
joined the North American countercultural movement in the 1960s both
continued to be influenced by its values at midlife and drew on these values
when they raised their children. The view of generational transformation to
emerge from these studies is a dialectical one—age mediates the impact of
particular historical and cultural events. At the same time, the manner in
which a particular generation is changed by historical experience shapes the
way in which social and cultural practices are subsequently transformed.

But generational change does not involve only the loss of some practices
and the adoption of others. Sometimes youth draw on old practices but enact
them in new circumstances, thus changing their effects, so that even the
reproduction of practices with long histories in a region can entail change. In
Tamatave, as I discuss below, young women's practices of transactional sex,
and particularly transactional sexual relations with Europeans, have a long
history reaching back to precolonial times. Nevertheless, the new context in
which these practices are enacted reciprocally works to shape the extent, the
content, and the effects of these practices in novel ways.

Nor is generational change a mechanical process that takes place similarly in all times and places. Youth's structural position between generations
may position them particularly well to contribute to processes of social change,
but this is more true in certain historical periods than others. In the context of
contemporary Tamatave, two factors contribute to youth's centrality in processes of social regeneration. First, the social and economic changes that have
accompanied Madagascar's move from state socialism to a liberalized economy have made normative paths to adulthood either irrelevant or impossible
to traverse. Second, and relatedly, the rise of consumerism that has accompanied these changes has made youth—particularly female youth—an increasingly visible category, everywhere used as part of the marked eroticizing of
consumer goods. Youth and the qualities of sexuality associated with youthful
bodies—particularly female youthful bodies—have been both discursively constructed and contested by a variety of different interests, a phenomenon that
restructures opportunities and shapes the ways in which youth think of themselves and their means of attaining adulthood. In youthful female sexuality, the
individual body and the social body come together in a particularly potent way
because it is through the individual bodies of young women and their changing practices that the social body may be reproduced and reconfigured.

In Tamatave, then, youth's experience of "fresh contact" not only forces
them to rethink received ideas and practices of generational growth through
kinship and marriage; accompanied by massive political inequalities on a
global scale, it also contributes to a process of class formation. This process has
the effect of encouraging the growth through kinship and marriage of certain
sectors of the population in Tamatave while rendering others tantamount to

prostitutes, bastards, and even slaves, an idiom of subordination that continues to structure how people imagine unequal social relations in Madagascar.[2]

The practices of transactional sex that I explore also put these young women at increasing risk for HIV/AIDS and other sexually transmitted diseases. However, this is not part of the story I focus on here, simply because during the main years of my fieldwork, from 1999 to 2002, HIV had not yet become a major concern among youth. Rates of HIV remained comparatively low, although not surprisingly, given the practices I describe, these statistics are changing.[3] The effects of neoliberal reform on middle-class young men are an important part of this story that I address elsewhere (Cole 2005); owing to lack of space I focus here primarily on the perspectives and experiences of young women. My argument is based on fieldwork from 1999 through 2003. I conducted research with both youth and their families in Tamatave, spending time with youth in the narrow, twisting sand paths of residential neighborhoods, attending church and neighborhood activities, and talking to both youth and their parents about practices surrounding marriage and family formation; love and sex; money, labor, and consumption.[4]

Prolonging Youth: Shifting Economies in Tamatave

Throughout the years of colonial rule (1895–1960) and the First Republic (1960–1972), the path to economic success lay through either international trade or government bureaucracy; often the two were tightly intertwined. Under these conditions, young Tamatavians sought success and upward mobility through schooling. Although access to schooling was a hotly contested political issue, and outcomes were always uneven, most people nevertheless believed that access to schooling was synonymous with social ascent.[5] However, with the general impoverishment that Madagascar experienced throughout the 1980s, increasing numbers of urbanites found that this was no longer the case. As the Malagasy franc was repeatedly devalued, once-prestigious jobs in the government administration and even jobs at the port no longer provided enough income to support a family. The impoverishment of the country also meant that schools were gradually emptied of books, supplies, and teachers; diplomas no longer guaranteed employment. These factors contributed to the prolongation of youth as an intermediate period between childhood and adulthood, as many youth were unable to find the employment that would enable them to form independent households and support dependents—the hallmark of adulthood in Tamatave.

In the early 1990s, these social and economic circumstances led to political unrest in many cities throughout Madagascar as protestors demanded that Ratsiraka, the president who had instituted the state-socialist Second Republic, allow new elections. In some cases, the demands were explicitly framed in terms of opportunities for youth. As one newspaper article, boldly entitled

"Crisis," read, "All the unhappiness of the world weighs on Malagasy youth and the situation is so bad that it needs to be dealt with before a catastrophe occurs. *Our youth want to become adult*" (*Tribune de Madagascar* 1991). Following these protests and nine months of general strikes throughout 1991 and early 1992, new elections were held. Beginning in 1993, the new government abandoned the state-socialist ideology that had guided government policy from 1975 to 1991 and, in the context of negotiations with the World Bank and the IMF, adopted the language (if not always the practices) of democracy and neoliberal economics in its place. Whereas the country was relatively closed to foreign influences throughout the socialist era of the late 1970s and 1980s, the economic and political changes that took place during the early 1990s created a wholesale "opening" of the country, with the creation of free-trade zones and the arrival of both foreigners (bent on business or tourism) and previously unavailable consumer goods. Whether people work as low-level government administrators, dockers at the port, or vegetable sellers at the bazaar, they now tend to think about success in terms of access to ideas, practices, and commodities that come from beyond Madagascar.

Wealth in Tamatave starts at the port and moves out, first in comparatively large chunks controlled by Malagasy, European, Chinese, and Indian merchants who own many of the import-export businesses located in the area around the port and who live in the villas stretched out around the large bazaar and along the shore, then dividing into somewhat smaller portions as it spreads among smaller-scale merchants who live on the larger streets, and then, finally, into the depths of the sand paths, where, if one goes deep enough, one might believe oneself in the Malagasy countryside. Here, if they are employed at all, people work as maids, watchmen, or very petty traders. The hierarchy of wealth created around the port is crosscut and intertwined in complex ways with the status and wealth that people receive from working in the state bureaucracy, whether as doctors, midwives, teachers, or secretaries.

Although the spatial map I have provided is important for illuminating the historical bases of wealth and status in Tamatave, this structure is in a constant state of transformation. Viewing it from a generational perspective, a recent study by the National Bureau of Statistics reports that whereas in the past one could easily classify people as either functionaries, managers, or employees, today this is no longer the case because more than half of the population works in the unpredictable informal sector, and people are more likely to end up in it than to be able to replicate their fathers' status (Projet Madio 2001, 59). This trend is paired with a movement away from farming and commerce and toward industry and service; it is in the city of Tamatave that the highest proportion of youth have left the agricultural livelihood of their parents. Despite the difficulties in replicating one's father's class status, Tamatave does offer some possible upward mobility, at least for those who already have some education: in Tamatave and Diego Suarez—the two largest ports in Madagascar—the children of skilled workers are more likely to attain managerial jobs than people in a comparable position in other cities.

Yet these social and economic changes have not resulted in the shortening of the period of youth that many people had hoped for. Rather, as in the latter part of the socialist period, youth continue to have difficulty finding jobs in the formal sector, and school leads to employment only for the privileged few. This phenomenon is particularly visible in Tamatave, where people who have completed more years of schooling have more difficulty finding work than those who have completed fewer (Projet Madio 2001). At the same time, however, youth have been increasingly drawn into the consumer economy. The combination of little expectation that schooling will lead to a job with an increase in the importance of consumption practices means that youth have been particularly quick to seize on the newly emergent fluid and often ephemeral forms of production and service available.

Youth who were still in school, like those I met on the boardwalk, rely, in part, on their parents and wider network of kin for money. Farida, for example, lived with her grandmother but was sent money by her mother, who had married a Comorian sailor and lived in Réunion. Many young people I knew who had college degrees tried to find work with the NGOs that flocked to Madagascar throughout the 1990s, largely as part of efforts to save the island's biodiversity. Young men with less education tried to get low-level jobs at the port unloading ships or worked in manual day jobs as mechanics or handymen. Many young men claimed that the only way to get money was to do *biznessy*, which means any kind of illegal traffic one can get one's hands on (breaking into the containers at the port, stealing gas, or even, some claimed, selling ancestral bones). Among young women, those who had more schooling sought jobs as cashiers or clerks in one of the several large supermarkets or import-export stores that had opened in the area. Poorer young women, particularly those who had just come from the countryside, inevitably worked as maids. Many young people also earned money during the lychee season, when they would work long night shifts packing lychees for export. During the period preceding the 2001 elections, another strategy that many Tamatavian youth used was to join political associations, usually funded by particular deputies who would pay them to work as their personal aides and to carry out small jobs. For young men, this job often entailed becoming someone's right-hand man on the spot, and they became involved in procuring services for and smoothing the way of the deputy. Young women also sometimes worked for powerful men by lending their beauty and sexual allure to particular campaign efforts.

Yet it remains the case that these sources of income are never enough: parents can almost never give their children the money that youth think they need, and rarely do the jobs that young people obtain provide them with enough income to support their own households. This, broadly, is the background for the emergence of a new category of consumer youth called *jeunes*, many of whom are intimately involved in the sexual economy. Before I can consider this phenomenon, however, let me briefly give some background on local ideas of girls, sex, and marriage in Madagascar.

Youth, Marriage, and Respectable Sexuality in Madagascar

In contemporary Tamatave, old and new understandings of youth coexist and intermingle in uneven and contested ways (see also Durham, this volume). The word for youth most frequently used in Tamatave is the official Malagasy word *tanora*; some people also use the words *gonalahy* and *gonavavy*, from the Betsimisaraka dialect of Malagasy, referring to males and females, respectively. All of these words connote growth; the word *tanora* is particularly closely associated with the growth of plants, so that one can also refer to rice that is *tanora*, meaning not yet ripe. In traditional terms, plant metaphors are regularly used to imagine human growth, so that a pubescent girl's breasts are described in the same words used for a plant sending out new shoots.

The period of youth is widely seen as one of searching (*mitady*). Adults expect youth to search—whether for fortune, fame, a friend, or a lover who could help them to unlock their *anjara*—a word that indicates one's personal lot or fate in life. Although the concept of *anjara* refers broadly to one's fate or fortune, it is also used more specifically with reference to marriage. For both men and women, searching for one's destiny in marriage includes sexual experimentation, because people believe that a successful marriage requires compatibility, which in turn means trying out many different paths—or people —before one settles down (see also Bloch 1998). In the Betsimisaraka village in which I worked previously, youth of the same sex would often sleep together in granaries or empty houses, slipping off for assignations. It is also normative for girls to receive gifts from their lovers (see also Bloch 1989b; Feeley-Harnik 1991). Despite the general acceptance of experimentation, it does not take place without adult knowledge (nor could it, in the rural context). Moreover, it is widely perceived by people as a process that should end with marriage, the formation of a household, and the birth of children.[6] Consequently, *tanora* is conceived of as a profoundly generative period that contributes to the growth of ancestries.

Although these practices of searching, including trying out many lovers before formalizing a relationship, are widespread both in rural areas and among the lower classes in urban contexts, middle-class urbanites are more concerned with controlling young women's sexuality, an attitude that reflects both the influence of missionary Christianity and a concern for consolidating or improving their own class position. This concern does not translate into a strict effort to maintain virginity. Nevertheless, middle-class families do want to attain at least a veneer of bourgeois respectability.[7] Claire, a fifty-year-old

Betsimisaraka woman married to a low-level functionary, described a middle-class version of how young girls got married in Tamatave in her youth at the end of the First Republic:

> Young girls before, they didn't leave the house or dress up. They were well behaved and they could find a spouse. There would be someone who lived nearby who would say, "There's a young girl in that household"—even if that girl never left the house! If they talked to someone who needed a spouse they would say, "There is a really nice girl over there." Like people doing business. They didn't need money, just talk. Often the parents would seek a wife for their son. And the parents would tell their son—go over to those people's house, for there is a really well behaved girl there. If you like her, then we'll make her your wife. And the boy would go to look at the girl. If he liked her, then he'd have to watch her and see what her character was like, and then after that they would get married and they would be a household for all time. But these days, if you just sat at home all the time you'd never find a spouse. It is those girls who flirt a lot and dress up who find spouses. Things are opposite these days.

Although Claire framed her story as a transparent account of what things "used to be like," the relationship of her narrative to past practice is complex—particularly her claim that parents used to control who married whom. According to more than twenty interviews I conducted with women and men in their late forties and early fifties—the parents of contemporary youth—the great majority had chosen their marriage partners; very few had had their spouses chosen for them. In fact, many people in their late forties and early fifties claimed that it was their parents (thus, contemporary youth's grandparents) who were more likely to have had arranged marriages.[8] When I later discussed with Claire how she had found her spouse, it was clear that hers, too, was a marriage of choice, despite her evocation of previous parental control. Her narrative is both a normative invocation borrowed from her parents' generation and an expression of anxiety over her own increasing lack of control over her children's sexual practices, and it may also express fear as to what unconstrained sexual experimentation in the contemporary urban context might lead to. Claire's observation, however, particularly her comment that nowadays girls need to "flirt a lot and dress up" to find a spouse, also points to the emergence of the new youth category *jeunes*. This group has emerged in the contradictory space created by partial employment and consumer desire.

Urban Youth Culture and the Emergence of *Jeunes*

In contrast to *tanora*, with its emphasis on productive labor and growth rooted in and, ultimately, contributing to the flourishing of families and ancestors, the concept of *jeunes* combines older rural ideas about the sexually playful nature of youth with a new emphasis on sophisticated individual consumption as a means to self-realization. Where *tanora* emphasizes productive labor and the local construction of value, *jeunes* highlights the role of consumption of foreign goods and the localization of value perceived to come from outside. And where *tanora* emphasizes generational growth, *jeunes* emphasizes an individual's improvement of his or her material circumstances.

To be *jeune* is to be always up-to-date, to follow the fashions, and to know the latest "new things." It is to be sophisticated and worldly and to have watched the latest Britney Spears video or to know about the latest platform shoes. It is to have watched the latest porn videos and learned new—ancestrally tabooed—sexual techniques, so that you really know how to make your partner "dream" (*mirevy*, from the French *rever*).[9] To be *jeune* also means to know how to obtain birth control or an abortion, so that one does not end up with an unwanted child. By contrast, young people in the country are *tanora*, bound to a miserable (in the eyes of my urban informants) life of planting rice, with nothing to do and no knowledge of progress. Youth is soon over for country girls, my urban informants claimed, because they quickly find themselves pregnant. Nor are the young maids that crowd the waterfront on Sunday afternoon truly *jeunes*—although it is possible that with time and good luck they will become so. Rather, only young urbanites who see themselves as sophisticated consumers—whether of sex or fashion—are truly *jeunes*. As youth's desire for novelty that Mannheim highlights took on a pervasively commodified form, people came to believe that what one consumes defines one's identity and that the trappings of modernity not only represent but are the essence of social power (Friedman 1990). Consequently people who literally "do not have" (*tsy manana*) are perceived as of lesser social value, unworthy of their peers' respect.

Part of what it means to be *jeune* is to want and know how to use modern things, and to use one's wits to get them. This is a view captured in Claire's statement that in earlier times a girl could just sit at home and get a spouse, whereas today a girl has to actively seek one out by "dressing well and flirting." The girl who doesn't go after what she wants is ridiculed. Her friends ask, "Aren't you young? Don't you want things? What are you doing? Do you want to be left behind?" At the heart of these statements is the assumption that desire for new, foreign things—styles, clothes, commodities—is both constitutive of what it means to be young and part of a new path to adulthood. Tamatavian youth I spoke with believe that adults are dissatisfied with their lot but—because of their increased responsibilities—less likely than youth to be able to change it. Many urban women—even those who had recently come from the country—complain that rural people do not know enough to desire.[10] Urban youth, however, believe that they yearn in a special, urgent way to improve their condition, and that this ceaseless searching can lead to progress or change. Their desire to achieve this goal leads them into the sexual economy.

Sex in the City: The Search for Money, Love, and (Maybe) Marriage

The practices of sex-for-money exchange that young women engage in are part of a complex sexual economy with many different ways of using sex to create relationships. In some cases this sexual and marriage economy has an institutionalized dimension. There is a large and thriving marriage market, via the Internet and postal correspondence, through which local women seek to meet foreign—often French or Réunionais—men. Usually, the woman pays a small fee and gives her photo to the people who run the agency (*agence matrimoniale*), who then place the photo on the Web; the woman waits for someone to contact her.[11] These practices of seeking a marriage partner through correspondence are accompanied by widespread participation in more informal practices of sex-for-money exchange.

Youth engage in transactional sex across a spectrum of possibilities, from short-term encounters with no long-term expectation of reciprocity—what most Malagasy I knew considered prostitution (*mivarotra tena*, literally "to sell oneself")—to more long-term liaisons characterized by the exchange of sex and caring services for material support, sometimes ending in formal marriage.[12] These different types of relationships are crosscut by different kinds of men with whom one forms relations. These men include the European or Réunionais (*vazaha*), who often come as tourists or French *coopérants*, or who work in private businesses, often associated with import-export; the wealthy Malagasy, who are almost always described as the *directeur de l'entreprise*, or the executive who worked at the port; the wealthy Indian traders; and finally the "simple Malagasy" (*gasy tsotra*), with whom, as one young woman put it, "you would just never make it."

As I noted earlier, these different kinds of transactional sexual relationships have a long history in Tamatave, reaching back beyond the colonial period to the late eighteenth and early nineteenth centuries. By the second half of the eighteenth century, many of the lineage heads in the region around Tamatave and just to the north were already the offspring of European pirates and local women (Deschamps 1949). Throughout the late eighteenth and nineteenth centuries, enough local women lived with European men who had come from the plantation islands of Mauritius and Réunion that the term *vadimbazaha*, or "spouses of Europeans," emerged in local parlance. In a dictionary from the late eighteenth century, the scholar-traveler Barthelemy Huet de Froberville defined the *vadimbazaha* thus:

> Literally the wife of the whites, the foreigners. It is not a question of referring to European women or foreign women ... rather the natives use the term *vadimbazaha* to refer to the Malagasy women that the foreigners take on their arrival to care for their homes; their [the *vadimbazaha*'s] prerogatives go as far as to include all the traditional conjugal rights (Bois 1997).

Practices more akin to Western notions of prostitution have long precedents as well. Indeed, over the course of the nineteenth century, Tamatave earned a reputation for immorality and debauchery because of the large numbers of women who went out to spend the night on European ships anchored in the harbor. Guillaume Grandidier recorded that women who engaged in sex-for-money exchanges were referred to as the *tsimihoririna*, or "those who do not sleep on their side" (Bois 1997). Today, this word has been replaced by the term *makorely*, possibly derived from *la maquerelle* or Madame, referring to a time when Réunionais women worked as madams in brothels,[13] although today women who engage in transactional sex keep the money primarily for themselves.[14] Early missionaries looked on both the *vadimbazaha* and the women who went out to the ships with horror, but European observers described the formation of liaisons with local women as essential if one wanted to settle in the area, and within Malagasy society both groups formed part of the local elite and even played a special role in local government ceremonies (Bois 1997).

Most contemporary young women first enter the sexual economy to gain the money that allows them to engage in the sophisticated consumption that is the hallmark of *jeunes*. Ultimately, they hope to use their beauty and sexy clothes to acquire a husband and perhaps, if they are lucky, a ticket overseas, although whether or not they succeed is another matter. Young women's desire to improve their situation through finding men who could help them was particularly visible in the cult-like following of *Marimar*, a Brazilian soap opera that features a young girl who becomes rich through marriage, but only after she has suffered cruelly at the hands of her elders. In the narrative, which unfolded over many episodes, the young, beautiful, and kind-hearted Marimar is the daughter of a wealthy man, but her mother dies without revealing to Marimar her true origins. One day, Marimar steals a chicken from the wealthy Baniz family to feed her starving grandparents. The watchman catches her and is ready to turn her in; however, her beauty and innocence capture the heart of Sergio, the son of the family. After a while, she and Sergio marry. The plot takes many twists and turns, but suffice it to say that Sergio's scheming stepmother hates Marimar because she is poor, and accuses her of stealing a bracelet, for which theft she is jailed. Eventually, Marimar is released from prison and goes to Mexico to work. Marimar and Sergio are finally reunited and the evil stepmother dies. As young women interpreted it, the story critiques both adults (and the ways in which they treat young people) and the relationship between classes. It also powerfully confirmed their view that finding a rich man could be a poor girl's salvation. As one young woman emphasized, "The lesson you can take from the film is this: poor people and rich people should love each other. And the lesson for parents is that they shouldn't hide things from their children. If Marimar had known who her father was, maybe she wouldn't have been poor. The things you see happen in *Marimar*, they are all things that happen in Madagascar!"

Most girls enter the sexual economy hoping to be like Marimar and find a rich man—preferably a *vazaha*. However, when they are unsuccessful or move too quickly from man to man, they move from the category of *jeune* to simple prostitute. People's views of those who slip into the category of prostitute are ambivalent, depending on how successful the women are in converting short-term relationships of sex-for-money exchanges into longer-term relationships that lead to the creation of wider networks and the investment of wealth in social and economic reproduction. For example, several middle-aged women I knew had set themselves up in business with money earned, so people claimed, from prostitution. When they were young women, just starting out, they were mocked; but once they gained money they also gained status. Their neighbors knew where the money came from but did not dare comment on it, fearing that any critical comments they made might be turned against them in the future. But less successful women were heavily criticized; in one case I encountered, a young woman who worked as a prostitute complained that the boys in her neighborhood mocked her and called her "the deformed Marimar." As these distinctions suggest, all girls who engage in the game of sex for money are constantly involved in a politics of reputation. They balance precariously between a basic cultural acceptance of youthful sexuality and a strong sense that after a short period of searching, young women should be married off and in the home. Although the idea of women married and in the home has always been more relevant to middle-class notions of adult femininity, it is an ideal that many urbanites seek to achieve, even if financial circumstances prevent most people from doing so. And while some women manage through their financial success to rewrite these norms, they are the minority.

Two vignettes convey the kinds of relationships that young women form by entering the sexual economy, as well as possible outcomes. I start with a story that Cathy, a fifteen-year-old girl who attended the local junior high school, told me about her older sister. Their parents came from southeastern Madagascar; the mother worked selling cooked food by the roadside, and the father worked as a docker. Cathy had not yet found a *vazaha* who might support her, but she exuberantly announced that she was sure she'd love one if she found one because "they have a lot of money." Her sister, however, had found a *vazaha*, and things had not turned out as she had hoped.

> My older sister already had a *vazaha* boyfriend. He had a motorcycle. But they have already broken up, and it was very sad the way he treated my older sibling. He was very mean. He liked to drink rum and go to nightclubs and when he was drunk he was cruel and liked to break glasses. They were together for a year, but during that time they often broke up because that *vazaha*, he liked too many women. They would break up because my older sister would get mad, but he'd come back to her and make up to her with gifts. My sister couldn't stand to see him grovel and would go out with him again. But when he went home he sold everything that he had bought for her house. The only things she got were the clothes she stole and a small

fan! But he lied to my sister! He told her, "We have to sell these things because we won't live here anymore. I've found new work and I have to return to France. When I've settled down, after a month or two, I'll send for you." He gave my sister money to go get her passport and she was very happy. But when he got to France, he wrote only once to my sister. He asked her if her passport was ready, but then he never wrote again nor did he send her anything. My sister just cried and cried. His name was Franck—he was short and balding.

Although most girls did not recount stories of drunken French men who smashed glasses in fits of rage, many were disappointed by *vazaha* who promised marriage or a ticket to Europe, but did not come through. Yet, despite her older sister's experience, Cathy remained optimistic about the possibilities of finding a man—a *vazaha* boyfriend or perhaps a husband—on the sexual marketplace. Her views seem to have been more influenced by accounts such as the one told to me by the fourteen-year-old Flavienne, who attended a private lycée and whose mother worked—sometimes—as a prostitute.

Flavienne's mother came from a town to the north; her grandmother was Betsimisaraka and her grandfather was Chinese and had a small shop. Her grandparents had cared for Flavienne when she was small while her mother pursued *vazaha*; then Flavienne's mother had come and claimed her. Flavienne explained,

> My mother doesn't like to bring her boyfriends here, except for the *vazaha*. That *vazaha*, he is already married overseas. He has two children. But he and my mother, they have been together a very long time. He has supported my mother for years. When he comes to Madagascar, he always comes to our house but doesn't go to the hotel. They are like a married couple. Some people think they are already married, but that Mama doesn't want to live overseas. There was a time when he brought Mama to France, but he didn't take Mama to the house where his wife lives. He brought her to another house. That *vazaha* really has a lot of money, and so he has a lot of houses. He really likes me. He treats me like his own child.

Each of these stories illustrates the ways in which young women use their sexuality to try to move from short-term transactional relationships, in which women receive gifts and money in exchange for sex, to more long-term bonds and social relationships that give them material support and enable them to both help their families of origin and form new families of their own. Flavienne's story about her mother suggests that in forming a stable relationship with a *vazaha*, and then by earning extra income through more casual prostitution when the *vazaha* was away, her mother was able to maintain a household and support her daughter, who attended a fee-paying school. Eventually, this *vazaha* took Flavienne and her mother back with him to France. But even in this very successful story, the fate of Flavienne and her mother remains ambiguous. All we know is that the *vazaha* brought them to France; we do not know if he divorced his wife to marry Flavienne's mother. Nor do we know if

Figure 3.2. This multigenerational photo is of a mother who participates in a sex-workers' association and sells handicrafts in the marketplace, her daughter, whose boyfriend is from Réunion Island, and her daughter's baby. *Photo by Jennifer Cole.*

Flavienne and her mother ended up abandoned and starving, as other women who had followed *vazaha* had reputedly done. And although by going to France Flavienne's mother rose up the social ladder, she did so by first risking her reputation to work as a prostitute. As I have noted, financial success, however, allowed her to rewrite the norms around what counted as respectable adulthood.

For Cathy's older sister, however, these same strategies subjected her to the risk of HIV/AIDS and other sexually transmitted diseases, the violence of Franck's hot temper, and, ultimately, disappointment when he left and took everything that he'd given her with him. As Cathy's case suggests, participation in the sexual economy can lead to downward mobility, as well. In talking about the possibilities for success in the sexual marketplace, many young people said that *anjara*, their lot or fate, would determine whether they were successful or not. For instance, it might be one's fate to marry a wealthy man but at a later age than is usually considered desirable. Viewed from the outside, however, there appears to be a window of opportunity—between about eighteen and one's late twenties, perhaps early thirties—in which girls can succeed. After a certain point, if they have little luck in the sexual economy, they will probably become ever poorer and more firmly entrenched in the category of prostitute, making it less likely that any local man will want to marry them. If a girl is unlucky enough to fall pregnant and bear the baby, and if there are no grandparents who are willing to raise the child, this movement down the social ladder becomes all the more likely.

Young Women and Social Regeneration

In their enthusiastic participation in the sexual economy of Tamatave, and particularly in their pursuit of *vazaha*, young women are clearly part of a long, historically constituted tradition in which women deploy their sexuality in the formation of relationships and in which women obtain prestige through transnational relationships with *vazaha* men. However, although these practices of transactional sex are old, the context in which they are taking place is doubly constituted as new, marked simultaneously by the changing social and economic circumstances brought about by neoliberal economic reform of the last ten years and by a particular generation coming into "fresh contact" with historically constituted practices. Many factors contribute to this new context: the inability of many young men to get jobs that will enable them to sustain a family; the concentration of wealth in the hands of a few, primarily older, men; the influx of images of Western style and opulence that girls want to emulate; and finally the arrival of (comparatively) wealthy men from abroad. The result is that young girls can use their sexuality to link people in partially new ways, disrupting social hierarchies along the axes of generation and gender.

Recrafting Families

Looking more closely at what young women do with the money they earn through sex gives some sense of the complex ways in which participation in the sexual economy disrupts and rearranges local family formations. It is difficult to generalize about how much money young women receive from men, because it varies so widely from case to case. Women may be paid as little as 5000 FMG (less than a dollar) for a quick encounter (*passe temps*), but one woman who worked as a maid for a European, earning 50,000 FMG a month (about seven dollars), recounted how all the prostitutes in her neighborhood mocked her, claiming that they earned in one night what she earned in a month. Another young woman I knew who had created a stable relationship with a *vazaha* received between 1,500,000 and 2,000,000 FMG (roughly between $200 and $300) a month to cover her expenses. As these examples suggest, many women who entered the sexual economy managed to just scrape by. For others, however, gifts and money from sex provided them with an important extra source of income, enabling them to purchase status-enhancing commodities, to invest in business, or to create new social relations on their own terms.

At least in the beginning of their entry into the sexual economy, many young women continue to live at home, using their money for clothes, cell phones, and other desired commodities. Fashionable clothes and cell phones are important forms of social capital, both marking out a girl as modern and increasing the chance that she will find either one of the rare jobs available or a wealthier man—or both. If a girl is young—say in her early teens and still in school—many parents object to her sexual activity because it increases the likelihood that the girl will end up pregnant and drop out of school. With slightly older girls, however, parents are often relieved to have the financial onus taken off them, and they expect that girls will be supported by their lovers; one way for a man to mark out a woman as a prospective wife is by giving her material support until a marriage can be arranged. Yet in both cases, the girl's acquisition of status-producing commodities, which the parents often do not have access to, symbolically enacts a reversal of power and authority within the household. The social status derived from control over commodities, however, competes against more normative modes of acquiring adult status through work and marriage, and young women are positioned uneasily between the two.

Girls unable to find a husband often set up houses of their own, either because their behavior causes fights with their parents and they want the freedom to do as they please, or because their parents do not have enough money to support them. Many of these young women have long-term ambitions and goals, but the need to perpetually keep abreast of fashions in clothes and prestigious consumer items can make such goals hard to fulfill. When they do earn enough money, many women use it to accumulate commodities, or they redistribute it to whomever they please, creating networks of patronage of which they are the center. When they are able to forge more long-term relationships of concubinage or marriage, young girls seek to use the money and connections they gain from their relationships with *vazaha* to help their families. Indeed, one young Malagasy man explicitly stated that women prefer *vazaha* because they do not come with big, needy families, thereby allowing the women to funnel resources to their own kin without dispute.

In seeking to use the money they gain through relationships with *vazaha* to help their parents, young girls, like young women in the nineteenth century, want to increase their social status and help their families. However, changes in the nature of the economy mean that these relationships may have different effects than they did then, making this dream harder to realize. After all, in the nineteenth century, *vazaha* were often immigrants to Tamatave who sought to run plantations; they needed the *vadimbazaha* not only for sex or domestic services but also because they provided access to productive resources—land and slaves—that were otherwise forbidden to them (Bois 1997).[15] By contrast, contemporary *vazaha* who come to Tamatave usually live there only temporarily and receive a salary. Although the woman may form a relationship with the intent of helping her kin, the desires and cultural expectations of the *vazaha*, less accustomed to the idea of an extended family who can make demands, mitigate against these plans.[16] More generally, what Tamatavian girls have to offer now is different from what their nineteenth-century counterparts had. In the nineteenth century, the *vadimbazaha* could provide Europeans with access to land and labor in addition to the "comforts of home" (White 1990). Today, these girls can only satisfy globally mediated fantasies about African sexuality and domesticity, because, with the exception of a few tourist spots, the economy no longer relies on access to land. As a consequence, these girls are at a disadvantage when compared to their nineteenth-century predecessors.

Even when families are able to gain some access to the capital brought by daughters' liaisons with *vazaha*, the relationships that crystallize around the wealth still lead to the splintering of local families. A story told to me by Maman Pasy, a woman who owned a hairdressing salon, gives some sense of this process. According to Maman Pasy, two of her younger sisters had married *vazaha*, Belgians whom they had met through a marriage agency (*koresy*), and a third sister was married to a local man. The Malagasy brother-in-law drove a truck, which was, in turn, owned by the Belgian brothers-in-law. Eventually, the Malagasy man lost a huge sum of money; the sisters married to the Belgians accused their Malagasy brother-in-law of theft and went so far as to bring him to court. When the case was tried, the Malagasy brother-in-law was eventually proved innocent, but in the meantime neighborly opinion sided with the sisters married to the Belgians and assumed the Malagasy brother-in-law's guilt. Remarking on the way in which popular opinion had sided with the *vadimbazahas'* position against the poorer Malagasy brother-in-law, Mama Pasy concluded, "People here, you know they like money, they like *vazaha*, so if the spouse of the *vazaha* does something wrong [like wrongly accusing her brother-in-law of theft], people protect her, because she has money. It makes me really sad to think that they no longer have what makes us kin because they are only thinking about money."

In observing that "they no longer have what makes them kin," Maman Pasy provides a powerful commentary on how the economic transactions that accompany the coveted relationships with powerful *vazaha* also lead to the violation of expected kinship norms. The introduction of wealth into family relationships created problems among kin in earlier periods, as well; it was certainly something I'd witnessed in the rural context in which I'd worked previously. But in the rural context, invoking the threat of ancestral anger to force people to remain together often mitigated, though it never erased, wealth's disruptive effects. In the contemporary urban context, the threat of ancestral anger or being cut off from kin did not carry as much moral weight, partly because once people managed to accumulate money, poor kin often ended up being more of a burden than a source of wealth.

People's perceptions of the ways in which participation in the sexual economy might transform kin relations were also embodied in another story that Rodrigue recounted that Sunday on the beach. (I heard versions of the story in other contexts as well, but I was never able to determine whether or not it was rooted in a true event.) According to Rodrigue, there was a pretty girl who loved a Malagasy boy. Her parents, however, wanted to capitalize on their daughter's beauty by forcing her to marry a *vazaha* against her will. In the event, the *vazaha* used the girl for his sexual pleasure, and then discarded her—when Rodrigue told the story he commented that it was the parents' fault that this girl had been "ruined." Other versions of the story I heard—similarly recounted by young men—ended with the parents using love magic to bind the girl to the man and to keep the money flowing to them. Although most people expect daughters to contribute some material support to their natal households, as we have seen, they also believe that girls have a right to choose their lovers. The use of love magic to enslave one's own child in a relationship that produced wealth for the parents against the child's will cogently bespeaks young people's fears about how sex and marriage for money could undermine proper social reproduction, nurture, and relations of authority within the household (see also Graeber 1996). That young men—precisely the kind of unemployed young Malagasy men that in the story the girl's parents did not want her to marry, and that many young girls I know also do not want to marry—should tell this story is worth emphasizing. As the next section makes clear, it makes sense that precisely those people most marginalized by changes in the economy, and who feel their own gendered positions to be threatened by women's relations with *vazaha* and other powerful men, should make the most telling comments about the ways in which relationships pursued mainly for material reasons could pervert the normative relations between parents and children.

Inversions: Women Supporting Men

The same economic forces that push women increasingly into the sexual economy also work to marginalize young men, so that women's practices of transactional sex have become associated with the disruption of local notions of proper gendered relations (cf. Livingston, this volume). Nowhere is this phenomenon more visible than in the emergence of the *jaombilo*, the man supported by the money that a woman earns through her relationships with *vazaha* men, or through prostitution more generally (Cole 2005). As one young man explained, echoing the story with which I began, "the *vazaha* gives money to the Malagasy girl, and she gives it to her Malagasy boyfriend—it's a parallel finance system." Although no one I knew was able to identify the origins of the word, the root *jao* means an uncastrated, powerful bull, and Gillian Feeley-Harnik tells me that it is also by extension frequently used as a man's name. The word had a previous analogue in *jaoloka*, a term used in western Madagascar to refer to a man who had the misfortune to live with his wife's family, which became more common as patterns of social reproduction changed after migrants came to the area following the introduction of wage labor (Waast 1980).

Whereas people view women's practices of transactional sex ambivalently, depending, in large part, on how successful women are in forging long-term relations, views of *jaombilo* are mainly negative, a fact reflected in the other term for the practice: *maladie legon*, which literally means "boy's illness." Girls like Farida bragged that they would certainly support a Malagasy lover if they received lots of money from a *vazaha*, but other girls I knew expressed distaste at the idea. Anita, the mistress of a rich political representative who was quite frank about how she made her living, explained why she found the practice unthinkable. "It is very painful to see women supporting men! Prostitutes might part with money to support the man they love but for me, it would be hard to support a man. People would make fun of me, and they would blame me." But one young woman who often "went out at night" (*mivoaka alina*), an expression often used to refer to prostitution, expressed distaste at the notion, as well: "Who, me," she said, "support a man? You've got to be joking." And for men, the practice was downright shaming, although many young men I spoke with admitted to having engaged in it for periods of time. As Beaumot, a man in his late twenties, said, slapping his muscles, "You, a young man, not work with the force of your own body? That won't do!"

Part of the reason that people find the *jaombilo* so deeply disturbing is that he inverts what people perceive the proper relationship between men and women to be. In criticizing *jaombilo*, people are basing their arguments on the deeply held notion that men should support women, and not the reverse. In the urban context, men are ideally supposed to work and give their spouses salaries for household use, while women, in turn, are supposed to perform domestic labor and use their spouses' money to maintain the household. And yet, in the case of the *jaombilo*, it is women who make a living for men by diverting the gifts or money they earn through sex with other men, a practice perceived as demeaning and emasculating for all the men involved: the *vazaha* because he is cuckolded and used only for his money; the *jaombilo* because he is supported by a woman's willingness to divert her earnings from sex work for *vazaha* men. As one young man explained,

> What makes it bad for a woman to support her man, is that God said in the days of Adam and Eve that it was the man who supports and not the woman. It is like the man has no pride if a woman supports him—he who should make his spouse a living is making a living by her! If you took the woman from her parents, then you should be ready to care for her. It is like you are dishonored if you do not support the woman. If you do not get along at home, then the man is crushed but he won't dare to speak. Because there is someone who supports him.

Moreover, the gender reversal is further elaborated because in some cases women expect their *jaombilo* to perform household tasks like washing clothes, doing dishes, or cooking: tasks that are explicitly marked as female. The woman's control over money means she can shame the *jaombilo* at any time: in one fight I witnessed, a furious woman stood outside her house, holding up the man's clothes and enumerating how much each item had cost and just where she, not he, had earned the money.

95

The gender inversion that *jaombilo* experience powerfully symbolizes the thwarted power of urban young men, who have historically been associated with the construction of Malagasy modernity (Ledoux 1951). In the past, at least some of these young men would have been able to find jobs in the government or even in business that would enable them to sustain the families and productive enterprises that signal a fruitful—but also modern—ancestral homeland. Although in theory it is possible that *jaombilo* could invest the money they are given or use it to start a business, thus possibly attaining the financial independence that is one aspect of legitimate adulthood, they are instead notorious for sponsoring the short-term pleasures of others.[17] As Beaumot elaborated, "*Jaombilo*, they are people whom girls support and they don't work. They won't take low wages. Whether they work or not, they are full from their lover's money. They are like the leaders of the gang in town, because they can finance many pleasures, like they can pay for their friends to go to discos, to drink or watch concerts." When these young men become "leaders of the gang," they are also involved in forging new measures of status by positioning themselves as patrons controlling other young men's access to pleasurable commodities like alcohol, and to activities like going to a concert. Like the women whose flaunting of status-producing commodities created a potentially new measure of adulthood, so too the *jaombilo* who distributed pleasures to their circles of friends marked a potentially new kind of adult man. But because their activities did not lead to the formation of households, which in turn might enable the buildup of capital among kin, and more kin-based collective endeavors, they were less successful than young women at converting their positions into more respected visions of adulthood.

Conclusion

So this is how "fresh contact" takes place in contemporary Tamatave, as youth's participation in the sexual economy disrupts existing social hierarchies in important ways. Although young men remain trapped in part-time jobs or are driven to live off theft, young women embrace the possibilities offered by the informal sexual economy, which links Tamatave to France, Réunion Island, and beyond, and creates complex redistributions of resources within Tamatave. As a result, young women have emerged at the forefront of a partially new body politics, by adopting a set of strategies that women in this region have historically used to advance their positions. These practices, however, have not been adopted wholesale but have become powerfully inflected with the consumerist values and practices that characterize contemporary Tamatave. Commodification may be a means to other ends, as Cornwall (2002), writing about Nigerian practices around sex and money, has argued, but in Tamatave it has pushed itself deeper into young women's lives, becoming a primary way in which many young women think about and attempt to achieve status and value.

This analysis of youthful practice around sex for money as part of a process of fresh contact and intergenerational transformation helps to extend and nuance recent anthropological discussions of youth culture by adding an important relational and temporal dimension to how we think about youthful practice. Not only do youth rework practices from the past, but the way in which they deploy these practices reshapes the ways in which families are currently being created and may be sustained in the future. Moreover, viewed through the lens of "fresh contact," the practices through which young women attempt to gain adulthood and form families are not simply one factor to be added to discussions of globalization and youth. Rather, because the changing demands of culture and economy reshape the ways in which people forge relations, youthful practice works to form new social hierarchies that constitute globalization locally. Both these points suggest that youth cannot be analytically separated from the network of social relations in which they are embedded. To argue this is not to say that youthful practice is devoid of any intrinsic meaning, a charge that has often been leveled at older anthropological and psychological studies of childhood and adolescence (Scheper-Hughes and Sargent 1998). Rather, it is to suggest that youth transform society because of the specific kind of agency bestowed on them by virtue of their position within a flow of generations.

But important questions follow. After all, the balance of generational and gendered power that I encountered may prove ephemeral. Some young girls may have gained a certain success for the moment, but it is difficult to tell how long this configuration will last. Not only would a rise in HIV/AIDS infection rates make young women's sex-for-money practices lethal but, on the basis of our knowledge of other parts of Africa, we can expect that the kinds of socioeconomic landscapes that I have described here may be accompanied by a combination of political instability and male violence. During the political crisis of 2002, the incumbent, Ratsiraka, created an economic barrier to choke off the capital city to try to defeat his rival, Ravalomanana. The barriers also severely disrupted the sexual economy in Tamatave, as people found themselves with less money. Those who could fled the instability, and Europeans stopped traveling to the region. Such contingencies point to how fragile young women's strategies are. Will these changes turn out to benefit a few lucky women, while others find themselves trapped in an endless round of sex for money? Or will the new ways of attaining adulthood provide an increased number of rural people who have come to the city with a means of social ascension, as several informants imply? In what ways might the shifts in women's role and power affect the conditions in which future generations are raised? This is a story that will play out in subsequent generations and is for future ethnographers to document, but doing so will require that they continue to look beyond synchronic notions of youth culture and youth agency to probe how economic demands shape the ways in which youth reshape how intimate bonds are forged.

Jennifer Cole

NOTES

This chapter is a slightly revised version of the paper that appeared in *American Ethnologist* 31 (4): 573–588. I am grateful to the American Anthropological Association for permitting me to reprint the paper here. The research on which it is based was funded by a U.S. Government Fulbright Grant, the American Philosophical Society, a Milton Grant from Harvard University, and the Wenner-Gren Foundation for Anthropological Research. I am grateful to the Randrianja family for their hospitality during my various stays in Tamatave, and to Solofo Randrianja for arranging my affiliation with the Université de Tamatave. Earlier versions of this chapter were presented at the Workshop on African Studies at the University of Chicago, the Department of Anthropology at the London School of Economics, McGill University, and the Medical Anthropology Seminar at Harvard University. I am grateful to the participants in all of these venues for their comments.

1. Presumably the *vazaha* was able to put the Malagasy man in jail by accusing him of theft; the European man essentially used his economic power to impose his will on the situation and get rid of his rival. Aurelie later told me, however, that once the *vazaha* left the police released the Malagasy man, which was how the wider community learned of the story.

2. I am grateful to Gillian Feeley-Harnik for suggesting this particular formulation.

3. According to UNAIDS (2002), in 2001 0.3 percent of adults and children between 15 and 49 were infected with HIV; HIV prevalence among sex workers tested in the capital city increased from 0.0 percent during 1991–1994 to 0.3 percent in 1995 to 1.3 percent in 1998. In the cities of Diego Suarez and Tamatave, HIV prevalence among sex workers in 1996 was 1 to 2 percent and less than 1 percent, respectively.

4. Building on my fieldwork conducted in rural East Madagascar (1992–1994, 1997), I carried out fieldwork in urban Tamatave (in Malagasy, Toamasina) over a total of ten months between 1999 and 2003. The interview segments provided here are only a selected few out of over a hundred interviews I have conducted.

5. So contentious was the question of access to schooling that it was one of the key issues in the demise of Tsiranana's First Republic and the switch to the state-socialist Second Republic under Ratsiraka (see Covell 1989). For a contemporary discussion of the politics of schooling in Madagascar, see Sharp 2002.

6. Once a household is formed women are supposed to be monogamous; men are not. The expression that most clearly expresses this double standard is "men can't be adulterous [even if they sleep around]" (*lehilahy tsy mba misengy*).

7. Families who have joined new evangelical churches represent an important exception to this rule. This group considers control over female virginity extremely important, and views girls who have lost their virginity as "spoiled" (*simba*).

8. Claire's reflections about the ideal type of courtship, in which parents at least partially shape their children's choice of spouse, are part of a wider set of ideas concerning how families become materially linked to one another at marriage. Only a small fraction of people actually get married in a civil ceremony, although it is only a civil ceremony that is legally recognized by the state. What is socially recognized, however, and what most people perform is a ceremony of the *vody ondry*, in which the groom gives a small sum of money to the woman's parents as a symbolic payment for their efforts in raising her (see also Bloch 1989a). However, it is only once a stable marriage forms that a girl's natal family may benefit from the relations created by it. In theory, at

least, marriage means that a woman handles the family finances, receiving her husband's pay and then using it to take care of household expenses. Because women control the purse strings, they are able to funnel money surreptitiously to their kin. Particularly in marriages of long duration and despite the fact that patrilineal links are ideologically prioritized, many married women hope to favor their kin, and often succeed in doing so at the expense of the man's.

9. Although I explicitly discussed sexual practices only with women who considered themselves prostitutes (as opposed to *jeunes*) and with men, who were less reticent about sexual matters, several people mentioned that oral sex—which people see in European porn films—is ancestrally taboo. Their logic was that it involved mixing the head, which is considered clean, with the genitals, which are considered dirty.

10. In accusing rural people of not wanting enough, urban youth sound uncannily like French administrators in the colonial era (see Cole 2001).

11. These "agencies" could be quite informal. Sometimes they were only a woman who had a relative living abroad who provided lists of men interested in marrying Malagasy women. Even more formal agencies often functioned via kin networks.

12. The appropriateness of the term "prostitute" in the African context is widely debated; many scholars have pointed out the problems of categorizing sex-for-money exchanges according to particular Western formulations (Hunter 2002; Schoepf 1992, 1995; Wojcicki 2002; Zalduondo 1991). In this chapter, I have used the broader and more neutral term "transactional sex"; however, in some cases, I have retained the word "prostitute" because it remained a very important category among my informants.

13. Personal communication from Solofo Randrianja, February 7, 2002.

14. Although there is no official institution of the pimp in Tamatave, occasionally people—for example, taxi drivers—do mediate between women and their clients and take some cut of the profits.

15. During the precolonial period, non-Malagasy were forbidden to own land, so that marrying a woman was one of the only ways that early settlers could obtain access to land.

16. Feeley-Harnik (1991, 294) reports that women in northwest Madagascar perceived *vazaha* as reluctant to establish kinship relations of the kind expected by local people.

17. Both the practices of, and others' attitudes toward, the *jaombilo* are similar to those described by Walsh (2003) for sapphire miners in northern Madagascar. In both cases, young men acquire money in ways that they believe marks the money as "hot" which means that it needs to be spent as quickly as possible.

WORKS CITED

Astuti, Rita. 1995. *People of the Sea: Identity and Descent among the Vezo of Madagascar.* Cambridge: Cambridge University Press.

Bloch, Maurice. 1989a. "Marriage amongst Equals: An Analysis of the Marriage Ceremony of the Merina of Madagascar." In *Ritual, History, and Power: Selected Papers in Anthropology.* Pp. 89–105. London: Athlone Press.

———. 1989b. "The Symbolism of Money in Imerina." In *Money and the Morality of Exchange.* J. Parry and M. Bloch, eds. Pp. 165–190. Cambridge: Cambridge University Press.

———. 1998. "The Resurrection of the House amongst the Zafimaniry of Madagascar."

In *How We Think They Think: Anthropological Approaches to Cognition, Memory, and Literacy*. Pp. 85–99. Boulder, Colo.: Westview Press.

Bois, Dominique. 1997. "Tamatave: La cité des femmes." *CLIO: Histoire, femmes et société* 6, numero spéciale: Femmes d'Afrique, 6: 61–86.

Bucholtz, Mary. 2002. "Youth and Cultural Practice." *Annual Review of Anthropology* 31: 525–552.

Cole, Jennifer. 2001. *Forget Colonialism? Sacrifice and the Art of Memory in Madagascar*. Berkeley: University of California Press.

———. 2005. "The Jaombilo of Tamatave (Madagascar), 1992–2004: Reflections on Youth and Globalization." *Journal of Social History* 38 (4): 891–914.

Cornwall, Andrea. 2002. "Spending Power: Love, Money, and the Reconfiguration of Gender Relations in Ado-Odo, Southwestern Nigeria." *American Ethnologist* 29 (4): 963–980.

Covell, Maureen. 1989. *Madagascar: Politics, Economics, Society*. New York: Frances Pinter.

Deschamps, Hubert. 1949. *Les pirates à Madagascar au XVII et XVIII siècles*. Paris: Berger-Levrault.

Durham, Deborah. 2000. "Youth and the Social Imagination in Africa." *Anthropological Quarterly* 73 (3): 113–120.

Elder, Glen, Jr. 1987. "The Life Course and Human Development." In *Handbook of Child Psychology*, vol. 1, *Theoretical Models of Human Development*. Richard M. Lerner, vol. ed. William Damon, editor in chief. Pp. 939–991. New York: Wiley.

———. 1999 [1974]. *Children of the Great Depression: Social Change in Life Experience*. Boulder, Colo.: Westview Press.

Feeley-Harnik, Gillian. 1991. *A Green Estate: Restoring Independence in Madagascar*. Washington, D.C.: Smithsonian Press.

Friedman, Jonathan. 1990. "The Political Economy of Elegance: An African Cult of Beauty." *Culture and History* 7: 101–125.

Graeber, David. 1996. "Love Magic and Political Morality in Central Madagascar, 1875–1990." *Gender and History* 8 (3): 416–439.

Hall, Stuart, and Tony Jefferson, eds. 1993 [1975]. *Resistance through Rituals: Youth Subcultures in Post-war Britain*. London: Routledge Press.

Hebdige, Dick. 1979. *Subculture: The Meaning of Style*. London: Methuen.

Hunter, Marc. 2002. "The Materiality of Everyday Sex: Thinking beyond Prostitution." *African Studies* 61 (1): 99–120.

Ledoux, Marc Andre. 1951. "La jeunesse malgache." *Cahiers Charles de Foucauld*, numero special sur Madagascar, 1ʳᵉ trimestre.

Liechty, Mark. 2002. *Suitably Modern: Making Middle-Class Culture in a New Consumer Society*. Princeton, N.J.: Princeton University Press.

Mannheim, Karl. 1972 [1952]. "The Problem of Generations." In *Essays on the Sociology of Knowledge*. Pp. 276–322. London: Routledge and Kegan Paul.

Mead, Margaret. 1928. *Coming of Age in Samoa: A Psychological Study of Primitive Youth for Western Civilization*. New York: Morrow.

Newman, Katherine. 1996. "Ethnography, Biography, and Cultural History: Generational Paradigms in Human Development." In *Ethnography and Human Development: Context and Meaning in Social Inquiry*. Richard Jessor, Anne Colby, and Richard Shweder, eds. Pp. 371–393. Chicago: University of Chicago Press.

Projet Madio. 2001. *L'emploi, le chomage et les conditions d'activité des ménages dans les sept grandes villes de Madagascar.* Antananarivo, Madagascar: Ministère des finances et de l'economie, Institut national de la statistique.

Rossy. 1994. "Bal Kabosy." On *Bal Kabosy,* music CD. MARS 1003.

Scheper-Hughes, Nancy, and Carolyn Sargent. 1998. "The Cultural Politics of Child-hood." Introduction to *Small Wars: The Cultural Politics of Childhood.* Nancy Scheper-Hughes and Carolyn Sargent, eds. Pp. 1–33. Berkeley: University of California Press.

Schoepf, Brooke Grundfest. 1992. "Women at Risk: Case Studies from Zaire." In *The Time of AIDS: Social Analysis, Theory, and Method.* Gilbert Herdt and Shirley Lindenbaum, eds. Pp. 259–286. London: Sage.

———. 1995. "Culture, Sex Research, and AIDS Prevention in Africa." In *Culture and Sexual Risk: Anthropological Perspectives on AIDS.* Han ten Brummelhuis and Gilbert Herdt, eds. Pp. 29–51. Luxembourg: Gordon and Breach.

Sharp, Lesley. 2002. *The Sacrificed Generation: Youth, History, and the Colonized Mind in Madagascar.* Berkeley: University of California Press.

Stephens, Sharon. 1995. *Children and the Politics of Culture.* Princeton, N.J.: Princeton University Press.

Tribune de Madagascar. 1991. "Crisis." January 7.

UNAIDS. 2002. "Epidemiological Fact Sheets on HIV/AIDS and Sexually Trans-mitted Infections: Madagascar." http://www.unaids.org, accessed August 10, 2003.

Waast, Roland. 1980. "Les concubins de Soalala." In *Changements sociaux dans l'ouest Malgache.* R. Waast, E. Fauroux, B. Schlemmer, F. Le Bourdic, J. P. Raison, and G. Dandoy, eds. Pp. 153–188. Paris: ORSTOM.

Walsh, Andrew. 2003. "'Hot Money' and Daring Consumption in a Northern Mala-gasy Sapphire-Mining Town." *American Ethnologist* 30 (2): 290–305.

Weisner, Thomas S., and Lucinda P. Bernheimer. 1998. "Children of the 1960s at Midlife: Generational Identity and the Family Adaptive Project." In *Welcome to Middle Age! (and Other Cultural Fictions).* Richard A. Shweder, ed. Pp. 211–257. Chicago: University of Chicago Press.

Weiss, Brad. 2002. "Thug Realism: Inhabiting Fantasy in Urban Tanzania." *Cultural Anthropology* 17 (1): 93–124.

White, Luise. 1990. *The Comforts of Home: Prostitution in Colonial Nairobi.* Chicago: University of Chicago Press.

Whiting, J. W. M., V. K. Burbank, and M. S. Ratner. 1986. "The Duration of Maiden-hood across Cultures." In *School-Age Pregnancy and Parenthood: Biosocial Dimen-sions.* Jane B. Lancaster and Beatrix A. Hamburg, eds. Pp. 273–302. New York: Aldine–De Gruyter.

Wojcicki, Janet Maia. 2002. "Commercial Sex Work or Ukuphanda? Sex-for-Money Exchange in Soweto and Hammanskraal Area, South Africa." *Culture, Medicine, and Psychiatry* 26 (3): 339–370.

Wulff, Helena. 1995. "Introducing Youth Culture in Its Own Right: The State of the Art and New Possibilities." In *Youth Cultures: A Cross-Cultural Perspective.* Vered Amit-Talai and Helena Wulff, eds. Pp. 1–18. London: Routledge Press.

Zalduondo, Barbara. 1991. "Prostitution Viewed Cross-Culturally: Toward Recontex-tualizing Sex Work in AIDS Intervention Research." *Journal of Sex Research* 28 (2): 223–248.

4

Empowering Youth

Making Youth Citizens in Botswana

DEBORAH DURHAM

Wake Up to Empowerment

The Botswana government is committed to empowering youth. So said President Festus Mogae in July 2002, addressing the Botswana Democratic Party Youth Wing.[1] The following September 30, President Mogae reiterated this commitment in his Independence Day message, which focused that year upon the nation's youth. While he again noted the government's commitment to empowering youth, in September he also told youth that "the world does not owe [them] a living" and that they "must work hard" to match and continue the achievements of their predecessors, now "retired from formal employment."[2] The recurrence of the word "empowerment" in the president's speeches and in wider government discourse on youth is striking—as is its linkage with the ideas of hard work, independence, and formal employment.

In this paper, I explore how the new youth development project in Botswana, using empowerment as its keyword[3] and linking work, self-development, and autonomy with ideal citizenship, revises notions of youth agency and citizenship in Botswana. The government's commitment to youth interprets a popular sense of crisis surrounding youth in terms of national development ideology, and in doing so resonates with rapidly changing social and economic experiences of young people. Nonetheless, in extending the official discourses of citizen empowerment and egalitarian liberalism to youth, the commitment to empower repeatedly runs up against other forms of social power historically associated with youth in Botswana, and other forms of belonging, still important in domains such as those of family and local community, that do not start with the idea of the independent actor. Here, the "power" of being a young person lies in one's ability to contribute to relations of caring for others within the family and, through activities associated specifically with youth, to extend those relations with other groups beyond the family, including lovers and future spouses, neighborhoods and local communities, and the nation and state. Through the intergenerational relations by which they are situated in the family, where their activities straddle work and play, youth have been key figures in regenerating not only new households, but also community interdependencies of work and care.[4]

Empowering youth takes place, in other words, in a dialogue with other forms of youth agency. An examination of the dialogue between youth empowerment programs and other forms of youth "power" illuminates the encounter between a global discourse of universal human subjectivity and agency (embedded in phenomena as diverse as human rights, development programs, and the spread of commodity consumerism) and other discourses of social agency (embedded in household relationships, interdependency, and highly specific capabilities associated with different ages).

The term "empowerment," relatively absent from public language in Botswana during my first period of fieldwork in 1989–1991, was suddenly everywhere by the middle or late 1990s, applied to citizens, women, local entrepreneurs, and youth. The term undoubtedly entered Botswana's powerful development apparatus from global discourses of development, human rights, social movements, and academic social sciences, cycling from one field to another. In the parking lot of my rural Virginia grocery store—not one of the government-mandated "Economic Empowerment Zones" of the early 1990s—an old man wears a ragged t-shirt emblazoned "Youth Empowered to Succeed." The idea of empowerment, for success or for "liberatory" purposes, has been carried around the world by international nongovernmental organizations (NGOs) attempting to improve women's status in Nepal (Leve 2001), the fates of street children in Ethiopia (Niewenhuys 2001), or the political role of marginalized peoples like the Bushmen of southern Africa (Hitchcock 2002). It has been carried by non-Western people who go to America to study sociology, development studies, political science, or health services, and return home to work in local NGOs or government ministries, or to teach in local universities or schools. The term, as exported from America, carries discursive implications for society and personhood. In the language of empowerment, as used by development programs and in political rhetoric, citizenship is recognized in a restricted set of activities, generally related to economic independence and the autonomous, self-determining, liberalist individual, and is not recognized in other forms of agency (see, for example, Cruikshank 1999 on discourses on welfare queens and empowerment in the U.S.). In some spheres where it is popular, such as education, "empowerment" refers to allowing the individual to build self-confidence, and with that anchor of selfhood to take control of his own learning and decisions, independent of the smothering disciplines of standardized texts, peer pressures, and course schedules (Weiss-berg 2000). Development and human service programs that take the idea of empowerment to new sites around the world focus upon creating independent, self-developing, and individualist people, freed from interdependencies and collective relations that constrain them as liberalist citizens of a nation or the world.[5] These projects are thus resolutely liberal, seeking equality and equivalent forms of economic, social, and personal power for their subjects.

The keyword "empowerment" fell on fertile terrain in Botswana, which has pursued an aggressively liberalist political-economic agenda since gaining independence in 1966. Two imperatives of this agenda have made the country particularly receptive, and constitute the groundwork for extending ideas of citizen empowerment to youth beginning in the later 1990s. On the one hand, the government has formally and fairly consistently tried to downplay difference among citizens, whether this difference arises from ethnic history, regional affiliations, gender, or, most recently, age. Of course, such a commitment to an undifferentiated citizenship has been repeatedly betrayed, at the level of political practice and in government policy, as well as in people's everyday encounters.[6] Nonetheless, the liberalist expectations of equality and equal opportunity for citizens are predominant at the level of official discourse, and are a powerful point of reference for people in villages and cities in Botswana. As such, liberalist ideals have provided the grounds for challenging inequality based on gender or ethnic background since the 1980s, and are now a reference point for young people and for those seeking to diagnose problems confronted by youth.

The second "liberalist imperative" that allowed "empowerment" to become such a powerful keyword in Botswana, which has guided government policy and political discourse and which is echoed strongly in citizen commentary in public forums, is an economic development policy that envisions individual initiative and work as the proper engine of economic well-being. While the government has used its tremendous diamond revenues to expand infrastructure, schools, and health care, it has consistently emphasized people's own responsibilities for "development." "Batswana must work hard to develop themselves," government ministers and bureaucrats have said to the people again and again over the decades.[7] The government has provided work relief and drought-related aid and seeks out "destitutes" for assistance programs; but it has also shown great reluctance to provide too much direct aid to those who are simply poor. While there are many government development projects, most programs in the 1980s and 1990s took the form of loans, reminding people that they and not the government must pay for (self-)development. While people continue to ask the government for money for this and that, they also generally support the idea that individuals are responsible for their own development, and attribute failures to individual faults (laziness, drunkenness, "just playing," or jealousies) and not to structural conditions or government failures. In 1999 the government opened up the question of whether people should pay school fees for primary and secondary education, which had been free. In the public discussions reported in the media, and letters to various private newspapers, many citizens, repeatedly and across the nation, agreed that it was right that they should pay. They agreed, it seems, with the president that "the world does not owe you a living." Similarly, in discussions of a possible value-added tax, people in villages are reported to have commented in public discussions that poorer people would thereby be allowed to pay taxes and feel equal citizenship with everyone else.[8]

At first, the term "empowerment" was publicly used in Botswana to urge the general citizenry to take advantage of the many government loan and development schemes, to "develop themselves." "Wake up to empowerment," called a newspaper headline, reporting a speech by the vice president. In it, he urged (sleeping? lazy?) people living near the Chobe Game Reserve to provide low-cost accommodations for tourists, as an alternative to the luxury hotels and camps that serve the reserve. The vice president said, "empowerment must not be taken to mean government giving handouts to its citizens for doing nothing," but that "empowerment entailed providing assistance to someone striving to uplift himself or herself."[9] Citizen empowerment has been promoted as the way in which Botswana will meet "global competition," which is most often understood in Botswana to take the form of foreigners snatching up business opportunities and employment.[10] The language of the citizen empowerment discourse continues in the twenty-first century in the Citizen Entrepreneurial Development Agency (CEDA), a centerpiece program offering start-up business loans to "empower" citizens, who are widely perceived to be less successful in such ventures than are foreigners (and non-African citizens). The term has spread, even appearing in claims such as the minister of health's statement that, by encouraging breastfeeding, Botswana is "empowering mothers" as well as "strengthening infants" with respect to the AIDS epidemic.[11] The term "empowerment" is now also frequently applied to youth, as the president used it in his speeches in 2002: in the following years, it appeared at least weekly in newspaper reports of the addresses of politicians, government officers, and elders to village *dikgotla* (chief's courts, which are spaces of public discussion).

A Commitment to Youth

The commitment to youth mentioned by the president takes the form of several policies and initiatives that have emerged since the mid-1990s, as the sense that youth were in crisis accelerated across the country. In his speech he referred to a National Youth Policy (published in 1996), a National Action Plan for Youth (1999–2005), and the Botswana National Youth Council. Each of these was designed or redesigned to address both the sense that youth, whose place in Botswana's liberalizing economy and society is unclear, are in crisis, and the threat that unemployed youth, on the streets or at home, pose to society.[12] While all acknowledge that youth are people who still need "support to realise their full potential" (Botswana 1996, 4), they also identify youth "problems" against an ideal image of an independent, self-supporting member of society.

Until fairly recently, how youth fit into Botswana's liberalist project had not been seen, publicly, as a problem. Youth worked, of course, to develop themselves—and their families. But as the latter implies, they were not really equal, independent actors in democratic society. While in the 1980s it could be asked whether, for example, ethnic minorities (such as Kalanga or Herero) or women were treated differently than Tswana men in government offices, when seeking loans, in hiring and retention, or as students in schools, the question of whether young people were enjoying equal opportunities was simply not asked. Childhood—which in the past and to some people today can continue into the early twenties—was seen as a time when one simply didn't have the knowledge or wisdom to manage enterprises or make informed analyses or decisions. Youth—a time that might start as early as the teens but could continue into the forties or later—was also a period in which one's abilities were different from those of mature adults, who managed complex sets of linked households, organized enterprises, and exercised wisdom and leadership in public forums (on changing ideas of youth, see Durham 2004). One might have asked, in the 1980s, why there were no women chairmen of business boards, or no Yei judges on the Supreme Court, but not why there were no twenty-five-year-olds. Since the mid-1990s, people—mostly university students and policy makers in government, education, and NGOs—have started asking such questions, and asking them loudly. While various government policy moves contributed to a new sense that youth are citizens, or citizens at risk, these policies responded to new concerns as much as they created them. (Such moves included lowering the voting age from twenty-one to eighteen, and producing a National Youth Policy that defined youth as those between the ages of twelve and twenty-nine and described youth primarily in terms of various risks.) Below, I will link the new questions about youth citizenship to changes occurring in the home, where questions about young people's opportunities and empowerment voiced by young elites are experienced more intimately and immediately across the entire population. But first, what was happening nationally to set the stage for the question of youth citizenship and youth empowerment?

In the mid-1980s, while Botswana's economy was still expanding at among the fastest rates in the world, young people who did work hard in school, found places in secondary schools, and finished the Cambridge exams or went to teacher training, technical, veterinary, or other institutes could expect to find employment in the government sector, or possibly in a growing private sector. (This is not to say, of course, that all did.) Those who finished junior secondary school also had fair employment prospects in the preferred white-collar sector, though formal educational paths at all levels leading to manual work remained (and remain) weak. A growing army and police force, mining ventures in potash and nickel-copper as well as diamonds, the slow but steady spread of shops of various sizes, and burgeoning construction offered opportunities to many who did not go far in school. In the 1980s, young people could believe that hard work would pay off, and parents could hope that one of their children at least would secure a good job and remit support to the family. The GDP was growing at an annual rate of 12 percent; per capita income, which had been $60 in 1966, had swelled to $3,000 in 1992 (Tsie 1996, 600). But some opportunities for young people started to shrink in the 1980s: migrant labor to South Africa fell off rapidly as South Africa turned more to its internal labor pool, and extended periods of drought undermined government efforts to stimulate the agricultural sector. In the 1990s, the rate of economic growth declined, and employment opportunities, especially those outside government and mining, failed to grow significantly. Whereas some teachers in the primary schools in the late 1980s had little more than a primary education themselves, by the 1990s specialized secondary education in a teacher training institute was becoming necessary to secure a teaching job. In 2003, the government announced that even graduates of such institutes could not expect guaranteed employment.[13] Official unemployment figures rocketed from 12.7 percent in 1987 to over 21 percent in 1994. Younger people, whose horizons are focused on formal employment prospects, were particularly affected: 51 percent of the unemployed were in the 15–24 age group, and a further 34 percent in the 25–39 age range (Hope 1996, 58–59). At the same time, the proportion of young people in the population swelled—more than half of Botswana's population is under sixteen—and the expanding school system is producing more educated young people who often compare their prospects with the guaranteed employment they believe existed in previous decades.

While the numbers do indicate problems confronting young people, the sense of crisis is far more nuanced. On the one hand, young people across the country are finding themselves acting with knowledge and responsibility and as managers, modes associated with adulthood. They are knowledgeable about government bureaucracy and programs, learn "scientific" agriculture in schools, and find themselves guiding their elders in many areas of life. High levels of internal job migration, coupled with earlier patterns of multiple dispersed households, often leave young people managing a family compound in a home village, or a cattlepost, while parents or uncles are in distant cities. By the late 1990s, young urban dwellers were seizing new consumerist opportunities, emphasizing their ability to reason and choose. On the other hand, in big villages like Mahalapye, residents began to say that they were afraid to walk about at night, because groups of unemployed, drunk young men wandered around causing mischief. They complained, as did officials in government ministries, about the pregnancies of schoolgirls too young to take care of themselves, let alone babies. Public pronouncements on youth crime, street youth, and uncontrollable youth sexuality and AIDS are now heard every-

Deborah Durham

where. Seemingly subject to neither the disciplines of the home nor the domain of employment, not "owed a living" (as the president said) and yet
seeking one by breaking into traditional households through crime and sexuality, youth are seen, by individuals and by society, as increasingly dangerous.
Suddenly, it is not clear where young people fit in society, if they are both
acting irresponsibly and yet taking on responsibilities, if they are not in school
with the expectation of working or actually employed. And so, against the
dangers of street life, crime, and sexuality, the government and other agencies
seek to "empower" them.

Youth Power and Empowering Youth

The problem of youth, and youth power or agency, is visible across Africa, both
in academic literature and in government discourses and news media. Aca-
demics are fascinated by the subversive activities of youth, as they respond
imaginatively and creatively to changing contexts and as they claim space in
traditional ones (see Argenti 1998, 2001; Bastian 2001; Diouf 1996; Durham
2000, 2005a; Fuglesang 1994; Gondola 1999; Honwana and De Boeck 2005;
Richards 1996; Sharp 2002; Weiss 2002). Liberalist empowerment programs,
however, are not generally sympathetic to the idea of the power of rebel-
liousness and social banditry (Hobsbawm 1965), the weapons of the weak
(Scott 1985), or the brandishing of stigmata as a form of resistance. They are
unimpressed with arguments that youth's "in-your-face" subcultural fashions
and leisure activities may be valuable commentary on social formations (Hall
and Jefferson 1976), seeing only the further marginalization these activities
produce.

A quick search of the *Africa News Service* archives for 2002 finds numerous political calls to "empower youth" in Zambia, Malawi, Uganda, Nigeria,
Niger, and Sierra Leone. If one recalls that in Sierra Leone's horrific civil war,
youth have perhaps been *overempowered* with guns and diamonds (see Richards 1996; also, for Uganda, Behrend 1997), it is clear that the kind of youth
empowerment envisioned in these calls is a highly specific one. They call for
youth to be given the means to participate in the legitimate economy and
political sphere of these countries, to be freed from the suasion of certain
political or other groups, to refocus and redirect energies that are currently
pouring into disruptive or nonproductive activities, or lack of any activity, all
of which drain families' resources. These are calls for a form of empowerment akin to the power described by Michel Foucault (1979, 1980) as diffused
in projects of governmentality that constitute disciplined subjects and self-
governing citizens, and not for power as the ability to exercise raw force to
influence others that underlies Hobbesian or Weberian ideas of governance
and citizenship and that needs to be surrendered to maintain social security
and a common good.[14]

But unlike the classic Western political model, which views all people as "naturally" endowed with a brutish but uniform power of violence, countries such as Sierra Leone, Nigeria, and Malawi have witnessed assertions by youth that are predicated on youth's different character and position—their power specifically as youth. The fear that children and adolescents, whose moral education is incomplete, are capable of greater cruelty than adults is a motif in the West (as in such fictional works as *Lord of the Flies*), and it made the use of child soldiers in Sierra Leone all the more horrific (see Boothby and Knudson 2000; Westerners are simultaneously horrified by the "loss of innocence" of child soldiers). In Nigeria, young men, uncorrupted by the various influences and interests that marriage brings, are "empowered" by that lack of corruption to guard the practices and tenets of Islam both against outsiders and against women and older men who have been distracted from the Islamic life (Last 1993). And in Malawi, Rijk van Dijk (1998) has discussed the ways in which youth have, through Pentecostalism, used their presumed ignorance of the past to challenge the gerontocratic sources of state authority. Such powers, distinctive to youth, can be highly disturbing to the rest of society. The fact that these countries witness calls specifically for *youth empowerment* projects at this time suggests, perhaps ironically, a lingering fear of the possible exercise of *youth power*, of the exercise of a social agency that is seen to be specific to youth. Instead, these are calls to remake youth as citizens, whose moral sphere of action is no different from that of other citizens.

With what kind of power, then, does the government of Botswana want to endow its youth, and how are these forms of power related to transformations taking place in Botswana society? What other kinds of power have youth had access to, situating them differently with reference to family, economy, and the political? What changes have made these forms of youth "power" seem unsatisfactory, or in other words, how have youth come to be understood to lack power in society? At a time when Botswana's socioeconomic landscape is rapidly shifting—or continues shifts begun or already under way at independence in 1966—and when the idea of citizenship and national participation is being scrutinized by "minorities," we should not be surprised to find both that ideas of youth empowerment go to the heart of citizenship and "the liberal imagination" in Botswana, and that the programs, and youth responses to them, are rife with contradictions. And how, amidst these contradictions, do youth respond? What power, and what disempowerment, do they find as citizens, and as youth, in Botswana? In what follows, I concentrate on one strand of the youth empowerment project, one that focuses on the fate of youth inside and outside the changing family.

Making Vinegar

In June 2000, I visited the Gaborone headquarters of the Botswana National Youth Council (BNYC) to interview staff about their mission, the problems facing youth, and programs to address them. The several offices of the BNYC, tucked into a dusty yard behind a church not far from the city center, bustled with plans and coordinators. People on phones answered questions about youth seminars scheduled across the country, mostly about paperwork, transportation, locations, and bureaucratic minutiae. The staff, all in their thirties or older, looked stressed, and some were working despite being clearly ill. A sense of serious purpose was more evident in this office than in many of the government and nongovernment offices I had visited over the years. The senior officer I interviewed described a wide range of programs sponsored directly by the BNYC, which both conducts programs of its own and serves as a central coordinator of government and NGO youth programming in the country. We talked about AIDS and sex, crime, low youth voting rates and political participation. In every sphere, empowerment was key. Poverty, said the officer, was what tempted young people to crime and prostitution. While she could have been referring to the poverty of households in which youth lived—for the unequal distribution of national wealth has been a growing concern in the country (see Fidzani 1997)—it was clear in our conversation that she was thinking, at that moment, of the poverty of youths as individuals.

The highlight of her presentation, the point at which she shrugged off the persistent flu that was troubling her and lit up with enthusiasm, was a description of Sechaba Youth Enterprises. (*Sechaba* is Setswana for "nation.") The original project of Sechaba Youth Enterprises had been a model farm program, which hoped to train youth to become independent farmers. But youth had shown little interest in the model farm. So a new project now planned to educate young people to make various goods in their homes, and then to sell them under the aegis of Sechaba Youth Enterprises to supermarkets and grocery stores nationwide. The project seemed to target young women who had left school early; the easily made goods included white and brown vinegar, petroleum jelly, candles, fruit juices and fruit-dairy mixes, tomato atchar, and sweets. The BNYC officer started the list with vinegar, and, coming back to it, left the room to bring back a sample bottle (the vinegar had not yet been made by young people in their homes, but was made at the Enterprises). Although they had not yet established any marketing agreements with shops or chains, the bottle bore a label with a bar code and a picture of a perky packet of french fries, overlaid by the words "White Spirit Vinegar 5% strength" and featuring the phrases "Sechaba Youth Enterprises" and "A Subsidiary Division of the Botswana National Youth Council" prominently on the front. I took the bottle back to my rooms with me, although like most people I knew in village Botswana I rarely if ever used vinegar in my daily cooking.

It is easy to be skeptical of this vinegar project, much as it is easy to be skeptical of the idea of impoverished villagers on the fringes of the Chobe Game Reserve, with few resources and poor English, setting up bed-and-breakfasts to serve nature-seeking but thrifty tourists, and thus becoming empowered as entrepreneurs and citizens. Both projects can, with little stretch of the imagination and with some accuracy, be analyzed as capturing their objects at the lowest level of a global system of difference and exploitation, and reproducing the villagers and young vinegar makers on the bottom rung of world underdevelopment (cf. Escobar 1995). The vinegar scheme, one suspects, might enrich the BNYC and give its staff valuable experience with marketing and managing, as Ferguson (1994) argues was true of development programs in Lesotho. Certainly the officer describing the plan to me was as excited about the labeling and the prospective marketing of the product, with its endorsement of the BNYC, as any other aspect. But she was genuinely concerned, too, about the plight of young unemployed people in Botswana, and in particular about homeless youth liable to resort to theft or prostitution. The project, with its notion of home-based enterprise for certain segments of Botswana youth, addressed seriously felt issues that were emerging in the 1990s, through studies and reports by sociologists, public complaints about youth heard in both causal conversations and *dikgotla*, and the complaints made by numerous young people to inquiring sociologists, sociology students, and reporters.

A story about the plight of modern youth, repeatedly told to me, lay behind the vinegar and other empowerment schemes. The basic ideas of the story were built out of the template that shaped the National Youth Policy and out of earlier concerns with urban street children (called *bo-bashi*), and are reflected in reports that "some of the youth, most of whom are school dropouts, have turned to drugs and alcohol as a way of drowning their life of misery and neglect" (in the words of the *Botswana Guardian*, August 9, 1996). Although I am going to deconstruct the narrative, and relate its motifs to other tales told about youth in Botswana, I do not doubt that there are many young people whose experiences match those in the story, nor that young people related it earnestly to researchers. The sense of youth in crisis is strong in Botswana, not only in the construction of the story and its uses, newspaper reporting, the discourse of NGOs, academia, and political rhetoric, but also in the day-to-day experiences of people looking for work, contending with family pressures, worrying over a lover's constancy, and watching the displays of wealth and status by their seniors or by those with wealthier connections. That suicide in Botswana is associated mostly with young males, who despair over success in school, jobs, and love, attests to the depths of experience.

The story is simple. One hears of a young person—while versions do sometimes feature a female protagonist, it is prototypically male—denied food or forced to leave home by parents who refuse to support him further, after he has left school but not yet found paid employment. The young person is told that, as he brings nothing into the household, he will get nothing from it, or that he will get scraps only after those who do contribute have consumed the food, clothing, soaps, and other needs of everyday life. While the story leads inevitably to comment on the problems of street or homeless youth, it speaks directly to changes in the family. It is a shocking story in Botswana, where the ability to make claims on people is the essence of kinship (see Durham 1995).

Deborah Durham

The story speaks to broad anxieties about the family, at a time when all relations within the family—from the core mother-child relations described by Livingston (this volume) to extended relations with aunts, uncles, and cousins —seem to be under stress. Making vinegar is subtly aimed at remaking youth into members of a problematic Botswana family, able to figure in its regeneration under stress, even while the project is more directly aimed, through its liberalist conceptualization of power as economic and independence as ideal, at making them into participating citizens in democratic Botswana.

Working and Caring for Others

The relationship of young people to their families has probably always been a point of some strain, even before the advent of missionaries, colonial government, and migrant labor opportunities in the nineteenth century. The strains may have been rooted in conflicts of material interests, such that senior males need to manage the juniority of others to command their labor and control the reproduction of domestic production, as described by Meillassoux in West Africa (1981). They may also have originated in a psychosocial or "oedipal" tension between fathers and their son-successors that put strain on their shared corporate interests as members of the same lineage (Fortes 1949, writing about Ghana). Benedict Carton (2000) has produced a finely nuanced history of how both such tensions became part of colonial history for a Zulu group in South Africa. Prior to British intervention, strong Zulu chiefs made youth part of military regiments and later arranged their marriages, usurping household authority. British colonial policies later reaffirmed patriarchal authority over sons, but undermined its internal sources of support in households, kin groups, and communities. Young people gained new opportunities for wealth, particularly through migrant labor, enabling them to form marriages and households independent of their fathers' or chiefs' approval. Money and goods, too, became important means of recruiting (or hiring) labor within African as well as white agricultural ventures, changing the dynamics of household work. Youth, desiring independence in many spheres, chafing against British authority and the patriarchy it supported, were easy recruits for colonial rebellion. Processes similar to those described by Carton characterized Botswana, although they did not culminate in rebellion by youth or others.[15] Processes that historically put strains on young people's relations with their families continue into the present: cash has replaced cattle in meeting day-to-day demands and even underwriting long-term planning for many, weakening the hold men have on their juniors; the rituals that sustain senior male authority have diminished, been diffused among other institutions, or disappeared; the education system and growing class difference have prepared certain people better to take advantage of the new economy; the articulation of family with the state, economy, and society is shifting and often contradictory.

Today, most young people in Botswana continue to grow up as members

Figure 4.1. Children playing in a village compound in Botswana, while an older woman and man look on. *Photo by Keith W. Adams.*

of complex extended families whose unity is indexed by a common cattlepost or cluster of cattleposts, common proximate ancestors, and a common compound or residential area in a village where members may build houses that are the sites of marriages, funerals, and seclusions after giving birth. Most of these young people cycle between households within the extended family: they spend time at a cattlepost with uncles or grandparents, live with grandmothers in the village while their parents are working elsewhere, and live with relatives while attending secondary schools or vocational schools or while looking for work or a place in school. A few children are now being raised predominantly in one household, as parents working in government service or the growing private sector increasingly have the means to pay maids or fees for crèches and to maintain stable households away from the family compounds. Growing class divisions are signaled by the efforts of some parents to give their children the advantages of a private English-language education, or access to the elite public schools in Gaborone or elsewhere, and a home life structured around study and exposure to the media of urban life, instead of allowing their children to be raised in villages.

Young people moving through different households are expected to contribute work to the household (including the elite household). While small children spend much time playing in the yards and streets, as they get older they are frequently reprimanded, and occasionally threatened, for "just playing" (Durham 2005a). Children may be sent to gather water or firewood, downtown to buy meat for the midday meal or milk for tea, or as messengers. They sweep the dusty yards, chop recalcitrant acacia wood for fires, scrub clothes and fire-blackened pots, prepare food and serve it. Boys are sent to cattleposts when they aren't in school, to help with livestock and maintenance; girls (and boys) are taken to the agricultural fields to weed, harvest, and thresh. One of the reasons young people are often raised by relatives is grandmothers' need for such labor as they age, single men's need for houseworkers and other labor as they build houses of their own, and urban relatives' need for household workers as they spend their days in jobs. Young people's ability to work is a highly valued and highly monitored moral quality that older people will comment on frequently. Work in Botswana is not, however, the work of Weber's Protestant ethic, a sign of God's individual blessing that singles the worker out from the sinning masses and a value in and of itself. Work is, instead, valued as a means of connecting oneself with others in various ways, and as a means of "developing oneself" through such connections. "I am going to marry you," an old man might say to a dusty young woman who has been scrubbing clothes in an old tin tub and sweeping the yard since 5:00 AM, pointing out to the anthropologist that her work for the household is a better attraction for marriage than physical beauty.

Young men's work for the household is also important, but is more visible at ritual events. At weddings, for example, young men slaughter, butcher, and cook the goats and cattle for the feast—an extension of the herding and assistance they are thought to provide at cattleposts, and that many do indeed provide during holidays or occasional weekends. Equally significant for a young man today, however, is his ability to control money gained through work outside the household: bringing home meat for dinner, a bag of mealie-meal, soap for the laundry his grandmother or sisters do; paying for younger relatives' school trips, clothing, or other small wants; participating in the network of loans and repayments that bind more distant kin together, as cousins and aunts look to meet various bills each month; and giving gifts to girlfriends and paternal support to children he has recognized but not adopted.[16] Young men may display their work by wearing shorts and stained shirts associated with "boys" and cattlepost workers, the overalls labeled "B.G.P." (Botswana Government Property) or Sefalana (a wholesaler), or the ties and suitcoats of their office jobs.[17]

The work that young people provide for their households is valued for the kinds of morality parents look to see in their children (and often say they do not see). This morality of household work has two dimensions. One is that the work that people do at home is part of a "household economy" of care, in which "love" and "caring" (as well as jealousy and desire) are manifest in the effects of one's own actions on others. Insofar as one's care/love is evident in

Figure 4.2. Young men slaughtering and butchering a goat for a feast, with older men watching. Note that the young men are wearing overalls. *Photo by Deborah Durham.*

the well-being of its objects, household work is an essential element of that love (see Durham 2002a, 2005b). While jural elements of family are still important—inheritance, rights, duties—Klaits (2001) has suggested that kinship in Botswana today is becoming organized around practices of caring, whereby shelter, clothing, food, and spiritual/medical practices are the physical manifestations of more ephemeral sentimental connections binding people's well-being together over time.[18] Because families and kin are often seen as *not* providing adequate care, or as actively jealous, many people seek alternative locations for care and housing—such as churches, as Klaits describes. People often see household work for married women as a tension-filled practice, preventing them from gadding about with natal kin, friends, and lovers and diverting their love/care toward their marital homes. It is from this perspective that youth are accused of "just playing" by various people when they work for groups outside the family, or outside the scope of the accusing group (see Durham 2005a).

Because household-directed work is a form of love and care, parents, too, ought to provide care for their children, and for their spouses and aging parents (see Livingston 2003). There is much public gossip and even public outrage over women who abandon their charges to fend for themselves at a cattlepost or in town, while they themselves (according to the gossip) go to beer drinks or to stay with boyfriends, and there is outrage over men who beat children too severely. The expectations that parents care for their children and that households are founded on mutual care/love make the accounts of parents refusing children food poignant; they are also part of a fairly common accusative formula used by young people and others. Secondary school students frequently stage protests and strikes, for example, claiming that their schools provide inadequate food for them, indicating a failure of care/caring for the children.

Unlike the situation described by Magazine and Ramírez Sánchez (this volume), there is no explicit calculation of long-term equivalent return for children's work, or for material and immaterial expressions of parental care. While women do note, wryly, that they may have to care for senile and incontinent elderly as if the elderly were children, I never heard anyone speak of this as a return for equivalent care she had been given as a child. It was simply what one did, and one ought to do it (or risk being the subject of gossip), whether the aging relative had been generous or stingy with his or her care years before.[19] The evaluations of caring work are immediate and reflect on present connectivity between people, although people tend to remember such care and connection. Grown men and women will often tell stories about how hard their mother or grandmother worked to get them food or clothing—the tricks used, the scavenging or labor; mothers, even those who give little care to their children, talk playfully about the Mercedes Benz their children will give them because they are their children, and not as a return on care. If the exchanges of care do balance out over a lifetime, it is not through any calculation.

I have written elsewhere that there are two ways of asking for things and responding to requests in Botswana (Durham 1995). In one, the asker and responder establish themselves as independent actors, free to initiate a relationship via the request and as free to deny it. But requests made invoking family relationships are different: if the responder acknowledges the relationship invoked by the asker, he or she is obliged to give what is reasonable and available. (Of course, within such relationships, there are numerous ways of deferring the response or enclaving resources, but these moves are made while recognizing the obligations involved.) The bonds forged in such requests recognize the constrained agency of those involved, and usually refer to or re-establish hierarchical dependencies. "Deniable requests" help construct people as the liberal independent contractors of democratic civil society; family and household care assumes a more dependent and constrained arena of agency. The idea that parents or guardians could deny food (or housing or clothing) to young people—that they do not "owe them a living" unless the young reciprocate—suggests a radically new conceptualization of households and the family aligned with the idea of the liberalist citizen of the developing state.

Making Selves and Society

But people do not restrict their sentimental fields to the households in which they are raised. Ideally, the work that children do in their households is early practice of moral behaviors that become more purposeful and creative of social ties as they get older and develop the capacity to reason and manage their own and others' lives. The process of developing relations with others, through "work" or other forms of care, and in so doing developing oneself, inevitably extends beyond a natal group, as the problematic cases of marriage, school, and community groups and churches mentioned above suggest. Whereas a child scrubbing pots, clothes, and households is admired for working hard and for household commitment, a young woman who is out of school and has no paid employment might often describe her extensive household labor as "doing nothing" (Burke 2000).[20]

Tensions arise, in part, from the second set of values embedded in notions of work, that work is a—or *the*—fundamental aspect of *go itirela*, making oneself. The word is cognate to the Setswana verb *go dira*, which means both "to do" and "to work"; the prefix *i-* is self-reflexive, and the suffix *-ela* indicates purpose or direction, as "work for." As both Alverson (1978) and the Comaroffs (1992) have discussed, *go itirela*, self-making, has long been a powerful core value for Tswana: to make oneself socially, as a person of influence and respect in a community of people.[21] In "traditional" Tswana society, one's work accumulated in material goods such as cattle, houses, and agricultural fields and produce, and in skills such as oratory, management, judgment, and the ability to care for others. But the goods and skills were meaningless in and of themselves. Both the material and immaterial aspects of self, the product of purposeful work toward them, allowed one to build relations with others, as kin to whom obligations could be fulfilled, as colleagues and friends with whom reciprocal exchanges could be negotiated, and as dependents whose support could be expected both as labor and in the ongoing politics of Tswana kin groups, communities, and polities.[22] The manifest product of one's work— work not dismissed as childlike, or as "just playing"—was the purposed well-being of others, much as small household duties, such as cooking and preparing baths, are expressions of love and are instrumental in constituting household bonds. On a larger scale, work at funerals or donations to community projects or feasts could lead to community respect and leadership.

General anthropological statements on the life cycle and age groups can leave the impression that movement from childhood to youth or adolescence, and from youth to adulthood, is clearly marked: an initiation ceremony or a birthday moves a person from childhood to youth; marriage, almost always depicted as resulting in a new household, marks the move to adulthood (see, e.g., Schlegel and Barry 1991; Schloss 1988). But in Botswana, more so perhaps than in many places, the movement from being a child to a youth, or a youth to an adult, is ambiguous, insofar as there are no clear markers, and a person's status tends to be situationally defined and not absolute. Who is or are youth is contested both on a society-wide basis, and for individuals as subjective beings (see Durham 2004). Marriage itself is an inadequate marker for several reasons: 1) marriage rates are in sharp decline, and many people remain single throughout life, although they may establish independent households and maintain several dependents (Gulbrandsen 1986; Solway 1990; Townsend 1997); 2) marriages, when they are contracted, very often take place long after claims to adulthood have been put forward; 3) while marriages are now clearly marked by "magistrate's court" registrations, these certified marriages are still part of processual unions that develop over entire lifespans, and whose status can be, and often is, renegotiated throughout people's lives and even after death.[23] While Burke (2000) has shown that being in school is the norm against which ideas of youth are being constructed, it does not follow that being out of school—as a graduate or dropout—allows a person to claim to be fully adult (or indeed even a youth and not a child). As Suggs (1987, 108) notes, adult status for Tswana women depends on others' believing they have "competence in decision making and judgement, motherhood, household provisioning, and the establishment of managerial household independence" —all capabilities and claims that shift with the situations in which a woman may find herself.[24] Men, too, find the grounds of adulthood constantly shifting: unmarried men in their mid-forties or even fifties with independent households including paid maids and unpaid dependents cannot always sustain claims to seniority or adulthood, and find themselves treated as youths in some situations, such as at funerals or weddings, in customary courts, or in public formal debates about community issues.

If children's work tends to be embedded for the most part within a guardian's household and is yet to be viewed as substantially invested in "self-making," and adulthood is indicated, situationally, by some form of household independence and demonstrated competences in judgment, managerial skills, and a directed self-making that encompasses others relationally in itself, then youth is the period in which one's work and self-making are located within a guardian's household and yet are beginning to be exercised outside of it. Exercised outside of home households, yet strongly located in them, young people's relationships transgress household borders in significant ways. Youth in the past have been among the most active parts of society in forming relations and interacting with others outside of kin and household groups. Schapera (1940) noted that young people in the 1930s left their houses in the evenings to join "concerts" of young people singing and dancing; this and other forms of evening gathering still take place in villages and, in more modern guise, in towns and cities. While the journeys of adults after dark can be viewed with suspicion—adultery, witchcraft, and secret deal-making are seen as common reasons for such trips—youth are expected to be mobile at night. As in daily trips through the streets, they form bonds with people from other households or towns as lovers and as friends: these bonds may lead to marriage, or to recognized children outside marriage, or to cooperative work ventures between the lovers' families, all of which link together formerly distinct households.

In the past, young men (and in some areas and times, women) were recruited to age regiments (*mephato*), which provided labor for tribal projects and for the chief, linking household laborers with national labor. After independence, Botswana introduced a form of national service for young people, called Tirelo Sechaba, the "work for the nation." Those who finished senior secondary school and sought government posts or further education were expected to undertake such service, in which they might be posted to a government office or village improvement project. They were not paid, but were "taken care of" by the sponsoring group, and more distantly by often-anxious natal families. These youth were situated, then, as household members receiving care, as engaging in self-development, and as forming links with and for the nation.[25] Today, young people, as members of choirs and youth groups, continue to form relationships with and between larger communities—with neighborhood wards, with villages, with schools and churches, and with political parties, and even with "the nation," as youth choirs and drama groups perform for various national events or raise money for flood victims or national hospitals. Youth choirs and drama groups represent Botswana, too, at regional competitions and on frequent international tours. The Herero Youth Association in Mahalapye clearly drew upon the expectations that youth would form these bridges and relationships when it set as one of its goals the facilitating of government development, education, and health programs among the Herero community of Mahalapye.

These liaisons youth form outside the household, while part of the processes of growing up and of realizing a complexly interrelated society, can be considered transgressive and dangerous. Young people outside of households may be as dangerous as the bands of young men now thought to be roaming village streets, but are more liable to be labeled "just playing" and dismissed as childish and selfish, diverting their attention and labor away from the various groups that try to claim it, such as families, ethnic communities, and neighborhoods or wards. Liaisons also, as in the past, may signal to household heads attempts to establish independent households. Such moves are often viewed with suspicion or ambivalence. For example, one young man (around thirty) told me how he had worked all his life with his uncle's cattle and livestock, and had been told that certain animals were his. The young man, having completed school and gotten a salaried, if low-level, position, still contributed to his uncle's household, in which he continued to live with his uncle's other children, although he was building a cattlepost near the family's set of cattleposts. He gave money to cousins, siblings, and half-siblings still in school for trips, fees, and clothing, and assisted them in other ways when called upon.

Although a member of youth associations and active in a church (to which his family belonged), he tended to forego concerts and meetings in favor of family rites and work on his cattlepost. Eventually, he asked his guardian for "his" cattle, which he wanted to use to purchase a motor vehicle (to aid in the development of his own cattlepost) and to start an agricultural business then being promoted by the Botswana government as an opportunity for citizen "self-development." His guardian refused to give up the cattle, implicitly suggesting that the young man had inadequate judgment to manage the cattle, or their vehicular equivalent, for appropriate self-making. When the young man impregnated a girl and acknowledged the child, even indicating an interest in marriage, his uncle (through his wife) brought food, soaps and lotions, and money to the girl's compound, undertaking the steps that both acknowledged responsibility for the child's welfare and opened a path of relationship that could culminate in marriage, or could simply set up a life-long mutual connection through the child. In doing so, his family supported the young man's youth, as it was manifested in bridging household economies. But the uncle would not support the move to independence suggested by the vehicle.[26]

Disempowered Citizens, Empowered Youth

So how does vinegar making fit into this? How will it empower youth? Possibly, such a project could help a young person who is berated by his household head for not contributing to the household. The small income from vinegar making might earn him a place at the table (so to speak), especially since households are no longer sustainable through household labor alone (food, furniture, toiletries, and clothes all must be purchased with cash). Indeed, such enterprises could enhance the powers associated specifically with youth in households, if the vinegar maker, or her parents or other household head, chose to interpret it that way. The vinegar enterprise might involve the work of others—nieces or nephews who ran errands or fetched water—and so enmesh them in the webs of household work and care. The enterprise would provide a link between the household and the government (although the BNYC is technically an NGO, people associate it with the government), and with a cooperative marketing venture that might offer other opportunities. Vinegar making might also provide the means to buy gifts for lovers, keeping the maker within the household and yet extending connections outside it. Vinegar making, under the auspices of Sechaba Youth Enterprises, might indeed empower young people as youth within households defined by mutual caring and the interdependence of well-being. But the president's commitment to empowering youth and the BNYC projects are not commitments to ensuring that youth continue to be fed by their families. They are commitments to liberate youth from such dependencies.

The most common direction given to youth by government officers and politicians, in addresses reported weekly in the newspapers, is to "empower yourselves" by taking advantage of CEDA or another loan program. Youth participation in these programs is envisioned, in political and government rhetoric, no differently from adult participation: "they [youth] are at liberty to apply for loans and start their own businesses like their parents," as one village councilor told a youth seminar.[27] Their businesses will establish them as citizens who "create employment opportunities for their peers"—instead of enmeshing them in webs of interdependencies of obligated care.[28] And, further, by taking out such loans and starting businesses, they would save Botswana from global competition: "they would be able to use their business skills to nullify perceptions that foreigners had robbed Batswana of their jobs and displaced them in the business world," one speaker told members of Junior Achievement Botswana in 2003.[29]

But CEDA, like other loan schemes, is particularly unsuited to most youth, as it is to the poorer majority in the country, and is as likely to lead to disempowerment as empowerment, by any measure. The forms for loans, like most government forms, are complicated well beyond the level of a junior secondary education; a young vinegar maker seeking to extend her business would need help in filling them out.[30] The loans demand up-front capital, something that youth are unlikely to have on their own, and news accounts suggest that, although the loans are supposed to empower citizens against global competitors, many borrowers form joint ventures with foreigners to secure capital. Youth might use the loans to reinsert themselves, as subordinates and constrained actors, into their natal households, of course, by requesting family assistance. And youth would have to resituate themselves again and again as household (inter)dependents, as they tried to repay the loans. One sees young people in the villages every month scrambling around between relatives', lovers', and friends' homes to find money to repay small furniture loans, and very often losing their furnishings after a few months. Only if they manage to repay loans from their own income (which many have already disbursed to relatives, lovers, and association dues), or have borrowed on business-like terms from someone, can they maintain the fragile sense of independence and free agency. While the default rate on CEDA loans to citizens of all ages has been fairly high,[31] youth defaults would undoubtedly draw comments about youthful inability to manage accounts. It is easy to see how government empowerment programs could, if embraced in their full by youth, disempower them both as citizens and, by pressing them back into accentuated dependencies, as youth.

Young people who interact with the youth programmers see the contradictions in the youth programs. Youth leaders often complain that they are not treated as adults, that the programs are all led by older people and youth cannot break into leadership positions. But at the same time that school graduates are increasingly being understood to be eligible for adulthood, many perhaps see the disadvantages most would face if they were treated fully as independent adult citizens. And so, while fairly small numbers of young people take the bread-making courses and look at the model farms, many young people seek to rewrite the youth programs to enhance a specifically youth agency, one that draws upon youth's abilities to transcend households and boundaries, and to suspend ideas of work in webs of "just playing." In the Youth Division of the Department of Culture and Youth, administrators complained to me that young people bring them endless proposals to perform and record music (traditional and modern pop music) and to put together plays on AIDS. The youth program administrators try to send these proposals to the culture division or to the Ministry of Health. But these are classic youth activities in which youth gather to form friendships outside their homes, to present themselves to the rest of the community, and to compose groups that will link their community with other communities in competition and travel.

Even more telling, perhaps, is the way in which youth expect to receive support from the government. Administrators complained, in 2000, that the young people are rude and refuse to complete application forms, which require details of proposed expenditure and management, and which imply that the requests may be denied (recall, deniable requests are a feature of egalitarianism and independence). "You're eating the money that was allocated for us," they say to the department bureaucrats. And so the youth had, in 2000, taken to going directly to the ministers and asking them for money for their activities (and, according to the frustrated administrator who told me this, getting it). This is not so different from a young woman asking a parent for a dress, a young man asking an aunt for help going to school, or students going on strike for more or better food or (as university students did in late 2000) increased allowances from the government.[32] In effect, the youth are constructing themselves as dependent on, or interdependent with, the nation or government—they are establishing themselves both as self-making and as making that self in a context where their own well-being and the well-being of others are intertwined. Because they are going to school, performing concerts, entertaining an audience, demonstrating care in the context of relation building, and preparing themselves to be adult citizens in the future, they *are* owed a living. But for now, they demand recognition—as youth.

Conclusions

Young people in Botswana are confronted with two discourses on self-development: one in which they are urged to pursue independence, another in which they must enlarge the circles of interdependence that constitute their well-being. The latter was the dominant discourse in Botswana until the later 1990s, although young people could read themselves into discourses on nondiscriminatory liberalism or the calls on Batswana to develop themselves. Throughout the 1980s and much of the 1990s, remarkably few of the young people who were sent to the United States, Britain, and elsewhere for education or training remained abroad when their training was complete. Self-development could not be achieved isolated from the community or communities of caring, in which relationships made self and development meaningful.[33] But by the turn of the century, as the country was flooded with calls for citizen empowerment, newspapers and "radio mall" (public, national gossip) began to express alarm at increasing rates of emigration by the educated young. While some argue that a lack of employment in the country is driving young people abroad, it is also true that for some young people now, the idea of self-development does not depend on creating webs of care (including dependents, and dependence) through work. The idea of work as a means of creating independence is increasingly coupled with the idea of the independent citizen, unconstrained by sentimental, cultural, and indebted affiliation with various groups—an ideal unmet but held up in public statements against regionalism, "tribalism," and nepotism. The ideal liberal citizen, free to make his or her own choices (much as he is free to develop himself), is neither disadvantaged nor advantaged by affiliations of tribe, village, or gender—or, as people are now exploring, age.

The language of empowerment, carried into Botswana by international development programs and by Batswana educated abroad, has exacerbated the tension between the two discourses of self-development, and between different ideas of the agentive subject. The global humanitarianism that carries the term, along with the liberalist political economics that motivates it in the United States, "couples," in the critical words of Mahmood (2001, 208), "the notion of self-realization [with] that of the autonomous will, as well as agency [with] the progressive goal of emancipatory politics." Talal Asad, in an article critiquing universalist notions of an essentialized human agency and its links to a celebration of self-empowerment and attacks on "traditional oppressions," notes that such celebrations presuppose "a teleological history and an essen-tialised human subject" (2000, 29). It is this teleological assumption, together with its connection with modernity, that allows "empowerment" to be carried so readily around the world, to break the chains of oppressive social relations and the constraints of cultural subjectivities.

One celebratory version of globalization suggests that as various ideas, images, and desires spread around the globe (and not just from the West to the rest), everyone will be forced to become an independent agent, because every-one will have to choose between the various moral visions, objects of desire, and ideologies available. Such an idea underlies some transnational develop-ment projects: educate women, goes the argument, provide them with alterna-tives, and they will develop their independence by having and making choices. Does this mean that, confronted with the two discourses of self-development, urged to be empowered, a young person in Botswana *chooses*, and thereby becomes, willy-nilly, an independent actor? No. For the vast majority of young people in Botswana, empowerment as independent agents, or citizenship un-marked by age, will remain elusive. Young people seeking the kind of em-powerment envisioned by the BNYC will remain dependent upon the webs of relationships through which they gather, monthly, the funds to repay business, furniture, and car loans, or through which they seek help with rent and with water and phone bills. Economic independence, the sort sought by empowerment schemes, is unlikely. But people, young as well as old, seek self-development across domains where empowerment is intertwined with interdependencies, where self-development involves both enmeshed circles of care and new links between old circles and new ones. Young people will remain interdependent with others as they negotiate child care, seek help with building or chores, and gain recognition of their steps toward establishing new households with new webs of interdependency. They will also insert themselves into the public spaces of Botswana in ways that accentuate their specifically youthful capacities to link the neighborhood with the nation, the household with the village, and Botswana with the world.

While Sarah Lamb, in this volume, argues convincingly that the various dilemmas associated with globalization confront people of all ages, and that people of all ages must address them creatively, ideas linking self-realization with liberatory empowerment, and with a uniform and independent human agent, may be particularly problematic for the young in a place like Botswana. They may wish to become the independent agents of liberalist government rhetoric, if they have the resources to do so—but for those who try and fail, the final effect may be genuine disempowerment. Or they may find self-realization, in Asad's words, in "a form of agency that doesn't seek self-empowerment but is, quite simply, the activity that reproduces and sustains human relationships" (2000, 48). Many of the Mahalapye youth whom I knew, still "youth" in their thirties and forties, had good jobs and exercised a great deal of economic influence in their parents' lives, but continued to cultivate their dependency as youth upon widening networks of people at home in the village. And yet, at the same time as they sang in choirs at political meetings and performed dramas at national festivals or in village courts, many other young people complained to me that they were being relegated to a condition of . . . youth, excluded from domains of power.

NOTES

Field research on which this chapter is based was conducted between 1988 and 2000 in Mahalapye and Gaborone, Botswana, and was funded by Fulbright-Hays, the National Science Foundation, Wenner-Gren, the National Endowment for the Humanities, the American Philosophical Society, and Sweet Briar College Faculty Grants. The ideas in the chapter have benefited from years of discussion about youth and about Botswana with many people, including Keith Adams, Nicholas Argenti, Charlanne Burke, Jennifer Cole, Jean and John Comaroff, Fred Klaits, Julie Livingston, Jackie Solway, and Dick Werbner.

1. *Botswana Daily News*, July 19, 2002, "Govt Still Committed to Empower Youth? Mogae," http://www.gov.bw/cgi-bin/news.cgi?d=20020719. The *Botswana Daily News* is a government paper that includes many reports of the speeches of the president, politicians, bureaucrats, and chiefs. Its print edition is distributed free across

the country. Its reports are often also given in briefer form on Radio Botswana, where they are widely heard.

2. The president's Independence Day message was posted on the government web page, http://www.gov.bw/cgi-bin/news.cgi, accessed June 2005.

3. I refer to Raymond Williams's (1983) idea of "keywords" as terms that ideologically carry political, economic, and social formations.

4. Chiefs and senior males are more often looked to as political actors who can "regenerate" society in formal ritual practices, through which households are controlled and individuals regulated. Here, I draw attention to regeneration from within the intimate space of domestic relations.

5. Lauren Leve has critiqued empowerment programs for women in Nepal for emphasizing their productive capacities instead of their reproductive roles (2001, 108), and notes critically of the programs that "empowerment is not a transformation that begins and ends with the individual" but rather must deal with collective relations (120). Niewenhuys (2001) similarly criticizes programs for street children in Addis Ababa for shifting from attempts to provide food to trying to empower children under the UN's "rights of the child" mandate, detaching children conceptually and in practice from the interdependencies in which they had lived (and so indirectly supporting such practices as child prostitution).

6. See, for example, Dow 1995 on challenges to legislation that allowed men to pass citizenship on to their children with foreign mothers, while women could not pass citizenship on to their children with foreign fathers; and Nyati-Ramahobo 2002 on how Yei are claiming recognition from the state, which gives only Tswana chiefs certain rights and roles in the state. In spite of these cases, and growing demands for recognition of ethnic minorities (Werbner 2002; Solway 2002; see below), many people and groups have seized onto liberalist discourse or the liberalist economic framework: see Durham 2002b; Motzafi-Haller 1998; Solway 1994).

7. "Batswana" are "Tswana people"; the term is used in public speeches to mean all citizens of Botswana regardless of ethnic (Tswana) background. Setswana, like all Bantu languages, uses prefixes and suffixes to modify noun stems: "Setswana" refers to Tswana language and culture; "Botswana" to the place of Tswana; "Motswana" to a single Tswana person; "Batswana" to Tswana people.

8. I have discussed elsewhere how in Botswana, donations of small amounts of change to public ventures help constitute people as equals and as independent contractors with society (whether village society or the nation) (Durham 1995).

9. *Botswana Daily News*, July 31, 2000, "Wake Up to Empowerment," http://www.gov.bw/cgi-bin/news.cgi?d=20000731.

10. "Localization," the replacement of foreign expertise (which was drawn upon heavily at independence) with that of Botswana citizens, has been a goal since the 1960s, and precedes the new rhetoric of responding to "globalization."

11. *Botswana Daily News*, June 9, 2003, "Ministry to Empower Mothers, Strengthen Infants," http://www.gov.bw/cgi-bin/news.cgi?d=20030609.

Kvinnoforum, a Swedish-based consultancy with projects on women around the world, including in Botswana, has, for example, noted that the term "empowerment" is becoming so popular in development programs for women that evaluation is becoming difficult, and the UNDP "Gender Empowerment Measure" of political, economic, and decision-making inequalities is now inadequate to the variety of local usages and goals (http://www.qweb.kvinnoforum.se/measuring.htm, accessed June 2002).

12. In this paper, I use the word "youth" vaguely. It is, of course, part of a "social imaginary" and as such is contested, especially in times of rapid social change. The National Youth Policy defines "youth" as people beween the ages of twelve and twenty-nine, along with others who share some of the predicaments of youth (being unemployed, out of school, and at risk seem to be the criteria). I have discussed elsewhere how the "imagined" category of "youth" is contested, as people who might be considered youth according to older local social schemas, and who may be as old as fifty-five, contend with people who had formerly been just children, possibly into their twenties, for the rights and positions associated with youth (see Durham 2004). I use the term "young people" to specifically indicate people below the age of twenty-nine.

13. *Botswana Daily News*, September 5, 2003, "New Teaching Jobs No Longer Guaranteed," http://www.gov.bw/cgi-bin/news.cgi?d=20030905. This is in spite of attrition because of AIDS, according to the article.

14. A recent *New York Times* article titled "Youth Power in Liberia: From Bullets to Ballots" (Polgreen 2005) captures many of these issues.

15. On the effects of missionization on Botswana's chiefships and household forms, see Comaroff 1985; Comaroff and Comaroff 1991, 1997; Landau 1995; Mafela 1994. On bureaucratic and new forms of governance, see Wylie 1990; Schapera 1970. On transformations in local and national systems of authority at independence, see Kuper 1970; Werbner 1982. On bureaucracy and subjectivities in Botswana, see Durham 2002b, 2003. On migrant labor, see Alverson 1978; Parson 1984; Parsons 1977; Schapera 1940; Townsend 1997; Wylie 1990. On economic opportunity, class, and youth frustrations today in neighboring South Africa, see Comaroff and Comaroff 1999; Niehaus 1998.

16. The process through which young men (and today, also many young women) relate to their households through cash as much as through cattle-labor began long ago, with migrant labor contracts to South Africa. See Alverson 1978.

17. Clothing is a polyvalent signifier (see Durham 1999), and carries multiple and sometimes contradictory meanings for wearer and observers. I have discussed elswhere how wearing shorts, which index youth and youthful labor, around his village compound subjected the Herero chief in Mahalapye to considerable comment—including from himself (Durham 2002b).

18. Indeed, court cases that appeal to jural rights are sometimes (but not always) as much about proofs of love and care. See Durham 1998.

19. But cf. Livingston, this volume, for a closer study of the care given to elders.

20. This is in spite of the fact that there is a good deal of labor involved, and, as noted in a preceding section, this labor could be considered important in attracting suitors for marriage. But marriage has been on a long decline in Botswana; women are more likely to have longer- or shorter-term lovers with whom they exchange forms of care, and whom they may marry later in life.

21. The term may also be used to suggest selfishness, a form of self-making that denies social connectivity and social relationship. Cf. my discussion of the Herero concept *oku vanga*, wanting for personal consumption/desire, which suggests some of the same selfish values, in Durham 2002a.

22. On the distinction between obligatory exchange and reciprocal exchange in Botswana, see Durham 1995; on politicking, see Comaroff and Roberts 1981.

23. Scholars of Tswana society have written extensively about the "processual" nature of marriage in the area, and about renegotiations and the uncertainty of mar-

riage in the past as well as recent times. For different but complementary studies, see Comaroff and Roberts 1981; Griffiths 1997; Gulbrandsen 1986; Klaits 2001; Solway 1990; Townsend 1997.

24. Even mature women with independent households may rely upon senior kin to manage spiritual affliction, or to bring claims about cattle or people to the chiefs' courts; see Burke 2001; Griffiths 1997.

25. Tirelo Sechaba was discontinued by 2000. People complained that the work was menial or purposeless and did not help them develop themselves, and parents were concerned about the neglect and abuse of their children.

26. The man's family was disturbed, however, when the young man named the child himself. In a "regular" marriage, the naming of children generally falls to senior family, usually a mother or grandmother. In naming the child himself, the man had either behaved irresponsibly, without judgment and hence childishly, or had failed to mobilize the various strands of relationship that are knit into marriages and new households. I wasn't surprised to hear, from one relative, that she thought he was "just playing." The girl belonged to a poor family that had lived as dependents on another person's cattlepost, and her mother was seen drunk in the mornings—while the man's family did foster the connection, they were not enthusiastic about it.

27. *Botswana Daily News*, November 19, 2001, "Youth Participation in Dev. Negligible," http://www.gov.bw/cgi-bin/news.cgi?d=20011119.

28. *Botswana Daily News*, August 7, 2003, "Earn Your Bread, Youth Told," http://www.gov.bw/cgi-bin/news.cgi?d=20030807.

29. *Botswana Daily News*, September 18, 2003, "Citizen Empowerment Can Be Achieved through JAB," http://www.gov.bw/cgi-bin/news.cgi?d=20030918.

30. In 2000 the head of the Botswana Democratic Party (BDP) Youth Wing, a thirty-five-year-old entrepreneur who spoke to me on his cell phone from the golf course, said in dismay and surprise that the BDP student association at the University "couldn't even" explain the Financial Assistance Policy, CEDA's predecessor.

31. In his 2003 budget speech to the National Assembly (February 3, 2003), the minister of finance and development planning noted that while 6.2 billion pula had been repaid by beneficiaries of CEDA loans at the end of November 2002, 3.6 billion pula were in arrears. (One pula equaled approximately 20–25 U.S. cents.) (Budget speech accessed June 2003, http://www.gov.bw.)

32. The university students' requests gained them the disdain of many—they were just playing, they were just irresponsible youth—in ways other than those I outline here, as well. Asking for a 60 percent increase, they pointed out that students overseas got higher stipends, and that government workers' salaries had increased whereas student allowances had not. Some students proposed a budget that included "gift to boy/girlfriend, P300; child payments P350; beer P400; rent P250; toiletry P250; transport P200; food P300." (*The Mmegi*, October 27–November 2, 2000, http://www.mmegi.bw. *The Mmegi* is a mainstream, somewhat liberal, weekly paper in Botswana.)

33. Some might also point out that the expanding economy and bureaucracy seemed to guarantee employment to those who returned.

WORKS CITED

Alverson, Hoyt. 1978. *Mind in the Heart of Darkness: Value and Self-Identity among the Tswana of Southern Africa*. New Haven, Conn.: Yale University Press.

Argenti, Nicholas. 1998. "Air Youth: Performance, Violence, and the State in Cameroon." *Journal of the Royal Anthropological Institute* 4 (4): 753–781.

———. 2001. "*Kesum-Body* and the Paces of the Gods: The Politics of Children's Masking and Second-World Realities in Oku (Cameroon)." *Journal of the Royal Anthropological Institute* 7 (1): 67–94.

Asad, Talal. 2000. "Agency and Pain: An Exploration." *Culture and Religion* 1 (1): 29–60.

Bastian, Misty. 2001. "Vulture Men, Campus Cultists, and Teenaged Witches: Modern Magics in the Nigerian Popular Press." In Henrietta L. Moore and Todd Sanders, eds., *Magical Interpretations, Material Realities: Modernity, Witchcraft, and the Occult in Postcolonial Africa.* Pp. 71–96. London: Routledge.

Behrend, Heike. 1997. *Alice Lakwena and the Holy Spirits: War in Northern Uganda, 1986–1997.* Oxford: James Currey.

Boothby, Neil G., and Christine M. Knudson. 2000. "Children of the Gun." *Scientific American* (June 2000): 60–65.

Botswana, Republic of. 1996. *National Youth Policy.* Dept. of Culture and Social Welfare, Ministry of Labour and Home Affairs.

Burke, Charlanne Leslie. 2000. "Dangerous Dependencies: The Power and Potential of Youth in Botswana." Ph.D. diss., Columbia University.

———. 2001. "They Cut Segametsi into Parts: Ritual Murder, Youth, and the Politics of Knowledge in Botswana." *Anthropological Quarterly* 73 (4): 204–214.

Carton, Benedict. 2000. *Blood from Your Children: The Colonial Origins of Generational Conflict in South Africa.* Charlottesville: University Press of Virginia.

Comaroff, Jean. 1985. *Body of Power, Spirit of Resistance: The Culture and History of a South African People.* Chicago: University of Chicago Press.

Comaroff, Jean, and John L. Comaroff. 1991. *Of Revelation and Revolution: Christianity, Colonialism, and Consciousness in South Africa.* Chicago: University of Chicago Press.

———. 1999. "Occult Economies and the Violence of Abstraction: Notes from the South African Postcolony." *American Ethnologist* 26 (2): 279–303.

Comaroff, John L., and Jean Comaroff. 1992. "The Madman and the Migrant." In *Ethnography and the Historical Imagination.* Pp. 155–178. Chicago: University of Chicago Press.

———. 1997. *Of Revelation and Revolution: The Dialectics of Modernity on a South African Frontier.* Chicago: University of Chicago Press.

Comaroff, John L., and Simon Roberts. 1981. *Rules and Processes: The Cultural Logic of Dispute in an African Context.* Chicago: University of Chicago Press.

Cruikshank, Barbara. 1999. *The Will to Empower: Democratic Citizens and Other Subjects.* Ithaca, N.Y.: Cornell University Press.

Diouf, Mamadou. 1996. "Urban Youth and Senegalese Politics: Dakar, 1988–1994." *Public Culture* 8 (2): 225–250.

Dow, Unity. 1995. *The Citizenship Case: The Attorney General of the Republic of Botswana v. Unity Dow.* Gaborone: Lentswe la Lesedi, Pty (on behalf of Metlhaetsile Women's Centre).

Durham, Deborah. 1995. "Soliciting Gifts and Negotiating Agency: The Spirit of Asking in Botswana." *Journal of the Royal Anthropological Institute* 1 (1): 111–128.

———. 1998. Review of Anne Griffiths, *In the Shadow of Marriage. American Ethnologist* 25 (4): 752–753.

———. 1999. "The Predicament of Dress: Polyvalency and the Ironies of a Cultural Identity." *American Ethnologist* 26 (2): 389–411.

———. 2000. "Youth and the Social Imagination in Africa." *Anthropological Quarterly* 73 (3): 113–120.

———. 2002a. "Love and Jealousy in the Space of Death." *Ethnos* 67 (2): 155–180.

———. 2002b. "Uncertain Citizens: The New Intercalary Subject in Postcolonial Botswana." In Richard Werbner, ed., *Postcolonial Subjectivities in Africa.* Pp. 139–170. London: Zed Books.

———. 2003. "Passports and Persons: The Insurrection of Subjugated Knowledges in Southern Africa." In Clifton Crais, ed., *The Culture of Power in Southern Africa: Essays on State Formation and the Political Imagination.* Pp. 151–181. Portsmouth, N.H.: Heinemann.

———. 2004. "Disappearing Youth: Youth as a Social Shifter in Botswana." *American Ethnologist* 31 (4): 589–605.

———. 2005a. "Just Playing: Choirs, Bureaucracy, and the Work of Youth in Botswana." In Alcinda Honwana and Filip De Boeck, eds., *Makers and Breakers: Children and Youth in Postcolonial Africa.* Pp. 150–171. Oxford: James Currey.

———. 2005b. "Did You Bathe this Morning? Baths and Morality in Botswana." In Adeline Masquelier, ed., *Dirt, Undress, and Difference: Critical Perspectives on the Body's Surface.* Pp. 190–212. Bloomington: Indiana University Press.

Escobar, Arturo. 1995. *Encountering Development: The Making and Unmaking of the Third World.* Princeton, N.J.: Princeton University Press.

Ferguson, James. 1994. *The Anti-politics Machine: "Development," Depoliticization, and Bureaucratic Power in Lesotho.* Minneapolis: University of Minnesota Press.

Fidzani, N. H. 1997. "Wealth Accumulation and Distribution in Botswana." In Doreen Nteta, Janet Hermans, and Pavla Jeskova, eds., *Poverty and Plenty: The Botswana Experience.* Pp. 83–102. Gaborone: The Botswana Society.

Fortes, Meyer. 1949. *The Web of Kinship among the Tallensi.* London: Oxford University Press.

Foucault, Michel. 1979. *Discipline and Punish: The Birth of the Prison.* Trans. Alan Sheridan. New York: Vintage Books.

———. 1980. *Power/Knowledge: Selected Interviews and Other Writings, 1972–1977.* Ed. and trans. Colin Gordon. New York: Pantheon Books.

Fuglesang, Minou. 1994. *Veils and Videos: Female Youth Culture on the Kenyan Coast.* Stockholm Studies in Social Anthropology 32. Stockholm: Department of Social Anthropology, Stockholm University.

Gondola, Ch. Didier. 1999. "Dream and Drama: The Search for Elegance among Congolese Youth." *African Studies Review* 42 (1): 23–48.

Griffiths, Anne. 1997. *In the Shadow of Marriage: Gender and Justice in an African Community.* Chicago: University of Chicago Press.

Gulbrandsen, Ornulf. 1986. "To Marry—or Not to Marry: Marital Strategies and Sexual Relations in a Tswana Society." *Ethnos* 51 (1–2): 7–28.

Hall, Stuart, and Tony Jefferson, eds. 1976. *Resistance through Rituals: Youth Subcultures in Post-war Britain.* London: HarperCollins Academic.

Hitchcock, Robert. 2002. "'We Are the First People': Land, Natural Resources, and Identity in the Central Kalahari, Botswana." *Journal of Southern African Studies* 28 (4): 797–824.

Hobsbawm, Eric. 1965 [1959]. *Primitive Rebels: Studies in Archaic Forms of Social Movements in the 19th and 20th Centuries.* New York: W. W. Norton.

Honwana, Alcinda, and Filip De Boeck, eds. 2005. *Makers and Breakers: Children and Youth in Postcolonial Africa.* Oxford: James Currey.

Hope, Ronald Kempe, Sr. 1996. "Growth, Unemployment, and Poverty in Botswana." *Journal of Contemporary African Studies* 14 (1): 53–67.

Klaits, Frederick. 2001. "Housing the Spirit, Hearing the Voice: Care and Kinship in an Apostolic Church during Botswana's Time of AIDS." Ph.D. diss., Johns Hopkins University.

Kuper, Adam. 1970. *Kalahari Village Politics: An African Democracy.* Cambridge: Cambridge University Press.

Landau, Paul. 1995. *The Realm of the Word: Language, Gender, and Christianity in a Southern African Kingdom.* Portsmouth, N.H.: Heinemann.

Last, Murray. 1993. "The Power of Youth, Youth of Power: Notes on the Religions of the Young in Northern Nigeria." In H. d'Almeida-Topor, C. Coquery-Vidrovitch, O. Georg, and F. Guitart, eds., *Les jeunes en Afrique.* Pp. 375–399. Paris: L'Harmattan.

Leve, Lauren. 2001. "Between Jesse Helms and Ram Bahadur: Participation and Empowerment in Women's Literacy Programming in Nepal." *PoLAR* 24 (1): 108–128.

Livingston, Julie. 2003. "Pregnant Children and Half-Dead Adults: Modern Living and the Quickening Life Cycle in Botswana." *Bulletin of the History of Medicine* 77 (1): 133–162.

Mafela, Lily. 1994. "Domesticity: The Basis for Missionary Education for Batswana Women to the End of the 19th Century." *Botswana Notes and Records* 26: 87–93.

Mahmood, Saba. 2001. "Feminist Theory, Embodiment, and the Docile Agent: Some Reflections on the Egyptian Islamic Revival." *Cultural Anthropology* 16 (2): 202–236.

Meillassoux, Claude. 1981. *Maidens, Meal, and Money: Capitalism and Domestic Community.* Cambridge: Cambridge University Press.

Motzafi-Haller, Pnina. 1998. "Beyond Textual Analysis: Practice, Interacting Discourses, and the Experience of Distinction in Botswana." *Cultural Anthropology* 13 (4): 522–547.

Niehaus, Isak. 1998. "The ANC's Dilemma: Three Witch-Hunts in the South African Lowveld." *African Studies Review* 41 (3): 93–118.

Niewenhuys, Olga. 2001. "By the Sweat of Their Brow? Street Children, NGOs, and Human Rights in Addis Ababa." *Africa* 71 (4): 539–557.

Nyati-Ramahobo, Lydia. 2002. "From a Phone Call to the High Court: Wayeyi Visibility and the Kamanakao Association's Campaign for Linguistic and Cultural Rights in Botswana." *Journal of Southern African Studies* 28 (4): 685–709.

Parson, Jack. 1984. *Botswana: Liberal Democracy and Labor Reserve in Southern Africa.* Boulder, Colo.: Westview Press.

Parsons, Neil. 1977. "The Economic History of Khama's Country in Botswana, 1844–1930." In Robin Palmer and Neil Parsons, eds., *The Roots of Rural Poverty in Central and Southern Africa.* Pp. 113–143. Berkeley: University of California Press.

Polgreen, Lydia. 2005. "Youth Power in Liberia: From Bullets to Ballots." *New York Times*, October 29. http://www.nytimes.com.

Richards, Paul. 1996. *Fighting for the Rainforest: War, Youth, and Resources in Sierra Leone*. Portsmouth, N.H.: Heinemann.

Schapera, Isaac. 1940. *Married Life in an African Tribe*. London: Faber and Faber.

———. 1970. *Tribal Innovators: Tribal Chiefs and Social Change, 1795–1940*. London: Athlone Press.

Schlegel, Alice, and Herbert Barry III. 1991. *Adolescence: An Anthropological Inquiry*. New York: Free Press.

Schloss, Marc R. 1988. *The Hatchet's Blood: Separation, Power, and Gender in Ehing Social Life*. Tucson: University of Arizona Press.

Scott, James C. 1985. *Weapons of the Weak: Everyday Forms of Peasant Resistance*. New Haven, Conn.: Yale University Press.

Sharp, Lesley. 2002. *The Sacrificed Generation: Youth, History, and the Colonized Mind in Madagascar*. Berkeley: University of California Press.

Solway, Jacqueline. 1990. "Affines and Spouses, Friends and Lovers: The Passing of Polygyny in Botswana." *Journal of Anthropological Research* 46 (1): 41–66.

———. 1994. "From Shame to Pride: Politicized Ethnicity in the Kalahari." *Canadian Journal of African Studies* 28 (2): 254–274.

———. 2002. "Navigating the 'Neutral State': 'Minority' Rights in Botswana." *Journal of Southern African Studies* 28 (4): 711–729.

Suggs, David. 1987. "Female Status and Role Transition in the Tswana Life Cycle." *Ethnology* 26 (2): 107–120.

Townsend, Nicholas. 1997. "Men, Migration, and Households in Botswana: An Exploration of Connections over Time and Space." *Journal of Southern African Studies* 23 (3): 405–420.

Tsie, Balefi. 1996. "The Political Context of Botswana's Development Performance." *Journal of Southern African Studies* 22 (4): 590–616.

van Dijk, Rijk. 1998. "Pentecostalism, Cultural Memory, and the State." In Richard Werbner, ed., *Memory and the Postcolony: African Anthropology and the Critique of Power*. Pp. 155–181. London: Zed Books.

Weiss, Brad. 2002. "Thug Realism: Inhabiting Fantasy in Urban Tanzania." *Cultural Anthropology* 17 (1): 93–125.

Weissberg, Robert. 2000. "The Vagaries of Empowerment." *Society* 37 (2): 15–21.

Werbner, Richard P. 1982. "The Quasi-judicial and the Experience of the Absurd: Remaking Land Law in North-Eastern Botswana." In Richard Werbner, ed., *Land Reform in the Making: Tradition, Public Policy, and Ideology in Botswana*. Pp. 131–150. London: Rex Collings.

———. 2002. "Introduction: Challenging Minorities, Difference, and Tribal Citizenship in Botswana." *Journal of Southern African Studies* 28 (4): 671–684.

Williams, Raymond. 1983. *Keywords: A Vocabulary of Culture and Society*. Rev. ed. New York: Oxford University Press.

Wylie, Diana. 1990. *A Little God: The Twilight of Patriarchy in a Southern African Chiefdom*. Hanover, N.H.: University Press of New England.

5

Aging across Worlds

Modern Seniors in an Indian Diaspora

SARAH LAMB

In Europe, it may be normal that children leave home. But in our society, we have roots, and suddenly, all these families have started sending their children abroad; the children lose contact with their past; they forget to come home.
—Jayaraj, director of Pathos, Kerala, India [1]

If we start depending on anyone these days it would lead to misery in old age.
—Suchita, commenting in an online Indian American chat group in a discussion of aging and loneliness [2]

Old age is a gift from God when spent in dignity, as in this country. I prefer an independent life. I like to live on my own instead of living with relatives. I am happy now.
—Gopal Singh, age 72, immigrant from the Punjab, Fremont, Calif.

It is no longer inevitable to age and decline. Ageing is now an option. It is entirely in your hands how happily and healthily you grow "older," not "get old." Productivity is the key to successful ageing.
—Dignity Foundation, Mumbai, India [3]

These quotations speak to some of the intense meanings accruing to aging among contemporary cosmopolitan Indians. Visions of aging are salient in the ways many, within India and abroad, reflect on and configure the contemporary era of global living. The Kerala film director Jayaraj created an award-winning film, *Pathos* (*Karunam*), about an aging Kerala couple, abandoned by their children who have settled in America. The couple prepare for a visit from their sons, cleaning the house, preparing food, and putting up a swing in the garden for the grandchildren. Then the news comes: the children have canceled in favor of a trip to Niagara Falls. Sujata is a young professional, settled in the U.S., with aging parents in India. Concerned about how to maintain ties with them from abroad, she joined an online chat group in which Indians in the United States and in India discuss aging and loneliness. The discussion began when one member asked, "Could you imagine the plight of aged parents when their kids settle abroad?" One participant advised Sujata to set up video cameras in both homes so that she could have videoconferences with her parents. Gopal Singh chose to leave India after all of his children migrated to the United States, and he lived for several years with his son and daughter-in-law in their Fremont, California, home. Facing intergenerational tensions there, however, and aware of a myriad of inviting American social services for the elderly, he decided ultimately to move with his wife into a separate (state-subsidized) apartment, and professes to very much enjoy such an independent, "American-style" mode of aging.[4] The Dignity Foundation is an NGO devoted to "Senior Citizens Life Enrichment Services" based in Mumbai, India, with chapters in Kolkata (formerly Calcutta) and several other major Indian cities. It caters primarily to retired professionals, many of whom have children settled abroad. One of the Foundation's key missions is to promote active and independent aging so that a new generation of Indian seniors can lead productive and fulfilling lives, even when they do not have nurturing families to depend on or live amidst.

Today, cosmopolitan Indians are participating in a kind of public moment of reflection: how to work out aging—and with it the reproduction of families and a valued, familiar society—in a terrain where family members are dispersed nationally and transnationally because of professional aspirations, and where the values of materialism, consumerism, and individualism, often associated with the West, modernity, or globalization, have taken center stage. Television serials, newspaper stories, films, and everyday conversations abound with such questions, not easy to answer, many of them concerned with the proliferation of old age homes in India's major cities—a startlingly new phenomenon in the nation. Indians living in the United States (who make up one of the fastest growing U.S. immigrant groups) are also vitally concerned with how to care for and maintain intimate ties with their elder parents, and thereby preserve prized dimensions of Indian family life and tradition, while the parents remain in India or are brought to America to attempt new lives here in their children's homes.

A vision of close multigenerational families, in which adult children (especially sons and nonworking daughters-in-law) care for their aging parents out of love, a general respect for elders, and a deep sense that they are obligated to attempt to repay the effort, expense, and affection their parents expended to produce and raise them, has long been a key part of an "Indian" identity. Such a system of long-term intergenerational reciprocity and intimacy implies not just care in old age, but a host of social values and meanings. Large, multi-generational joint families are commonly associated with morality, fellow-feeling, tradition, a time when kinship was more important than material success, warm rambling households, a connection to village lands, spirituality, patriarchy, and, again, "Indianness." Of course, scholarly and popular narra-tives have also long depicted age-old tensions between mothers-in-law and daughters-in-law, elders' complaints of filial disrespect, and poverty so grueling that children cannot support parents even when they would like to; so we should keep in mind that practices of intergenerational reciprocity and elder respect have always been performed and enjoyed to varying extents. However, prevalent contemporary discourses in India are that "traditional," quintessen-tially "Indian" family-based modes of aging are now undergoing especially striking transformations: the partly desired and (even if not desired) inevitable flows of modernity, globalization, and Westernization mean that kin now live all over the nation and even the world, joint families break up to become nuclear families, people live in modern small flats, and careerism, individual-ism, materialism, consumerism, and gender and age egalitarianism become overwhelmingly alluring. With all these social changes, the system of life-long intergenerational reciprocity within the family disintegrates, and the old per-son left in an old age home or across the oceans separating India and America becomes a quintessential sign of the new age.[5]

Old people themselves are not all simply passive victims of modernity and global living, though; many actively participate in its making. This chapter examines the ways such competing lifeways and values, making up a new era of global cosmopolitanism, are worked out by those living in Indian American multigenerational transnational families—families in which children settle in the United States and the parents opt to remain in India, or join their children in America, or move back and forth between the two nations/cultures/homes.[6] It focuses particularly on how seniors and their kin practice, experience, and reconfigure aging in such a milieu. New modes of aging are, in turn, wrapped up with broader challenges of social reproduction: is it possible to maintain and reproduce the best of the esteemed "Indian" social values—such as family intimacy, respect for elders, and tradition—at the same time that individuals, and the wider society and nation, pursue cosmopolitan living and modern success?

Through this ethnography, this chapter makes a broader argument—that aging is a fruitful lens through which to examine globalization and social change. Scholars have long thought of social change in generational terms. Karl Mannheim speculated that cultural transformation comes about through the continuous emergence of new generations: as each generation comes into "fresh contact" with its social and cultural heritage, it remodels what it finds (1952, 293). Meyer Fortes mused a few decades later that a generational model is an "apt imagery by means of which to depict continuities and discontinuities in a community's social and cultural life over a stretch of time" (1984, 106). Studies of global modernity frequently portray change in terms of generational conflict as well, with the young representing modernity, contemporaneity, and the global or transnational, while the old represent tradition, the past, the local and nation-bound.[7] In such models, it is the young who are the primary vectors of change, moving away from a static, staid old. The popular and scholarly idiom of the "generation gap" likewise carries an image of change occurring because the young move forward, leaving the old behind—fixed in time and culture.

This chapter suggests, however, that it is inappropriate to think of the young as the only or primary site where globalization inserts itself into culture and society. Old people themselves construct globalization in significant ways, as well as serving as potent signs of global modernity. At the same time, the old indeed are often taken to be—by others, and by themselves—quintessentially representative of "tradition." Aging and old age thus become illuminating sites through which to scrutinize the paradoxes and conflicts of globalization—the tensions and interplay between modernity and tradition, the global and the local—and the challenges of social reproduction in such fraught times.

This chapter argues further that aging is an illuminating lens through which to examine not only the macro but also the critical micro—experienced, particular, everyday—dimensions of the global and transnational. This is because while aging is irrefutably intimate and local, embodied and experienced, it is at the same time wrapped up with broader national, transnational, and global forces, such as state welfare policies and diasporic flows of ideas, images, and people. The processes we are labeling transnational and global are not only produced through the kinds of macro forces that are receiving so much scholarly attention today. They are also—crucially—produced and experienced through the daily life practices and intimate relationships of particular people, as they address questions such as how to age meaningfully in lives that span national-cultural worlds.[8]

Fieldwork for this project was conducted in India and the United States, primarily in the urban areas of San Francisco, Boston, and Kolkata. Over an eighteen-month period in 1994 and 1995, and during annual summer visits after that, I spent time with Indian American[9] families in the San Francisco region (largely in the South Bay, near Silicon Valley), where I accompanied older immigrants to local seniors' meetings; volunteered (as a member of the board and chauffeur) in an Indo-American community senior center; attended family gatherings, religious ceremonies, and late-morning tea breaks; and interviewed people about their life stories, hopes, dreams, losses, and struggles. From 1996 on I did much the same in the Boston region. In both the San Francisco and Boston areas, Indian Americans live largely in mixed-ethnic (often primarily white) urban and suburban neighborhoods, in comfortable middle-class and upper-middle-class homes.[10] My Indian American infor-

Sarah Lamb

mants are mostly Hindu (though with some Sikhs and Jains) and largely Bengali and Gujarati (though with some Punjabis, other North Indians, and South Indians).[11] Most of the people I have grown to know have been associated in some way, as members or friends of members, with the Indo-American community center in California where I volunteered, or with an organization for Bengalis overseas, Prabasi. Others are simply neighbors, colleagues, or friends of friends. Fieldwork in the United States was complemented by extensive research on aging in India, in 1989–1990, 2003, and 2004, during which I interviewed and spent time with families, residents of old age homes, and members and directors of aging-related NGOs, as well as perusing the surge of media stories on old age.[12]

"Traditional" Indian Aging and Family, through the Lens of Modernity

People in India and abroad often contrast modern aging to a traditional Indian past. Modernity is perceived as entailing a cluster of concepts and terms, including the English "modern" (*adhunik* in Bengali) and other terms conveying the temporal present, such as "these days" and "now." It is regularly associated with features of globalization, such as the global spread of Western values and lifeways, a (Western-dominated) global economy and media, and transnational or diasporic living. Modernity entails as well a host of other facets of contemporary life, including urban residence, nuclear families, small flats, individualism, consumerism, careerism, a persistent lack of time, weak family ties, and old age homes. In such discourses, the English term "tradition" is often used to convey a more quintessentially Indian past. Family is key here. The joint, multigenerational, intimate family, more than almost anything else, represents a traditional Indian past in contrast to an emerging modernity. For my purposes, I do not claim (or deny) that this past "really was"; I am interested in people's representations of the past as a backdrop to understanding how they work through the present.

In visions of traditional Indian society, aging itself is a family matter, and parents and children construct their relationship according to a long-term model of intergenerational reciprocity. In this model, juniors provide care for their senior parents, in old age and after death (when they are venerated as ancestors), in return for all the effort, expense, and love their parents expended to bear them and raise them through infancy and childhood.[13] Although the common discourse is that "children" repay their parents, traditionally it has been sons and daughters-in-law who take on this duty, while daughters assume responsibility for their husbands' parents.

A number of modes of exchange, both material and sentimental, are perceived to make up such a system of intergenerational reciprocity. Parents and children each in turn provide material support (parents first giving to young children, and adult children reciprocating years later to elder parents)—

food, clothing, money, shelter, funding for education, and often (within to-day's professional classes) passage to America or another site abroad. Equally as important, parents and children provide each other with caring services: cook-ing, serving food, cleaning, massaging tired limbs, bathing, and cleaning up urine and excrement—a service parents inevitably provide for infant children, and which children can be required to provide for incontinent elderly parents. Parents and children also perform for each other important life cycle rituals: parents process their children through the whole cycle of rituals from birth through marriage (*samskars* for Hindus), and after death children construct ancestral bodies for their parents, just as parents gave their children bodies via birth.

Gopal Singh explains his immigration to the United States quite precisely in terms of his and his children's expectations of participating in such a system of long-term intergenerational reciprocity. He describes intergenerational ex-changes not only of forms of material support, but also of bodies (via birth), affection, talk, and the "shar[ing of] sorrows and happinesses."

> My wife and I were living in India. Our children [two daughters and one son, all of whom had become naturalized American citizens] thought that there was nobody to take care of us, as we had brought up our children. We . . . gave birth to them, provided a house for them, brought them up, gave them an education, and sent them to the United States for [a] better life. . . . So we came here to join our children, to spend the evening of our life with our children. Because if we give to someone, we [in turn] need someone to care for us, to talk to us, to share our sorrows and happinesses. We shared the sorrows and happinesses of our children, and they share our sorrows and happinesses. . . . This is why we have come here, to live with our children and spend our old age.

The parental form of such providing is frequently described by older and younger Indians as requiring vast expenditures of effort, money, and emotion. Parents do so much to raise their children, and children owe everything to them—more than they could ever repay. Although in later life parents are on the receiving end of the relationship and thus dependent on their children, when viewed in the context of the whole life cycle, and taking their earlier gifts into account, the elders remain productive and highly significant members of the family.[14]

Representations of aging in a "traditional Indian" society further empha-size that elders are respected in the society as a whole, not merely by members of their family. Thus the director of the Agewell Foundation, a New Delhi–based NGO, commented to me that if given the choice between the junior Bush and the senior Bush, Indians would never have selected the junior Bush; they would have unquestionably gone with the senior. Shri Atal Bihari Vaj-payee, then the prime minister of India, was eighty years old, he added with a smile. He went on, "If there is a seventy-eight-year-old person within an Indian family, most likely that person would be respected, although perhaps now relegated to the side due to modern pressures. In traditional India, the older person's opinions were sought before any family decisions were made, such as marriage or spending money. The seniormost person—of whatever age or medical condition—would be asked for his or her opinion and counsel." Elders are even at times compared to deities, because of their seniority and ability to bless and curse, and are bowed down to—given *pranam*—in respect and in hope of blessings (Lamb 2000, 59–66).

It should be noted that aging and seniority are defined in such a family and social system not so much by having lived a certain number of years, but rather in terms of family position, the relationship between senior and junior generations. Old age begins as one moves into the senior generation, when one's children—especially sons—marry, bring daughters-in-law into the home, and have children of their own (Lamb 2000, 43–46; Vatuk 1990). This is in contrast to "modern" reckonings of seniority, in which individual chronological age is key—as many nations in which Indians now live (such as the United States) offer benefits to "senior citizens" of specified ages. Such benefits programs for seniors are now also emerging in India, including small pension schemes for the destitute elderly and discounted rail fares for those over sixty. Further, Indians with government and other professional jobs are being assigned prescribed retirement ages (sixty is the most common) and awarded pensions. Calculating one's seniority according to chronological age rather than family relationships is a highly individualistic mode of reckoning one's place in the social world.

There is most certainly a sense in traditional representations of aging and family that generational conflict—particularly between mother-in-law and daughter-in-law—was always present (e.g., Lamb 2000, 71–87; Davis 1983, 129–130). But, my informants surmise, such conflict could in earlier times be worked through without dissolving the family (as happens "now"), mostly because seniors held the ultimate authority and were immensely respected, juniors lived in their seniors' household (or the family household) rather than vice versa, and the "generation gap" was not as vast as it is now—that is, social change was not as rapid or profound—and so the senior and junior generations held more values and lifeways in common. In their musings, then, elders, their juniors, and NGO workers frequently remark that the whole system of intergenerational reciprocity and respect for elders is now rapidly changing. Devaki, a social worker at Kolkata's Dignity Foundation, reflected, "In Indian thinking, you can't leave your parents just because of a career. Parents give *everything* to raise their children. But nonetheless, such things are happening in India now." Under the category "Calling NRIs (Non-Resident Indians)"[15] on its website, the NGO Help Age India proclaims, "25 years ago, when you left India, families looked up to the Patriarch. Even at 80, he controlled things, managing relations with the most amazing dexterity and maturity. . . . Things changed. You left them in the care of others. Those others have moved on, in search of better opportunities."[16]

How are people working out the social changes of the modern, global era? I will turn first to look at the lives of those Indian seniors who migrate to the United States late in life to be with their children, and then at some strikingly similar experiences and reflections among those who remain in India, while their children live abroad. Indians in transnational families are self-consciously engaged in a demanding project of constructing radically different but hopefully meaningful futures out of overlapping national-cultural worlds and eras. Marshall Berman, in *All That Is Solid Melts into Air*, presents the central task and dilemma of modernism as the struggle "to make ourselves at home in a constantly changing world," one characterized profoundly right now by global capitalism (1988, 6). This struggle is a never-ending creative project, one that many cosmopolitan Indians at home and in the diaspora are engaging in by intensely reflecting upon and practicing novel modes of aging.

Global Aging across India and America: Families, the State, Prosperity, and Time

The working out of aging across India and America entails not only new ways of thinking about old age per se, but also profound reconfigurations of the proper social-moral relationship between individuals, families, and the state, and of the very shape and aims of the human life course.

The 1965 U.S. Immigration and Naturalization Act vastly increased immigration opportunities for people from Asia, and since then Indians have been one of the fastest-growing U.S. immigrant groups.[17] Especially at first, the majority of Indians came as young professionals with preferred occupational skills, or as students in graduate and professional schools. Thus the Indian American population has been very "young" as a whole.[18] However, as earlier migrants have matured and put down roots here, they have increasingly begun to express a deeply felt social-moral obligation or desire to bring their aging parents over from India. Many elders also speak of finding it natural to come to America to be with their children in old age. Parents and children are both striving to sustain the long-term bonds of intergenerational reciprocity and affection that so many see as crucial to an "Indian" and "good" family and old age. But life in America can never be the same as it is envisioned in India. People move back and forth between geographic and conceptual worlds, and in so doing create new, complex forms of family and aging across what can appear as gaping divides between generations, nations, and eras. Let me begin by looking at the tension between material prosperity and family intimacy when time is limited.

Material Prosperity, Intimacy, and Time

When I first met Matilal Majmundar, at an Indo-American seniors' meeting,[19] and he found out that I was interested in Indian American perspectives on aging, he insisted, "Well, you must visit me!" He had spent the past several years reflecting attentively on the topic, writing a column on Indian American aging for a local newspaper, and becoming active in the senior center as a counselor for more newly arrived immigrants. When I arrived at his home, he apologized for having no tea (his wife was visiting their other daughter, and his daughter and son-in-law were of course at work), and then he launched into his account, opening with an anecdote about the difficulties of getting a cup of tea in America:

> One gentleman came from India, old man, just to find out whether he would be comfortable here with his children. I met him. I said, "How are you?" "Oh, I'm not happy." . . . He gets up at six o'clock, he requires a cup of tea, he is moving here and there, waiting for a cup of tea. The children, they get up at 8:00, or 7:30, busy with all their activities. . . . At 9:00 or at 8:00–8:30 there will be a breakfast table, so many cups of tea and all these things. "But what is the use of all this? Early in the morning I don't get it." I told him that it's very bad of your children, to lock up the tea and the sugar material. He said, "No, no, they're not locking." I said, "Then why don't you prepare?" He said, "No, I don't like." Then I said, "You better go to India. You better go back to India. In India, if you take a second cup, or a third cup of tea, they will object, they will object. Here, you can take even *ten* cups of tea, prepare yourself, any material you use, your children will never object. But, if you want their *time*, they will object. They will object if you want their time. So, better go to India. Here is not the place for you."

His narrative says that even if there is less material prosperity in India (i.e., people cannot always afford as many cups of tea as they might want), at least families in India are closer, and old people are better served. America is the land of material prosperity; India is the land of intimacy and time. American children give their parents commodities, but they cannot give their time.

Lata Parikh's story of her arrival in America also tells of neglect by children who lack time: "It was the month of December. And it was in Columbus, Ohio. Full of snow—all over. . . . Arrived, and absolutely a new country, new things. And in the morning, you look out, and all you see is white white white white white white everywhere, nothing else!" She took a deep breath, recalling her shock, "And I said, 'Oh, my God! What are we going to *do*?' And the children were busy! They didn't have any time!"

The junior generation is severely lacking in time, elders and some of their children muse, because of both the nature of work and the urgent tempo of life in the U.S. cultural milieu. In most cases, younger people from India—both women and men—have come to the United States in pursuit of professional development and material success. This means that even daughters-in-law are not regularly available to perform domestic chores, as they would often be in a more traditional middle-class Indian household, along with servants. Although many elite and middle-class women in India have also developed professional careers, my informants tend to believe that it is more common for Indian women in the United States to work outside of the home. Further, the "24/7" work style of America is simply more demanding, they say, and one cannot depend on servants to take care of household labor. And somehow time just gets eaten up in America, although each minute is supposed to be accounted for. Recent popular and scholarly books reflect on this urgently accelerated pace of time in the modern West, as people feel that they've never had so much to do in so little time (e.g., Brennan 2003; Gleick 1999; Hochschild 1997).

So, even if they can offer plentiful material goods, juniors in the United States do not have the time to provide the services ordinarily owed a senior parent in the Indian system as it is envisioned, such as companionship, meal preparation and serving, and the intensive care needed when an elder becomes ill, bedridden, or incontinent. Lata Parikh's husband, Ajit, reflected, "What happens is, with the people working, and there being no servants, it is a very difficult thing for the children to look after the ailing elderly. And so the nursing homes play a very important role in looking after the elderly." The Parikhs live now in a senior apartment complex, and friends of theirs, another Indian couple, were recently admitted to a nursing home. "And in fact," Ajit Parikh went on, "you get used to that type of living."

Indeed, older Indians see themselves as, even if ambivalently, actively supportive of, and largely responsible for, their children's modern, material success, having raised them in cosmopolitan households, sent them to elite English-language schools, funded their sojourns in America for higher education and professional opportunity, and selected spouses for them who had professional degrees. Through their professional children, they gain both prestige and material comfort. Matilal Majmundar explained quite precisely why Indian seniors wish to join their children in America: "What they feel is that they had brought up their children, spent so much money on them. And then, when they [the children] become prosperous, their wives or their husbands will get the benefit, they [the parents] won't get it! You understand? That particular idea is there: Why should *we* not share the prosperity of our children, for which *we* were accountable?" Swapna Goswami concurs that senior Indians come to the United States "out of attachment to their kids, and out of attachment to material things." Although they often long for wonderful features of life in India—old friends, sweet mangoes, familiar soil, streets teeming with comforting noises and people—elders say that if one doesn't return to India within a few years of arriving, one won't be able to go back, having grown too accustomed to all the material amenities of daily life in America.

Nonetheless, most Indian American seniors feel keenly aware that the pursuit of material prosperity thwarts intimate intergenerational relationships. Swapna-di says that she never stops wondering, "My kids have a better life here [i.e., a more materially prosperous one—one is a doctor, another a chemistry professor, the third an engineer], but if we had stayed in India, would we have been *happier*? *closer*?" She and her husband live alone, in an apartment next door to her younger son, who (she feels) only rarely visits. Children are also aware of the irony: their parents pursue material, cosmopolitan success through them, which in turn means that they are not able to care for their parents. Manju, a young participant in the "Ageing and Loneliness" chat group, commented, "One of the primary aims of Indian parents is to see that their children are well-educated and achieve good positions in life. What happens afterwards is that bcoz of their 'positions' the kids are unable to look after their parents in old age. Sad twist of affairs!"[20]

Generational Divides, across Cultures

Perceived cultural divides between the two generations can also obstruct intimate intergenerational ties within Indian American families. What those in India tend to label a "generation gap"—differences between persons born of different eras due to social change over time—those in the United States tend to explain more in terms of a cultural divide between India and America and thus between seniors and juniors. Most seniors expect such a cultural-generational divide to exist, and say that it's only natural that their children and especially grandchildren should become very "American," while they stay more indelibly "Indian," having migrated so late in life. Thus, they make a point of stating that they're not really opposed to their children's ways, or to their children's and grandchildren's being culturally different from them; but they can still find it difficult to live together across such divides.

Tensions around food—which powerfully symbolizes home, relatedness, tradition—are rampant. Elders wince seeing their kids eat ready-made cold food on the go—like sandwiches or protein drinks in the car for lunch—without stopping for a "real" face-to-face meal. Traditionally Bengalis, in fact, consider it "fasting" not to have hot rice at noon. Rajata, of the younger generation, was planning a casual party one Friday evening for several friends. She came home from work carrying bags of ready-made appetizers, snacks, and drinks only to find that her mother-in-law had already prepared an elaborate, multicourse Indian meal. "It's not that kind of party," Rajata exclaimed in irritation, appalled at her mother-in-law's interference.

Seniors are disturbed as well by other practices of their juniors associated with American living, like divorce, drinking alcohol, mixed-gender dancing at parties in the home, their daughters-in-law wearing shorts and miniskirts, and a lack of fundamental respect for elders and for "Indian traditions." One man's young grandson asked, "Are you an Indian? Then why don't you have a bow and arrow?" The boy's parents laughed, thinking it funny, but the senior man was deeply hurt.

On their part, some juniors cannot stand the vast expectations and family orientation of their seniors. Justine, a Euro-American woman married into an Indian family, finds the traditional role of the Indian daughter-in-law—humble and subservient—to be "a saintly one, but impossible." "I don't—I somehow don't have it in me to be a *saint*," she said with firm resignation. She had been driven to a nervous breakdown, in fact, after several years of living with her in-laws, and so they have moved into a nearby senior apartment complex. (Her husband still jumps to serve them whenever they call, she says, and they still all get together a few times each week.) Pranab Das Gupta has been in the United States since college, for more than thirty years, and views himself as "absolutely American." He cuttingly describes his widowed mother's expectations that her son will care for her in her old age as "old-fashioned" and part of a "medieval view of life," but imperative nonetheless. "There's no question I have to do it," he said. She lives half of the year with him and his wife in their San Francisco flat and half the year in a Kolkata old age home. Sipra, a history professor, invited her mother-in-law to come over from India to help care for her first-born, but found that Ma desired so much care and companionship herself that Sipra had to hire a sitter anyway just to be with Ma; and later all three (Sipra, her husband, and Ma) decided that it would be best if Ma returned to her home in India, making trips to the United States only for visits.

Independent Selves and State Support

Because of such generational and cultural divides between seniors and juniors, and because the U.S. government offers services to the elderly in order to facilitate independent living, quite a few multigenerational Indian American families ultimately decide to separate into independent households. In such arrangements, the state and the seniors themselves end up shouldering a good deal of the seniors' material and social needs. Senior immigrants take advantage of age-based welfare benefits, Medicare, state-subsidized senior apartments, senior bus passes and transportation services, subsidized lunches and gatherings at senior centers, and the like, resulting in whole new forms of social reproduction: the displacement of key dimensions of family sustenance from the family and onto the state and private individuals.

At first, many are perplexed by a system of state support of the elderly. Vitalbhai Gujar, for instance, described to me the confusion he experienced during his initial interview with welfare agents. Nearing seventy, he had come to the U.S. from Gujarat, India, several years earlier to live with his only son, a naturalized American citizen and engineer who was married to a Gujarati-born woman and who had one daughter. Gujar regularly attended a nearby multiethnic senior center, where once or twice a year social service agents would come to speak about the federal Supplemental Security Income (SSI) program for the elderly.[21] He inquired about it at the local social service office, and recalls the puzzlement he felt: "Why are they defining me as indigent, when my son makes money?" Vitalbhai Gujar in fact had no resources "of his own" in the United States, having come to this country too late in life to begin new work here, and having had (like most of his compatriots) to leave behind any resources in India, because the Indian government restricts the outflow of money from the nation. But he had considered himself appropriately well provided for in the household of his son. If he were in India, he stressed, he would not consider himself, nor be considered by others (the community or the state), to be "indigent." He was also bewildered when asked to check the box on the SSI application form indicating "I am living in another person's household." I asked, "In India, would you call it 'your' house?" "No," he answered decisively, "the *family* house."

Vitalbhai Gujar went on, though: "If the American government defines things this way, and if we are living in America, then why not accept?" In fact, many like Gujar who immigrated to America late in life do end up accepting age-based SSI benefits. The directors of the Indo-American community center where I volunteered estimated that from 50 to 75 percent of the senior members were receiving SSI. Of the thirty-two people I worked with most closely who are over sixty-five, twenty-four received SSI.[22] One active member of the Bay Area Indian American seniors community and a primary informant, eighty-four-year-old Harikrishna Majmundar, proudly wrote a book, *Mapping the Maze: A Guide to Welfare for Elderly Immigrants* (2003), in which he draws on years of giving informal advice to senior Indians about SSI, Medicare, and other programs of the U.S. welfare system. The cover of the book promises a complicated yet happy journey to an independent home.

Many older immigrants come to see SSI and other such state programs for the elderly as part of a quintessentially "American" way of doing things, including aging. In America, many Indians explain, children do not provide for their parents—and this is not due (necessarily) to moral laxity on the part of children. Rather, older parents do not even expect or want their children to support them. They value independence and self-sufficiency, and are averse to being "burdens" on their children.[23] Nor does the state ordinarily expect adult children to care for their parents, as immigrants discover in their interactions with state agencies.[24]

Some Indians are disturbed by this novel mode of imagining the relationship between an old parent, an adult child, and the government. Vitalbhai Gujar, who nonetheless was accepting SSI payments, said to me,

> Have you heard of the *buro ashram*? old age home? . . . Seniors from India are using the U.S. government like an old age home. They come here, and the U.S. government takes care of all medical expenses, food. [*I asked, "Do you think that's wrong?"*] Yes! And it's bad for families, too. My son is not taking on his responsibility of caring for me! And then their children are not learning from them—they think just that the government should do it. . . . They're forgetting the Indian system.

Many, however, have gradually come to admire and enjoy dimensions of what they see as an American mode of aging, in which elders support themselves or are supported by the state, rather than being dependent on their children. A good proportion of senior Indian immigrants, especially those who are still married, end up using their SSI money to rent their own apartments, some in state-subsidized senior complexes. One morning in 1994 I discussed such modes of aging with two older Punjabi Sikh men, Gopal Singh and Teja Singh, two good friends who had been in the United States for more than ten

Figure 5.1. The cover of *Mapping the Maze*, by Harikrishna Majmundar, shows an elderly immigrant couple cheerfully making their way through the maze of the U.S. welfare system to an independent home. © 2003 *Harikrishna Majmundar. Artist: Mukund Talwalkar.*

years. At the time, I did not yet know either of them well. I had only recently begun my research and still assumed that most Indian seniors would prefer to live with their children.

> Gopal Singh: So, the [Indian] seniors have decided that they would like to live close to their family, but prefer their independence and freedom. We prefer our independence and personal freedom.
>
> Teja Singh: As the American seniors.
>
> SL: So, some decide to live separately?
>
> TS: Yes, yes. Independent living means respectable living. But [only those] who are getting this SSI, who are getting medical coverage—then only one can live independently here.
>
> GS: Yes, Indian elderly see the American elderly living in the senior homes [subsidized senior apartment complexes] in U.S.A., and their lives are *excellent.*
>
> SL: Oh, you think their lives are excellent? [*surprised*]
>
> GS and TS: Yes!
>
> SL: Would you like to do that also?
>
> GS: Yeah, we would like to!
>
> TS: I'm living that way! I'm living that way right now!

On another occasion, Gopal Singh spoke to me eagerly about how one doesn't even need to depend on children here, since the state provides so much—SSI, Medicare, senior centers. "Why, we can even call 911 if something goes wrong. We tried it once," he said with delight. "Why would we have to live with our children?"

A senior Gujarati man, Manubhai Daiya, explained his transition to such an "American" mode of living. When he and his wife first came to this country in 1986, they came to be with their daughter (a naturalized citizen) and help care for her children while she and her husband worked. Six years after arriving in the U.S., he turned sixty-five. He explained, "After we became senior in American parlance—that is, age sixty-five—we received SSI. So we thought we might as well launch out on our own, and accustom ourselves to American life." He and his wife moved into a separate apartment (still near their daughter), where they are supported almost entirely by SSI. He describes with enthusiasm the "independence" and "freedom," and the reduction in family conflict, that they have enjoyed since moving into their own home.

Indian seniors who live alone or with busy working offspring must also learn to cook and clean for themselves, a challenge that many men in particular find daunting, in the absence of both servants and solicitous daughters-in-law. Some who had never even learned to prepare a cup of tea for themselves in India take up cooking, vacuuming, laundry. Vitalbhai Gujar not infrequently boasted at the Indo-American senior center meetings that he had never once asked his daughter-in-law to make him even one cup of tea. (In her conversations with me, she disagreed. Nonetheless, she concurred that her father-in-law had acquired a good deal of self-sufficiency since moving to the

United States.) Every morning after his son and daughter-in-law go to work, Gujar looks in the refrigerator to see if there are any leftovers there for his lunch. Usually there are none, so he has learned to boil up a pot of rice and dal for himself or to take a bus to an Indian restaurant, using his SSI funds as "pocket money" to pay for the meal.

Other seniors get part-time jobs in order not to have to depend entirely on their children. Lata Parikh, who was able to earn a little money by working in a child-care center while also receiving some SSI income and living with her son and daughter-in-law, said of life in the United States, "You have to earn your pocket money! You know, if you don't have any other and have to beg from your children. [*She laughed a little, sheepishly.*] Of course, they don't mind, but any time, you don't, you don't feel like asking them for *every* penny you spend."[25]

SSI money and part-time jobs cannot make seniors independently wealthy or even, in most cases, fully independent of their children. Most adult children continue, whatever the circumstances, to provide their parents a substantial degree of material and social support. About two-thirds of my closest informants live in the homes of their children (and thus receive a smaller SSI allowance, if they are on SSI). Those who do not live with children tend at least to receive quite a lot of material support from them, such as money, cars, medical expenses, and airplane tickets to and from India. Nonetheless, their independent income makes it possible for senior immigrants to support themselves to an important extent, as well as to participate as independent consumers in the nation. The senior immigrants thus become in some ways like American perceptions of teenagers with discretionary income to spend— betwixt dependence and independence—although this is not an analogy I have heard Indians make themselves. They begin to cultivate a kind of egalitarian autonomy, still fused with hierarchical interdependence, made possible in part by working with American policies that displace the management of aging from the family onto individuals and the state.

Death, Technology, Materiality: Individuality and the Body

Finally, the structure and meaning of family relationships are reshaped as Indian seniors negotiate dying across India and America. Older Indian immigrants are struck most of all by American attempts to control and preserve the body as long as possible, coupled with the construction of death as an end to the individual body and self, rather than a means for expressing, reshaping, and extending family relationships. American strivings for bodily immortality are apparent in the pervasive popular cultural techniques for keeping even the very old body fit and young-looking—hair dyes, face lifts, anti-wrinkle creams, exercise routines, sporty youthful clothing, and the like. These strivings are also manifest, even more powerfully, in America's elaborate, advanced medical technologies geared toward keeping the body alive seemingly indefinitely. Medical anthropologist Byron Good reflects on the key soteriological role that biomedicine plays in American culture, where death and finitude are found in the human body, and "salvation, or at least some partial representation of it, is present in the technical efficacy of medicine" (1994, 86). "In this country, we spend an astounding proportion of our health care dollars on the last several weeks of life," he observes, "so great is our commitment and our technological capacity for extending life" (87).

Many of my informants contrast such practices to an "Indian" system, in which one thinks of the body as something that naturally fades and passes away at the end of life, much as a tree loses its leaves, or a rice plant drops its seeds and withers to the earth. An important part of the Hindu funeral ritual is cremation, the final dissolution of the body, which frees the soul to take new paths—to ancestorhood, and to reincarnation in a new body or, perhaps, ultimate liberation (*moksha, mukti*). Sons or other close descendants ritually reconstruct an ancestral body for the parent, and then continue to remember, honor, and nurture the ancestor, ideally for generations, through ongoing ritual performances or *sraddhas*. In such a system, death is an important means of expressing and extending intergenerational family ties (cf. Lamb 2000, 144–180; Parry 1994) and a passage on to important new existences.

Indian Americans struggle to sort through these intermingling practices and attitudes, to construct an acceptable mode of aging and dying out of the interplay of India and America. It turns out that the ritual of reconstructing bodies for parents after death is very often abandoned by Indians living in America. Although Hindu funeral rites can be performed in the United States (most large metropolitan areas now house a Hindu temple or two), many (especially juniors) feel that such ritual attention to ancestors is no longer important in the American context. Many seniors state that even if they would like these rituals to be practiced, they cannot expect their children to do so here, because of factors such as lack of time and good available priests, and what they see as very different cultural systems. Some say they doubt whether the elaborate Hindu funereal transactions between sons and parents really amount to anything anyway. Suresh Trivedi, a man from Gujarat in his eighties, one morning irritatedly asked a gathering of a few friends at the Indo-American senior center, "What is this boy? When I go, he will put flowers, he will put my photo, and flowers and all these things on the photo. He will pray and all these things. What is the use of all this when in normal life he has been maltreating me?"

Some, who say they have always had quite secular views anyway, embrace what they see as not merely an "American," but a more broadly modern, rational, secular way of approaching dying. Matilal Majmundar, for instance, mused, "If you go to India, they will definitely talk to you, 'Oh, there is life after death' and all these things. Nothing. In their heart they know that there is no life. Once you go, then you are completely forgotten out of history. There will be no trace." His whole family has cultivated a "secular outlook on life that fits very well in America," and he does not expect his children to perform *sraddhas* for him.

However, some remain very keen on finding ways to be ritually processed after death as a Hindu. Some make plans to return to India to die—though realizing that maybe "just when you need to go the most is when you are unable to go!" as Lata exclaimed, imagining future infirmities. Others plan explicitly transnational funerals, instructing their children to send their ashes back to relatives remaining in India, so that proper funeral and ancestral rites can be at least minimally practiced there, ensuring their insertion into a ritual economy that promises ancestral eternity, and—in a very literal way—dying on a global scale.[26]

Confrontations with American medicine provoke intensely ambivalent feelings. Many (juniors and seniors) consider the state-of-the-art medical care available for elders to be one of the main benefits of living in America. However, they fear becoming overly embroiled in life-prolonging technology. Tarun Mukherjee exclaimed, "I have visited nursing homes. I have visited, yes. I have seen people suffering. I tell you, such a bad situation has come over here. That because of medical facilities, we are living too long." One medicalized death was discussed at Indo-American seniors' meetings over a period of several months. A senior Gujarati man (whom I had not known personally) had had a heart attack. His son called 911, so he was taken to the hospital. There he was put on life support and died over a period of weeks. The ordinary Hindu dying rituals, such as lying on the floor—intended to help purify the person and body, loosen worldly ties, and help the soul (or *atma*) leave at the moment of death (Lamb 2000, 158–160; Madan 1987, 134–135)—could not be practiced in the hospital. At one point, the man's son and wife indicated that he should be put on the floor, but the nurses either did not understand or could not accept the request. So he died in the hospital, in bed, hooked up to machines. In musing over the event, people reflected that in the "Hindu" way, the body would be discarded when old and used, like old clothing; but in the American system, a call to 911 results in attempting to keep the body alive as long as possible.

As death and dying in America become less family affairs, moments for expressing and extending intergenerational family ties, they become increasingly medicalized and bodily events. Dying in the United States is perceived to be located outside of the family and in hospitals (and in the state, through services such as Medicare and 911), and managed through a highly advanced, admired, at times welcomed, and yet disturbingly binding and individualizing medicine.

So seniors in Indian American transnational families strive, with an ambivalent mixture of nostalgia and creative resourcefulness, to construct a meaningful aging through the competing expectations and values traversing India and America, generations and eras—of family and individualism, time and material prosperity, intimacy and professional success, the spirit and technology, locality and cosmopolitanism, tradition and modernity. Indians living in America take some symbols, practices, and policies from what they see as India, some from America, and some from a more broadly dispersed global modernity, in the process both reciprocally constructing and creatively intermingling these diverse overlapping worlds. Much changes in the passage from India: Familial economies become less multiplex, and key aspects of reproduction are displaced onto the state. An ethos of freedom and egalitarianism is fostered, in part, by state support of individuals, which works toward leveling status differences of age and gender but which simultaneously erodes the moral density that dependency engenders. Here, semi-autonomy is partly symbolized by the ability to exercise the power to consume (even if thanks to a state subsidy), in a context in which material prosperity and consumption are eminent values. An immediate, present time and individualistic focus is cultivated, too, by powerful practices of preserving the body and self of this life as long as possible, in the face of uncertainty that life and its relationships will hold any value or continuance afterward. At the same time, most Indian American seniors, in diverse ways and to varying degrees, also nurture precious images and values of a dearly remembered India, such as of intimate intergenerational reciprocity, a slowness of daily time, and an acceptance of worldly, bodily, transience. Thus, senior Indian Americans may brew their own cup of tea, while acquiring the supplies from their juniors' coffers; they may enjoy SSI welfare payments, but reside intimately with their families; they may die in an American hospital hooked up to medical technologies, but as a Hindu striving to be put on the floor where worldly attachments are fewer. In these ways, they forge their lives, reinterpreting India and America and the complex meanings of aging through intricately multivalent global processes of cultural production.

Aging and Cosmopolitan Modernity in India

Strikingly, very similar transformations of aging and family are occurring in India. What those in the United States frequently label "American," in contrast to an "India" of timeless tradition, those in India attribute to more globally dispersed and locally occurring forces of profound social change, tied to "modernity," "Westernization," and "globalization." During trips in 2003 and 2004 to Kolkata and New Delhi to investigate such cosmopolitan discourses of aging, I continually heard about the careerism, materialism, and consumerism taking over India; the fact that young women and men now both work out of the home; a persistent lack of time (so that even if elders live in their children's homes, the children can't stop to ask, "Ma, how are you doing?"); a deep generation gap (due to the accelerated pace and vastness of social change); and the commonness of transnational migration, so that, people commonly say, most elders among the middle or professional classes have NRI ("nonresident Indian") children living abroad. State programs to support the elderly are not nearly as extensive in India as they are in the United States—although gerontologists, governmental officials, and NGOs such as Help Age India hope that India will be able to develop comprehensive programs for the elderly, including pension schemes and state-supported old age homes (see, e.g., Rajan, Mishra, and Sarma 1999). State support for the elderly is internationally considered one of the signs of a "developed" or "advanced" nation, after all. Nonetheless, many institutions pertaining to old age care have sprung up in India over recent years, some funded partially by the state and others by NGOs, charitable organizations, and private businesses. All these factors add up to mean that close intergenerational relationships within "traditional Indian" joint families are being seriously tried and transformed as India, too, witnesses a profound transition from family to individual and institutional modes of aging—a global trend in "modern" nations.

Perhaps the single most striking dimension of this new mode of modern aging is the near flood of old age homes opening in India's major urban centers. Over the past two decades, the number of old age homes in Kolkata alone has climbed from about three (largely catering to the Anglo-Indian community) to over thirty. In 1995 Help Age India began publishing a directory of old age homes in India, the most recent edition of which has now reached 409 pages (Help Age India 2002). Most of the homes were opened after 1980, and each directory becomes outdated almost as soon as it is printed, with new homes continually being founded. One resident of a home commented, "If I were to open an old age home today, tomorrow it would be filled, such is the demand now." People speak of old age homes as a distinctly modern mode of managing aging, influenced by Westernization (the institutional form itself, as well as the values promoting it, are widely regarded as specifically Western), careerism (working children with no time), and globalization (dispersed families and pervasive global and Western cultural values). Many of the homes cater to parents of NRI children, and in fact publish separate rates for those with and without children living abroad: those with NRI children pay about double.

Other organizations have also sprung up to offer support services for the financially well-off elderly, whose busy professional children live abroad, in modern nuclear apartments, or with their parents but with no time to care for them. A couple in the Delhi suburbs, Mr. and Mrs. Saksena, have started a business looking in on the elderly parents of NRI children. It is the children who are the paying "clients" (at $5.00/hour), and the Saksenas visit the senior parents as "friends of their son or daughter overseas." Their motto is "to do whatever we are asked to do, provided it is not illegal," including routine visits to chat over tea; escorting seniors to doctors' appointments, railway stations, airports, and late-night wedding receptions; taking them out on special occasions—to dinner, the movies, concerts, or religious festivals; arranging cakes, flowers, etc. for birthdays or anniversaries; and, finally, being present at the time of death. "Typically, it takes anywhere between twenty-four to forty-eight hours for our nonresident clients to arrive in India. As such we have to be present with the [dying] elderly to provide emotional support and make arrangements for the funeral. Not a very pleasant task, but it has to be done,"

Mr. Saksena told me. The Agewell Foundation, an NGO launched in 1999 in New Delhi, offers similar services: home visits, a telephone help line, escorting, assistance filling out tax forms, places to socialize with fellow seniors, and the like. NRI children can sponsor their parents, paying Rs. 5,000 (a little over $100) for a lifetime membership. Himanshu Rath, the founder and director of Agewell, compares the hired counselors to surrogate sons, explaining, "Imagine the counselor to be like a son (all counselors are males between the ages of 21 to 35) who takes the place of the natural child and performs the same duties for his elderly charge as a son would do. The presence of a younger person in the house gives these old people something to look forward to." Rath added that the response from children who can't spend time with their parents has been overwhelming. "Agewell allows children to gift the membership to their parents. A sad situation indeed where children cannot gift their parents time. But this is a contemporary reality that has to be faced."[27] Sons and elder care by hire: market intimacy in the modern era.

Indian gerontologists frequently advocate the development of such individual self-sufficiency and institutional (nonfamily) means of elder support, often presenting "traditional" family-centered modes of aging as "backward." S. Irudaya Rajan, U. S. Mishra, and P. Sankara Sarma (1999) recommend, for instance, that the Indian government should support old age homes and pension plans, and that aging individuals should cultivate self-reliance—through savings, exercise, and an open-mindedness about living in old age homes— because they can no longer count on (and should no longer count on, if they are modern and educated, it is implied) depending on their children in old age (cf. Lamb 2001b). Shovana Narayana comments, "The self-sufficiency of the elderly is a very healthy trend. . . . The *problem* lies in the *rural mind set* where people consider their children as a support system for their old age" (Gupta 2001, emphasis added).

Media representations, though, tend to be less sanguine, portraying today's modern Indian elders as pathetic victims, helplessly trapped in old age homes and isolated apartments as if in jail, their stories peppered with what sound like urban legends. For example, "The old couple are even forced [by their children] to go without food, unless they do odd jobs in the house" (Ghosh 1999); "Delhi's seniors have come to dread their own children, who in their greed for money and ancestral property are terrorizing their aged parents" (Shakeel 1999). "No one is allowed to go in or out" of old age homes, claims another, and the cost is exorbitant. "They are actually paying to be in a prison!" (Sharma and Menon 2000).[28]

On their part, some seniors do deplore such contemporary modes of aging. Ranjan Banerjee, a retired psychiatrist living in an exclusive Kolkata old age home, muses thoughtfully about how old age homes reflect not only a new form of aging, but also much broader—and regrettable—social, cultural, and national transformations:

Old age homes are not a concept of our country. These days, we are throwing away our culture. The U.S. is the richest nation in the world and therefore has won us over. Now we, too, are only after material wealth as a nation and have become very unhappy. Some are here [in the old age home] because their families dumped them here, and there are others whose children are living abroad and can easily afford the money. But old age homes are not our way of life. My parents died *right with us*. . . . I have a granddaughter and my world revolves around her. I miss her so much when I don't see her for a few days. [*He paused, with glistening eyes.*] Here [in the old age home], there is a little hardship regarding food and all, but that's OK. I have time to read and such. The real hardship comes from missing loved family, like my granddaughter. . . . We as a nation have become very unhappy. Material wealth [*artha*] used not to be the prime value in life; rather, family and social closeness were. But now it has become so. I myself am against the old age home concept—but old age homes will stay and increase in India.

However, other elderly residents of old age homes and senior members of NGOs on aging present themselves as quite resourceful and even optimistic in dealing with modern social changes, now that the changes are occurring. I think that many would have liked to retain much of the past; but since the past is gone, they work creatively to carve out a new life and mode of aging in the present. Quite a few residents of old age homes were the ones to decide firmly on their own that they would be moving in—clipping out newspaper advertisements (which some still carefully save and pull out with pride), making enquiries, and then moving in (often while their families protested, they say[29]), adjusting to the new way of life, making friends among peers, playing cards, sewing, chatting as they fall asleep (for those who live dormitory-style), even speaking of other residents as their new family. Many also see institutional living as better than other options, such as keeping their children from succeeding in their careers, or living with children and confronting the vast generation gap, or following their children to alien lands such as America. Some acknowledge, as well, that the past itself wasn't as rosy as many people now make it out to be, that of course generational tensions existed then, too, and that joint families used to be particularly difficult for young women and daughters-in-law, who had to serve their elders while foregoing higher education and rewarding work.

In such ways, cosmopolitan Indians of senior and junior generations actively negotiate the competing worlds of tradition and modernity, locality and globalization, family intimacy and material success, intergenerational reciprocity and elder care by hire. The meanings and experiences of old age are key here. New modes of aging work in some ways as fundamental signs of social degeneracy, and in others as intrinsic parts of a valued—rational, cosmopolitan, contemporary, egalitarian—global modernity.

Concluding Reflections:
Age, Generation, and Global Modernity

We have seen, then, that aging is a powerful set of idioms and practices through which many people in India and abroad imagine and experience the changes of the global era. Discourses and practices of aging are significant ways in which people strive to construct valued forms of family, society, and nation, as they forge lives across India and America and in a global sociocultural milieu. Elderly cosmopolitan Indians and their communities construct aging by drawing from three overlapping domains: tradition and modernity, then and now; the divergent national-cultural worlds of India and America, here and there; and globally dispersed shifts in cosmopolitan family life. Such globally emerging forms of family are not tied specifically to either India or America, or to any single national-cultural place (though many believe that they originally emanated from "the West"), and entail features such as urban and transnational migration, 24/7 work lives, individual self-sufficiency, dependence (when necessary) on the state or on private institutions rather than on kin, and a consumerism that stresses the creation of personal value and the maintenance of bodies with commodities and modern technologies. Indians engage in such processes with ambivalence, grappling with what they perceive as a major challenge of social reproduction, as they abandon many "traditional" Indian values while embracing modern, global social forms.

Such a focus on Indian American and cosmopolitan aging speaks to two interconnected ways of studying and conceptualizing aging and globalization. First, I suggest that aging is a fruitful lens through which to bring into focus the crucially interrelated macro and micro dimensions of globalization, which are too often dichotomized and overlooked. In making tea (or not), moving into apartments and old age homes, hiring surrogate sons, and dying in hospitals, older Indians are creatively forging new ways of aging that are quintessentially both intimate (experienced, embodied, particular) and part of enormously large-scale processes of economic, social, and cultural globalization. To study the micro, local, particular, and experienced is to be steeped in the global or macro, and vice versa; and thus we must challenge ourselves to do ethnography while transecting the intimate and far-flung, here and there, local and global.

Second, aging is also a productive lens through which to scrutinize the ways we think about social and generational change in the context of such contemporary global flows. It is striking that anxieties attendant on social and cultural reproduction—the production of recognizable and valued futures—so often express themselves right now, in scholarly literature and in popular consciousness, in terms of intergenerational divides, in which only the young represent the rapidly changing global and modern, and the old stand for stalwart locality and tradition. With the loss of older patterns of social, political, and economic identity, generation often comes to signify, even naturalize, new oppositions, playing on the fact that the old and young might now live in very different experiential worlds or "ages." The idiom of generation in such conceptualizations represents not merely change across time, but change across space or place, as different generations are perceived as being tied not only to distinct eras but also to different places, entailing discrete, even opposing, values, lifeways, cultures.

Yet, when examining generations or generational "gaps" as a means of representing global social change, one cannot assume that it is best to associate old age with tradition and a fixed past, and youth with changing modernity— to envision the young as the only site where globalization penetrates society and culture. For, among the cosmopolitan and transnational Indians I know, what is as striking as such perceived oppositions between generations and eras (which are, certainly, also expressed) is the variety of ways older people creatively rework their worlds, through participating in an inventive mélange of places, traditions, and modes of family, state, body, purposefully carving out new forms of aging on a global scale. In the discourses explored here, in fact, one of the key ways for individuals, families, and societies to be modern is to forge new, global modes of aging. Thus, old age itself—in its new forms— comes to represent, and illuminate, a contemporary era of global modernity.

NOTES

The research on which this chapter is based was supported by a postdoctoral fellowship in Socio-Cultural Gerontology through the Medical Anthropology Program at the University of California–San Francisco, and by a Mazer Award for Faculty Research and the Sachar Fund at Brandeis University. I would like to thank several friends and colleagues for perceptive comments and insightful discussions that strengthened the piece immensely, including Amy Borovoy, Jennifer Cole, Jean Comaroff, Deborah Durham, Nita Kumar, Harikrishna Majmundar, McKim Marriott, Diane Mines, Linda Mitteness, anonymous reviewers for Indiana University Press, and my remarkable research assistant Hena Basu. Most of all I am indebted to the people and families of this study, who enabled me to work among and learn from them. A few parts of this essay appeared in "Intimacy in a Transnational Era: The Remaking of Aging among Indian Americans" by Sarah Lamb, *Diaspora* 11 (3): 299–330. Copyright © 2002 University of Toronto Press, Incorporated. Used by permission.

1. *Pathos* (*Karunam*) was awarded the Golden Peacock in the Thirty-First International Film Festival of India in 2000. Jayaraj's comments appear in an interview in Dupont 2000.

2. Suchita lives in the U.S. while her aging parents remain in India. She is concerned about how to maintain close contact with them, and also about her own future old age. Discussion posted November 7, 2000 (in my files).

3. This statement appears on the Dignity Foundation's main web page, at http:// www.dignityfoundation.com/, accessed November 9, 2005.

4. Personal interview. This gentleman's story will be explored further below. All informants from my own fieldwork are identified by pseudonyms.

5. Lawrence Cohen's important 1998 study similarly examines discourses of mo-

dernity and the "bad family" in India, revealing how the powerful image of the disintegrating "modern" family has been around for a long time (cf. Lamb 2000, 88–99). This chapter focuses on some of the newest forms of such discourse: the impact of global or transnational living.

6. Of course, not all emigrant Indians move to the United States. Many also migrate to Canada, Britain, the Middle East, Singapore, Hong Kong, and other places. This chapter focuses on families split between India and the U.S.

7. In her *Television, Ethnicity, and Cultural Change* (1995), for instance, Marie Gillespie suggests that older South Asians in Britain signify and partake in tradition, while only the young participate in change and transnational modes of experience. Jean and John Comaroff (1999) investigate how generation is used as one of the dominant idioms through which youths in postcolonial South Africa frame their identities and place in the world. Widespread anxiety over the hardening materialities of life in an era of global capital translates frequently into bitter generational opposition. Jennifer Cole (this volume) similarly scrutinizes youth's transformative power, arguing that their "structural liminality . . . makes them uniquely positioned to take advantage of new social and economic conditions." See also Lamb 2001a.

8. A surge of academic work has been produced on transnationalism and globalization over recent years (e.g., Appadurai 1990, 1991, 1996, 2001; Appadurai and Breckenridge 1988; Clifford 1994; Foner 1997; Freeman 2001; Gupta and Ferguson 1997; Hannerz 1989, 1996; Inda and Rosaldo 2002; Itzigsohn 2001; Kearney 1995; Marchand and Runyan 2000; Marcus 1995; Ong 1999; Portes, Guarnizo, and Landolt 1999; Sassen 1998; Schiller, Basch, and Blanc-Szanton 1992; Shukla 2001; Tololyan 1996; Vertovec 1999). Most of this work has concentrated on macro processes, such as the global flows of capital, circulating media images, and mass movements of bodies across borders. Such a focus on macro processes has meant that little serious, careful consideration in transnational and global studies is being given to the kinds of issues that have long been crucial to anthropology: thick ethnographic fieldwork, human practices, and the ways broader forces play out in and via the lives of particular people. Notable recent exceptions to this trend are being produced, however—works that seek specifically to produce rich, ethnographic accounts of global and transnational processes (e.g., Constable 2003; Gamburd 2000; Mills 2001). The anthropological pendulum has swung from earlier accounts of local, bounded wholes; to studies of the highly broad, macro, detached, global; and now back to a more nuanced, integrated center in which scholars examine the ways local and global, micro and macro, intimate and broad or abstract human phenomena are inextricably intertwined. I discuss this in further depth in Lamb 2002a.

9. There is no uniformly accepted term for people from the Indian subcontinent living in the United States. "South Asian," the phrase most widely used in academic circles, refers to persons from the contemporary nations of India, Pakistan, Bangladesh, Sri Lanka, Nepal, and Bhutan (although it veils what many perceive to be deep differences of language, religion, ethnicity, etc.). People of Indian descent in the United States refer to themselves by a variety of labels, including "Indian American," "Indo-American," *Desi* (of the *des* or homeland; primarily used by youth), and simply "Indian." "Asian Indian" has been the official U.S. Census category since 1980. See Anand 1994; George 1997, 52 n.3; Kibria 1996; Leonard 1997, 2000; Natarajan 1993; Nelson 1992; Prashad 1999; Radhakrishnan 1996; and Shankar 1998 for further discussions of these labels and their social-political ramifications.

10. Since the passage of the 1965 U.S. Immigration and Naturalization Act, which allowed Asian immigrants with preferred occupational skills to enter the United States, immigrants from India have, on the whole, had high socioeconomic status. The class backgrounds of Indian Americans are gradually becoming somewhat more varied, however, as family members (who are not all professionals) immigrate under the Family Reunification Act, and as second-generation children pursue a variety of careers. For discussions of the history of South Asian immigration to the United States, see Agrawal 1991; Hing 1993, 69–73; Jensen 1988; Leonard 1997; Lessinger 1995; and Visweswaran 1997.

11. In my U.S. fieldwork, I conversed primarily in Bengali with Bengali seniors, and primarily in English with younger Bengalis and non-Bengali Indians. Younger first- and second-generation Indians in the United States are almost all entirely fluent in English and tend to prefer English even in their homes. Most older immigrants from India also speak English, coming as they do largely from middle- and upper-class backgrounds. However, several of my informants, especially older women, were more comfortable expressing the nuances of their perspectives and experiences in their mother tongues. Thus, English was regrettably an imperfect medium of communication in some cases.

12. My earlier 1989–1990 fieldwork focused on what many Indians would consider more "traditional" forms of aging, within rural, largely multigenerational families (Lamb 1993, 1997a, 1997b, 2000, 2002b). The 2003 and 2004 research trips to Kolkata and New Delhi focused on contemporary cosmopolitan discourses of aging within old age homes, NGOs, the media, and everyday talk.

13. Compare this model to Tlalcuapan models of generational interdependence described by Magazine and Ramírez Sánchez (this volume), in which young children work hard as one half of an "exchange" with parents in which parents provide children with nurturance, shelter, material support, and eventually an inheritance, and children provide labor and "help" (*ayuda*).

14. A more detailed discussion of the ways Bengalis perceive such traditional intergenerational relationships can be found in Lamb 2000, 42–69.

15. In January 2003, the government of India changed the official term for Indians living abroad from "Non-Resident Indian" (NRI) to "Person of Indian Origin" (PIO); however, NRI is still the term in popular use.

16. http://helpageindia.org/nris_more.html, accessed February 28, 2003. See also Livingston (this volume) and Woronov (this volume), who examine the ways values surrounding "traditional" intergenerational reciprocity are being complexly reconfigured in modern, global times in Botswana and China, respectively.

17. See Agrawal 1991; Hing 1993, 69–73; Jensen 1988; Leonard 1997; Lessinger 1995; and Visweswaran 1997.

18. The 1990 U.S. Census counted Asian Indians age sixty-five and over at only 1.6 percent of the Asian Indian population (Winokur 1994, 12). The 2000 U.S. Census counted them at 4.0 percent. Many older Indians, however, move back and forth between India and the United States, often retaining Indian nationality and legal residency, and thus are not included in the U.S. census.

19. The Indo-American Community Center, located in the San Francisco South Bay region and at which I volunteered, holds regular meetings for seniors. This center was, in fact, originally called the Indo-American Community Senior Center, but later the "senior" was dropped from the name, as the directors wished to convey that in the

Indian community, seniors are not distinct, isolated persons but rather an intrinsic part of the community as a whole.

20. T. E. Woronov (this volume) scrutinizes similar tensions in contemporary Chinese families, whose parents seek to foster modern "American-style" economic success in their children, while at the same time realizing with distress the need, then, to release their children from "traditional" Chinese modes of parent-child relations.

21. The Supplemental Security Income (SSI) program is a federal program established in 1974 to provide a nationally uniform guaranteed minimum income for the aged, blind, and disabled. Until 1996, both citizens and legal immigrants could receive benefits under this program, provided they met eligibility requirements. Since the passing of Welfare Reform Bill #H.R.3507, now Public Law 104–193, immigrants arriving after 1996 are only eligible for the program if they become citizens.

22. It is important to note that of all the Indian immigrant seniors I knew who were receiving SSI, each was a recent immigrant. That is, they had come to the United States late in life to be with their children. Of the fewer senior Indian Americans I know who migrated to the United States sufficiently early in their lives to work here, and thus earn Social Security credits and amass retirement funds, none are receiving SSI. Among Indian American households in general (not just households including recent immigrants age sixty-five and over), welfare use is low: in California in 1990, only 7.4% of Asian Indian households received any form of public assistance (U.S. Dept. of Commerce 1993: table 116, p. 256).

23. Anthropological research has similarly found that Americans, especially among the white middle classes, expect resources to flow in a unidirectional manner from parents to children throughout a lifetime: parents support their children as minors, and then often continue to provide some financial assistance to children as adults, ending perhaps with leaving an inheritance at death. However, most find it anathema to think of reversing the direction of transactional flows to become financially dependent on children in old age (e.g., Clark 1972; Hashimoto 1996; Hunt 2002; Kalish 1967; Monahan 1998; Simic 1983; Vatuk 1990; Vesperi 1985). Of course, America is a highly diverse nation. Carol Stack, for instance, writes of the deeply felt obligations among African Americans in the rural South to provide and care for the aging grandparents and parents who raised them (1996, 107–121).

24. Congress's ten-year assessment of SSI, published in 1984, includes a brief discussion of the transition from family to state support of the elderly, although without specifically marking children's potential responsibilities. In early America, the report reads, influenced by the Poor Laws of England, "relatives were to be held responsible for the support of their needy kinsmen" (U.S. Congress, Senate 1984, 3). Such a system disappeared, the document suggests, because of economic forces: industrialization "undermined traditional economic structures and the family," and the Great Depression "seriously affected the ability of families to support aged relatives in need" (3). The document contains no further discussion of the cultural or moral issues surrounding care of the elderly by children or families, however, and no indication that contemporary lawmakers ever considered the possibility of requiring children (with adequate resources) to provide support for elderly parents.

25. Note that even in a "traditional" Indian system where it is expected that seniors will depend on their juniors in late life, generally the seniors (in particular men) will maintain some control over financial resources until death (unless they are impover-

ished and have none)—with a home or land in their name, a retirement pension, or savings in a bank account.

26. Writer Tahira Naqvi's short story "Dying in a Strange Country" (2001) poignantly portrays an older Pakistani woman's gripping fears of dying in America when she visits her son, who has settled in Connecticut. See also Firth 1997 for a rich look at beliefs and practices surrounding death and dying in a British Hindu community.

27. Rath's comments were published in Sokhal 2000, one of about twenty newspaper clippings he offered me when I met with him for several hours in March 2003 to discuss the Agewell Foundation and his general views about aging. Other similar organizations include the Dignity Foundation, founded in 1995 with branches in Mumbai, Kolkata, Pune, Navi Numbai, and Chennai; and private, for-profit groups—Sawantarni and Sandiparni—in the posh Salt Lake region of Kolkata. See also Sundaram 2001 for a discussion of the Saksenas' business.

28. This claim—that no one is allowed to go in or out—is not at all true of most old age homes in India, where people come and go regularly, and which in general are less rule-bound than the American old age homes I know.

29. Most residents of old age homes feel compelled to publicly state that their families did not want them to move in (whether or not the assertion is fully true). This saves the family's prestige and represents the elder as loved and served.

WORKS CITED

Agrawal, Priya. 1991. *Passage from India: Post-1965 Immigrants and Their Children.* Palos Verdes, Calif.: Yuvati.

Anand, Rajen S. 1994. "What Should We Call Ourselves: Let's Debate." *India-West,* February 18.

Appadurai, Arjun. 1990. "Disjuncture and Difference in the Global Cultural Economy." *Public Culture* 2 (2): 1–24.

———. 1991. "Global Ethnoscapes: Notes and Queries for a Transnational Anthropology." In *Recapturing Anthropology: Working in the Present.* Richard G. Fox, ed. Pp. 191–210. Santa Fe, N.M.: School of American Research Press.

———. 1996. *Modernity at Large: Cultural Dimensions of Globalization.* Minneapolis: University of Minnesota Press.

———, ed. 2001. *Globalization.* Durham, N.C.: Duke University Press.

Appadurai, Arjun, and Carol A. Breckenridge. 1988. "Why Public Culture?" *Public Culture* 1 (1): 5–9.

Berman, Marshall. 1988. *All That Is Solid Melts into Air: The Experience of Modernity.* New York: Penguin.

Brennan, Teresa. 2003. *Globalization and Its Terrors: Daily Life in the West.* New York: Routledge.

Clark, Margaret. 1972. "Cultural Values and Dependency in Later Life." In *Aging and Modernization.* Donald O. Cowgill and Lowell D. Holmes, eds. Pp. 263–274. New York: Appleton-Century-Crofts.

Clifford, James. 1994. "Diasporas." *Cultural Anthropology* 9: 302–338.

Cohen, Lawrence. 1998. *No Aging in India: Alzheimer's, the Bad Family, and Other Modern Things.* Berkeley: University of California Press.

Comaroff, Jean, and John L. Comaroff. 1999. "Occult Economies and the Violence of

Abstraction: Notes from the South African Postcolony." *American Ethnologist* 26 (2): 279–303.

Constable, Nicole. 2003. *Romance on a Global Stage: Pen Pals, Virtual Ethnography, and "Mail Order" Marriages.* Berkeley: University of California Press.

Davis, Marvin. 1983. *Rank and Rivalry: The Politics of Inequality in Rural West Bengal.* Cambridge: Cambridge University Press.

Dupont, Joan. 2000. "An Indian Director's Stirring Vision of Old Age." *International Herald Tribune,* January 28.

Firth, Shirley. 1997. *Dying, Death, and Bereavement in a British Hindu Community.* New Religious Identities in the Western World 1. Leuven, Belgium: Peeters.

Foner, Nancy. 1997. "What's New about Transnationalism? New York Immigrants Today and at the Turn of the Century." *Diaspora* 6: 355–375.

Fortes, Meyer. 1984. "Age, Generation, and Social Structure." In *Age and Anthropological Theory.* David I. Kertzer and Jennie Keith, eds. Pp. 99–122. Ithaca, N.Y.: Cornell University Press.

Freeman, Carla. 2001. "Is Local : Global as Feminine : Masculine? Rethinking the Gender of Globalization." *Signs: Journal of Women in Culture and Society* 26 (4): 1007–1037.

Gamburd, Michele Ruth. 2000. *The Kitchen Spoon's Handle: Transnationalism and Sri Lanka's Migrant Housemaids.* Ithaca, N.Y.: Cornell University Press.

George, Rosemary Marangoly. 1997. "From Expatriate Aristocrat to Immigrant Nobody: South Asian Racial Strategies in the Southern Californian Context." *Diaspora* 6 (1): 31–60.

Ghosh, Deepshikha. 1999. "Search for New Horizons after 60." *The Statesman,* April 22.

Gillespie, Marie. 1995. *Television, Ethnicity, and Cultural Change.* New York: Routledge.

Gleick, James. 1999. *Faster: The Acceleration of Just About Everything.* New York: Pantheon.

Good, Byron J. 1994. *Medicine, Rationality, and Experience: An Anthropological Perspective.* Cambridge: Cambridge University Press.

Gupta, Akhil, and James Ferguson. 1997. "Culture, Power, Place: Ethnography at the End of an Era." In *Culture, Power, Place: Explorations in Critical Anthropology.* Akhil Gupta and James Ferguson, eds. Pp. 1–29. Durham, N.C.: Duke University Press.

Gupta, Aparna. 2001. "To Light Up That Wrinkled Face." *Asian Age,* October 2.

Hannerz, Ulf. 1989. "Notes on the Global Ecumene." *Public Culture* 1 (2): 66–75.

———. 1996. *Transnational Connections: Culture, People, Places.* New York: Routledge.

Hashimoto, Akiko. 1996. *The Gift of Generations: Japanese and American Perspectives on Aging and the Social Contract.* Cambridge: Cambridge University Press.

Help Age India. 2002. *Directory of Old Age Homes in India: 2002.* (First edition published in 1995.) New Delhi: Help Age India.

Hing, Bill Ong. 1993. *Making and Remaking Asian America through Immigration Policy, 1850–1990.* Stanford, Calif.: Stanford University Press.

Hochschild, Arlie Russell. 1997. *The Time Bind: When Work Becomes Home and Home Becomes Work.* New York: Metropolitan Books.

Hunt, Robert. 2002. "Economic Transfers and Exchanges: Concepts for Describing

Allocations." In *Theory in Economic Anthropology.* Jean Ensminger, ed. Pp. 105–118. Walnut Creek, Calif.: Alta Mira Press.

Inda, Jonathan Xavier, and Renato Rosaldo, eds. 2002. *The Anthropology of Globalization: A Reader.* Malden, Mass.: Blackwell.

Itzigsohn, Jose. 2001. "Living Transnational Lives." *Diaspora* 10: 281–296.

Jensen, Joan M. 1988. *Passage from India: Asian Indian Immigrants in North America.* New Haven, Conn.: Yale University Press.

Kalish, Robert. 1967. "Of Children and Grandfathers: A Speculative Essay on Dependency." *Gerontologist* 7: 65–69.

Kearney, Michael. 1995. "The Local and the Global: The Anthropology of Globalization and Transnationalism." *Annual Review of Anthropology* 24: 547–565.

Kibria, Nazli. 1996. "Not Asian, Black, or White? Reflections on South Asian American Racial Identity." *Amerasia Journal* 22 (2): 77–86.

Lamb, Sarah. 1993. "Growing in the Net of *Maya*: Persons, Gender, and Life Processes in a Bengali Society." Ph.D. diss., University of Chicago.

———. 1997a. "The Beggared Mother: Older Women's Narratives in West Bengal." *Oral Tradition* 12 (1): 54–75.

———. 1997b. "The Making and Unmaking of Persons: Notes on Aging and Gender in North India." *Ethos* 25 (3): 279–302.

———. 2000. *White Saris and Sweet Mangoes: Aging, Gender, and Body in North India.* Berkeley: University of California Press.

———. 2001a. "Generation in Anthropology." In *International Encyclopedia of the Social and Behavioral Sciences.* N. J. Smelser and Paul B. Baltes, eds. Pp. 6043–6046. Oxford: Pergamon.

———. 2001b. Review of *Social Aging in a Delhi Neighborhood,* by John van Willigen and Narender K. Chadha, and *India's Elderly: Burden or Challenge?* by S. Irudaya Rajan, U. S. Mishra, and P. Sankara Sarma. *Journal of Asian Studies* 60 (2): 589–591.

———. 2002a. "Intimacy in a Transnational Era: The Remaking of Aging among Indian Americans." *Diaspora* 11 (3): 299–330.

———. 2002b. "Love and Aging in Bengali Families." In *Everyday Life in South Asia.* Diane P. Mines and Sarah Lamb, eds. Pp. 56–68. Bloomington: Indiana University Press.

Leonard, Karen Isaksen. 1997. *The South Asian Americans.* Westport, Conn.: Greenwood Press.

———. 2000. "State, Culture, and Religion: Political Action and Representation among South Asians in North America." *Diaspora* 9: 21–38.

Lessinger, Johanna. 1995. *From the Ganges to the Hudson: Indian Immigrants in New York City.* Boston: Allyn and Bacon.

Madan, T. N. 1987. *Non-renunciation: Themes and Interpretations of Hindu Culture.* Delhi: Oxford University Press.

Majmundar, Harikrishna. 2003. *Mapping the Maze: A Guide to Welfare for Elderly Immigrants.* http://www.geocities.com/mappingthemaze/Mapping-the-Maze.htm.

Mannheim, Karl. 1952. "The Problem of Generations." In *Essays on the Sociology of Knowledge.* Pp. 276–320. London: Routledge.

Marchand, Marianne H., and Anne Sisson Runyan, eds. 2000. *Gender and Global Restructuring: Sightings, Sites, and Resistances.* New York: Routledge.

Marcus, George E. 1995. "Ethnography in/of the World System: The Emergence of Multi-sited Ethnography." *Annual Review of Anthropology* 24: 95–117.

Mills, Mary Beth. 2001. *Thai Women in the Global Labor Force: Consuming Desires, Contested Selves.* New Brunswick, N.J.: Rutgers University Press.

Monahan, Shannon. 1998. " 'Perfectly Happy to Live Alone': The Choices and Constraints Affecting Elderly Living Alone in a Local Housing Complex." M.A. research paper, Anthropology Department, Brandeis University.

Naqvi, Tahira. 2001. "Dying in a Strange Country." In *Dying in a Strange Country: Stories.* Pp. 1–16. Toronto: TSAR Publications.

Natarajan, Nalini. 1993. "Reading Diaspora." Introduction to *Writers of the Indian Diaspora: A Bio-bibliographical Sourcebook.* Emmanuel Nelson, ed. Pp. xii–xix. New York: Greenwood Press.

Nelson, Emmanuel S. 1992. Introduction to *Reworlding: The Literature of the Indian Diaspora.* Emmanuel Nelson, ed. Pp. ix–xvi. New York: Greenwood Press.

Ong, Aihwa. 1999. *Flexible Citizenship: The Cultural Logics of Transnationality.* Durham, N.C.: Duke University Press.

Parry, Jonathan P. 1994. *Death in Banaras.* Cambridge: Cambridge University Press.

Portes, Alejandro, Luis E. Guarnizo, and Patricia Landolt. 1999. "The Study of Transnationalism: Pitfalls and Promise of an Emergent Research Field." *Ethnic and Racial Studies* 22: 217–237.

Prashad, Vijay. 1999. "From Multiculture to Polyculture in South Asian American Studies." *Diaspora* 8: 185–204.

Radhakrishnan, R. 1996. "Is the Ethnic 'Authentic' in the Diaspora?" In *Diasporic Mediations: Between Home and Location.* Pp. 203–214. Minneapolis: University of Minnesota Press.

Rajan, S. Irudaya, U. S. Mishra, and P. Sankara Sarma. 1999. *India's Elderly: Burden or Challenge?* New Delhi: Sage Publications.

Sassen, Saskia. 1998. *Globalization and Its Discontents: Essays on the New Mobility of People and Money.* New York: New Press.

Schiller, Nina Glick, Linda Basch, and Cristina Blanc-Szanton. 1992. "Transnationalism: A New Analytic Framework for Understanding Migration." In *Towards a Transnational Perspective on Migration: Race, Class, Ethnicity, and Nationalism Reconsidered.* Nina Glick Schiller, Linda Basch, and Cristina Blanc-Szanton, eds. Pp. 1–24. New York: New York Academy of Sciences.

Shakeel, Sujata B. 1999. "Like Father, Unlike Son." *Hindustan Times,* June 5.

Shankar, Lavina Dhingra. 1998. "The Limits of (South Asian) Names and Labels: Postcolonial or Asian American?" In *A Part, Yet Apart: South Asians in Asian America.* Lavina Dhingra Shankar and Rajini Srikanth, eds. Pp. 49–66. Philadelphia: Temple University Press.

Sharma, Aruna, and Vinay Menon. 2000. "Senior Citizens' Homes: Life in a Cocoon." *Hindustan Times,* November 14.

Shukla, Sandhya. 2001. "Locations for South Asian Diasporas." *Annual Review of Anthropology* 30: 551–572.

Simic, Andrei. 1983. "Aging in the United States and in Yugoslavia: Contrasting Models of Intergenerational Relationships." In *Growing Old in Different Societies: Cross-Cultural Perspectives.* Jay Sokolovsky, ed. Belmont, Calif.: Wadsworth.

Sokhal, Sonali. 2000. "Bright Twilight." *Cardmembers' EXPRESSION India.* June: 54–55.

Stack, Carol. 1996. *Call to Home: African Americans Reclaim the Rural South.* New York: Basic Books.

Sundaram, Viji. 2001. "Delhi Couple Fill On for Absent NRI Children." *India-West* 26, no. 30 (June 1): A36.

Tololyan, Khachig. 1996. "Rethinking Diaspora(s): Stateless Power in the Transnational Moment." *Diaspora* 5: 3–36.

U.S. Congress. Senate. Special Committee on Aging. 1984. *The Supplemental Security Income Program: A 10-Year Overview.* 98th Congress, 2nd session. Committee Print.

U.S. Department of Commerce, Bureau of the Census. 1993. *1990 Census of Population: Social and Economic Characteristics: California, Section 1 of 4.* Washington, D.C.: Government Publishing Office.

Vatuk, Sylvia. 1990. "'To Be a Burden on Others': Dependency Anxiety among the Elderly in India." In *Divine Passions: The Social Construction of Emotion in India.* Owen Lynch, ed. Pp. 64–88. Berkeley: University of California Press.

Vertovec, Steven. 1999. "Conceiving and Researching Transnationalism." *Ethnic and Racial Studies* 22: 447–461.

Vesperi, Maria. 1985. *City of Green Benches: Growing Old in a New Downtown.* Ithaca, N.Y.: Cornell University Press.

Visweswaran, Kamala. 1997. "Diaspora by Design: Flexible Citizenship and South Asians in U.S. Racial Formations." *Diaspora* 6 (1): 5–29.

Winokur, Julie. 1994. "Cowboys and Indians: Indo-Americans Have Made Great Strides in the West, but Now They Are Returning to Traditional Values." *San Jose Mercury News*, May 15.

6

Maintaining Local Dependencies

*Elderly Women and Global Rehabilitation Agendas
in Southeastern Botswana*

JULIE LIVINGSTON

David

I met David[1] in August of 1997, during my first timid weeks of field-work. It was quite cold and windy that day, and David sat huddled with his great-grandmother near the small fire she had built in the cooking enclosure. I was accompanying Dikeledi, a very experienced rehabilitation technician in her early thirties, who worked with a community-based rehabilitation (CBR) program in southeastern Botswana. We moved among three villages and their surrounding agricultural lands, where she provided a range of services to de-bilitated persons in their homes: physical therapy, stimulation, speech therapy, occupational therapy, surgical referrals, social work, employment generation, and technical aids (wheelchairs, walking frames, etc).

Community-based rehabilitation in Botswana is managed and run by a number of NGOs with support from the Ministry of Health, as part of a global program spearheaded by the World Health Organization. WHO began pro-moting CBR in the mid-1970s, as part of its "Health for All by the Year 2000" initiative. The initiative began with pilot programs in nine developing coun-tries, Botswana among them. By the late 1980s, the program had been repli-cated in many countries throughout the developing world. Ideally, CBR uses professional rehabilitation workers to train local people to provide rehabilita-tion services to their relatives, neighbors, and friends who require them. The low cost of the program (a small fraction of a dollar a day per capita) made it attractive to many participant countries, though in southern Africa CBR, like many public health programs, increasingly competes with HIV/AIDS programs for funds.[2]

David was five years old at the time, and a very small boy—to me he looked more like a three-year-old, and a skinny one at that. He suffered from cerebral palsy brought on by birth trauma during a vacuum extraction at the local primary hospital.[3] David was clearly a bright little boy, a keen observer of life around him, but he had communication problems that made him difficult to understand. Yet Neo, his great-grandmother, and Dikeledi could usually grasp the gist of what he was saying. His legs were twisted and their joints contracted, and one of his hands had clawed from lack of use. He could move quickly about the compound by shuffling on his bottom, but he could neither sit upright for more than an extended moment, nor walk, nor "toilet," nor feed himself. With his skinny body and tattered clothing, he was a stark contrast to his three-year-old cousin who also lived in the compound. She was usually well dressed (if dusty), and was a plump and smiling little girl. On one visit we found that David was too dirty to be treated, and so we bathed him. Afterward we asked for a clean change of clothing, and his grandmother gave us a tattered, flowered dress, a castoff from his younger cousin, and not something I had ever seen a small boy wearing in Botswana.

Over the course of many visits I could see that Neo and her great-grandson David were deeply connected. They seemed always to be touching somehow, sitting or lying up against one another while Neo performed various light household chores, like shelling beans, or as they napped together in the shade. Neo welcomed our CBR visits, and had even traveled in the past to a neighboring village to attend the meetings of a cerebral palsy mother's group that Dikeledi had organized. By contrast, her daughter Florence, David's grandmother and the head of the household, wanted nothing to do with CBR. For her, the problem was not David but the relationship with her daughter that the little boy indexed. This was a problem that CBR highlighted, rather than solved.

On most visits, Florence would not even talk to Dikeledi, and would often leave the compound altogether when we arrived. Things had come to a head several times as Dikeledi tried to make the family follow the rehabilitation program of daily exercises, hand splints, speech therapy, and the like, and even raised the highly sensitive issue of David's being stinted during family meals.[4] But Florence continually referred back to her daughter. David's mother was at loose ends, without a permanent home, drinking too much, contributing neither to the household income nor to the care of her elders, her daughter (age ten, who also lived in the compound), or her son. Dikeledi would complain to the family that she spent a lot of effort teaching them skills, providing CBR, but when she came back each time to check up on David's progress, the family had not followed through, they had not worked on the rehabilitation program. Florence would inevitably reply, "But the mother is not also making an effort that she does that rehabilitation work. So now we can't do it." Producing a more "independent," healthy, and "highly functioning" grandson could not be her priority. In order for David to be brought back into the moral universe of the family for meaningful care, his own mother had to open the door.

Mother-daughter relationships have become increasingly central to the domestic economy of care in southeastern Botswana in recent decades, but these relationships are also experiencing new strains. Ideally, over the life course, the early sacrifices of motherhood are later rewarded with meaningful care in elderhood, but this dynamic is increasingly uncertain, a fact which instances of disability can aggravate.[5] Novel socioeconomic and epidemiological pressures brought, in part, by the movement of global capital pose new challenges to mother-daughter dynamics that are already being reconfigured. Disability in grandchildren, and in elderly women themselves, has become a key site where women's intergenerational tensions are played out. Global disability discourse and practices implemented through CBR are caught up in these domestic struggles, which have bodily implications for disabled children and elderly women. Elderly women subordinate the rehabilitative goals and processes of CBR to their efforts at maintaining and reproducing their relationships with their daughters. This strongly affects the outcome of these programs.

This chapter does two things. It shows how the effects of global capital, in this case the mineral boom in Botswana, foster novel pressures in mother-daughter relationships by providing wage work for young women, usually requiring migration to towns and cities. It also probes elderly women's responses to CBR, to see how Tswana women negotiate global care agendas. Elderly women's approaches to CBR provide a means to explore the range of women's intergenerational tensions in action, and to understand how such stresses are sustained through and amidst multiple global currents of ideas and capital.

Mothers, Daughters, and Disability

In the months and years after that early encounter with David's family, I met many small boys and girls with impairments like David's, as well as many frail or disabled elderly women who were CBR clients themselves. I learned how their stories necessitated the kind of "rewriting" of kinship that is so apparent among disabled families in Botswana and elsewhere (Rapp and Ginsburg 2001). Female kinship is already at issue in contemporary Botswana, where socioeconomic transformations have combined with epidemiological changes to make women's social reproduction a central tension in Tswana kinship. Negotiations around disability, which merge economic and caregiving responsibilities into an overarching moral framework, produce and highlight differences among three generations of women, exposing central tensions over social reproduction.

Social reproduction in this case centers on the ways that older women (those who are grandmothers and great-grandmothers) attempt to shape their daughters into particular kinds of mothers. Older women in southeastern Botswana focus their efforts on creating a moral imagination in their daughters, one that fosters a shared understanding of the responsibilities and rewards of motherhood. Women's sexual, social, nursing, and economic practices are all, in part, understood and managed through this idiom of motherhood. Motherhood and daughterhood are linked across generations, and so reproduction of mothering norms and values is central to older women's own continuing status as mothers. In other words, successful mothers produce well-behaved daughters, and those well-behaved daughters are themselves well-behaved mothers. Women who care for their seniors and their children through their nurturing economic and social practices, daughters who give money and gifts, who bathe children, who visit regularly, who whisk flies and move patients into the shade validate the moral status of their own mothers. Motherhood entails certain forms of bodily concern—sexual restraint and nursing care—which reaffirm the intersubjective nature of human bodies and their needs. Furthermore, older women deploy their motherhood, with all its benign meanings and associations, to shelter them from pathologizing or stigmatizing popular suspicions of witchcraft, which has long been associated with older women. Yet these efforts by older women to shape their daughters into mothers strike at the heart of long-standing tensions between the personal possibilities for liberal individualism and the priorities of the gerontocratic and social hierarchies that characterize Tswana society (Durham this volume, 1995, 1999a, 2005). In recent years, these tensions are increasingly manifest in mother-daughter relationships, and, as we will see below, often enacted around cases of disability.

The pervasive bodily perils, together with the social dislocations of the AIDS epidemic, mean that elderly women struggle to manage their own bodily impairments and those of their grandchildren in a context in which care is at a premium (Livingston 2003b; Klaits 2001; Durham and Klaits 2002). And yet the demand for long-term care for disabled children and elderly women has grown. Beginning in the 1970s the government of Botswana enjoyed rising revenues from mineral wealth, and it began implementing food transfers and primary health care initiatives, which, along with rising general incomes, fostered an epidemiological transition. Infectious disease and malnutrition (though still present) began to give way to chronic and debilitating illnesses. More children have survived longer with disabling impairments (whether the result of congenital problems, birth trauma, infectious disease, or accidents), and more adults began to experience "diseases of development"—chronic conditions like hypertension, diabetes, and cancer, and eventually the frailties of age (Livingston 2003b).[6] In 1991 (the most recent census data to which I have access), the elderly (persons sixty-five and over) accounted for 4.7 percent of the national population. Of the 62,531 people that represents, a little less than 17 percent were listed as disabled (Coombes, Khulumani, and Ngome 1994, 24–25).[7] The census further found that 10.5 percent of households housed at least one disabled resident (Central Statistics Office 1996, 55).[8]

Disability does not automatically imply dependency or a need for particular forms of care, but in children and the elderly it often highlights and exacerbates existing relations of dependency. Meanwhile, the AIDS epidemic has reached critical proportions in Botswana, undermining the youth and adult populations and creating new responsibilities for older women as caregivers to AIDS patients and their children. Estimates from 2001 suggest that 330,000 people in Botswana are living with HIV/AIDS (though not all of them are experiencing symptoms and requiring care). A more telling figure for purposes of this discussion is the 26,000 AIDS deaths in 2001, each of which suggests a history of illnesses that required nursing care (UNAIDS 2002). Older women, as both providers and seekers of care, occupy a pivotal position in the networks of caregiving these combined figures suggest. These networks are rife with intergenerational tensions, whose pressures are especially evident in relation to global disability discourse and programs.

Global rehabilitation programs imagine their "clients" located within communities of parent-centered extended families, imbued with a cooperative ethos of caregiving. These families, in turn, are supposedly nested in villages that may willingly mobilize labor and material resources to promote the bodily independence and civic participation of impaired residents. However, elderly women, both as caregivers and as people with aging bodies, live in grandmother-centered families. They struggle to retain authority over their daughters in tenuous interdependencies that exchange grandmother's child care and patient care for daughter's food and wages. For grandmothers, the strength and ease of these exchanges reflect a moral ethos of care and mothering they either share or contest with their daughters. Because their experiences of and priorities in domestic life diverge from globally imagined norms, often older women do not respond to the rehabilitation programs in the ways CBR planners hope, an issue to which I will return later.

Elderly women are caught up in multiple relations of dependency that produce particular tensions. They must rely heavily on husbands, sons, and brothers to protect their jural rights. For those recently widowed or divorced, this may entail leveraging one relationship to fend off the predations of another. For example, a brother may be needed to help a sister retain her property in the event of a divorce (Griffiths 1997). For those with married sons, daughters-in-law may provide valuable domestic and agricultural labor, but problems may also arise over, say, the distribution of a son's wages. But for elderly women in the late 1990s, tensions bred in the rapidity of recent economic, epidemiological, and social change aggregate in the dynamic between mothers and adult daughters, in particular. Some men, as fathers, sons, brothers, and uncles, do play important caregiving roles in the lives of their disabled relatives, but they are not considered primarily responsible for basic nursing tasks. Many men with children born outside marriage (a very common occurrence) are only minimally involved, if at all, in their children's lives. In all the discussions of who would help provide for David's needs, I never heard anyone mention his father. This was not unusual. In practice CBR efforts focused on mobilizing women's caregiving (to disabled persons of all ages), though in the cases where male help was forthcoming it was appreciated and enlisted.

Global Agendas: Rehabilitation

CBR planners promote their goals as universal, indeed global. Influenced by the international disability rights movement and orchestrated by agencies like the Red Cross and WHO, their agendas have global reach (Kohrman 1999, 2003; Devliger 1999; Priestley 2001). Yet local rehabilitation workers like Dikeledi know that the realities on the ground are far more complex than CBR rhetoric suggests. The priorities of the older women in Botswana who orchestrate care in their families can differ greatly from the purportedly global rehabilitative aims of CBR. Through biological and rights-based language and aims, global rehabilitation agendas stress independence and individualism in ways that do not always resonate with elderly women, either as caretakers of disabled grandchildren or as disabled subjects themselves. This produces paradoxical and wide-ranging results.

CBR provides an important set of alternative ideas, practices, and moral frameworks that disabled persons and caregivers respond to and utilize in diverse fashions as they seek to navigate the contingencies of embodied life in southeastern Botswana. The reasons why individuals embrace or reject elements of CBR are incredibly complex and cannot be distilled into singular explanations. Human and material resources, emotions, personalities, personal histories, religion, family histories, architecture, terrain (which affects mobility), moral orientations, the nature of particular impairments, and the institutional challenges faced by the varied NGOs that provide CBR services can combine in so many ways that it is difficult to think in terms of "typical" responses to CBR. My goal here, therefore, is not so much to explain why rehabilitation works or fails in general as it is to highlight how elderly women in Botswana in villages served by CBR programs incorporate globally marketed ideas about disability and the rehabilitation practices built around them into their efforts at mediating interdependencies between themselves and their daughters.[9]

CBR seeks to intervene in and shape the social facets of disability in strategic ways. With the admirable aim of extending the reach of medical and social services to people with disabilities by promoting a decentralized approach, CBR programs throughout the developing world seek to empower disabled persons to access political, social, economic, and cultural rights and opportunities. This emphasis draws on a liberal tradition that values autonomy (for which bodily autonomy is an assumed foundation) as an essential element of citizenship and personhood. To this end, CBR encompasses a package of services designed to maximize bodily function and to minimize or erase social stigma. Rehabilitation strategies stress developing or regaining proficiency in activities of daily living, with the ultimate goal of living an "independent" life. Rehabilitation workers train local health workers, family members, and community groups in the concepts and skills of rehabilitation. They also provide stimulation, physical therapy, speech therapy, social work, and a range of other services to their disabled clients. Nordholm and Lundgren-Lindquist (1999) provide a good thumbnail description of CBR (see also Ingstad 1992):

> In 1976 the member countries of WHO adopted an approach to rehabilitation called community-based rehabilitation. Rehabilitation is defined as "a process aimed at enabling persons with disabilities to reach and maintain their optimal physical, sensory, intellectual, psychiatric and/or social functional levels, thus providing them with tools to change their lives towards a higher level of independence." In CBR the emphasis traditionally placed on an institutional approach has been shifted to a community oriented approach. This approach has been described by Helander as "a strategy for enhancing the quality of life of disabled people by improving service delivery, by providing more equitable opportunities and by promoting and protecting their human rights. It calls for the full and coordinated involvement of all levels of society: community, intermediate and national."
>
> At the *community level* CBR is seen as a component of community development. It involves mobilization of local resources such as the family. The community should support the families who carry out rehabilitation at home. . . . Self-actualization, self-determination, social integration and empowerment are key concepts. (Nordholm and Lundgren-Linquist 1999, 515, emphasis theirs)

As Stacy Pigg (2001) has noted for globally modeled AIDS prevention programs, international health projects attempt to intervene in bodies and social relationships simultaneously, through reference to a set of goals that are taken to be obvious and universal. This is certainly true for CBR. Embodied human rights, optimal functional levels, and maximal independence and self-determination are presented here as fundamentally desirable modern projects, yet ones that are most appropriately tackled at the "community level." Because of their desire to engage "the community," CBR programs, like AIDS prevention programs, place emphasis on the need for "cultural sensitivity." "Culture" in these programs appears either as an obstacle to be overcome through reference to rationality and the patent desirability of biosocial empowerment, or as a resource to be edited through, sifted for values, ideas, and tools that could be of use. But as Pigg explains, neither the biological "facts" promoted through global health initiatives nor the idealized social relationships in which those "facts" are envisioned are universally understood and agreed upon. Therefore, such programs struggle to establish a common epistemological and moral terrain and language upon which to build their efforts. In the absence of such common ground, disjunctures arise between the agendas of rehabilitation programs and elderly women, which not only makes for many cases of CBR "failure" but also throws into question globalized rhetoric and practices

Figure 6.1. Day of the Disabled community meeting organized by a CBR worker. *Photo by Thatcher Ulrich.*

around "independence" as a locally desirable biosocial state (see also Lamb, this volume).

The fundamental epistemological and moral grounding of Tswana and global rehabilitative approaches to disability diverge greatly. Tswana approaches to disability stress an underlying sense of impairment as misfortune, and do not separate individual bodies from their wider sociomoral network. In these approaches instances of impairment generate debates over root causes, which inevitably mean debates over impaired social and spiritual relationships. While there is some sense of the body as mechanized, this is only a superficial mapping of physiology. Because witchcraft, negative sentiments, sexually polluted breast milk, and illicit abortions, among other things, can cause impairments in distant bodies, it is difficult to separate an individual's disability from the social field of potential toxins that may have engendered it. For example, one man I knew, according to his medical records, had suffered a cerebral hemorrhage that left him with brain damage while working in the South African mines. His mother and uncles accused his wife of having had an abortion in his absence, thus causing his sudden seizure and ensuing impairments. An aborted fetus (a toxin emanating from a grave moral lapse) in southeastern Botswana could generate disabling misfortune several hundred miles to the south on the Witwatersrand.

But amidst the social and economic reconfigurations of recent decades, and despite fundamentally different ways of conceptualizing disability, many elderly women (both as disabled subjects and as caregivers) do find some elements of CBR quite useful and desirable, while they disregard or resist others.[10] Elderly women are not passively convinced by the stunning logic of Western biology and liberal rhetoric; instead, they approach CBR as a potential tool in their own attempts to intervene in bodies and social relationships simultaneously.[11] They sift through CBR's "culture" for tools and values that are useful and they discard or ignore the rest.

Likewise, as Veena Das and Renu Addlakha (2001, 512) remind us, "disability and impairment [are] located not in (or only in) individual bodies, but rather 'off' the body of the individual and within a network of social and kin relationships." In Botswana, the social character described by Das and Addlakha combines with the spatial and gendered nature of care to place elderly women at the center of many negotiations and practices around disability. Their responses to CBR, in turn, are forged in this grandmother-centered dynamic, in which elderly women seek to cobble together and direct coping strategies that reinforce their interdependencies with their daughters, and remind their daughters of them. Elderly women in southeastern Botswana often stress intersubjective rather than individual aspects of personhood, because doing so affirms the nexus of mothering relationships through which they create status and security within the family. For married women it reminds in-laws and husbands of past biosocial work building families and lineages. For all women it reminds daughters and sons (with their potential wages, labor, and emotional concerns) of the history of their mother's sacrifices of labor, blood, milk, and love (Bledsoe 2002).

For some elderly women, this emphasis on intersubjectivity entails a flat rejection of CBR, with its disruptive messages of individualism and neatly bounded bodies. Others, depending upon their particular situations, can better stress social interdependencies and the ideals of mothering by promoting CBR than by rejecting it. Neo put it well when she explained her take on disability and CBR:

> Having a disabled child at home can bring peace, and sometimes can bring problems. It depends on how one actually tackles it. Sometimes it brings peace—you start learning to work together. Sometimes it brings problems— you are scattered, you are no longer helping one another.

Global Capital, Local Priorities: Women's Work

In recent decades, mother-daughter relationships in contemporary southeastern Botswana have faced new pressures brought by an increase in women's wage work and labor migration, combined with ongoing responsibilities around caregiving and mothering. Disability in children and in elderly women exacerbates these pressures and highlights motherhood as an arena in which economic and caregiving activities are imbued with moral currency.

Scholars of southern Africa have long recognized how the historical pene-tration of global capital into the region fostered intergenerational conflicts between fathers and sons over control of wages, labor, and marriage decisions (Schapera 1940; Carton 2000). But over time, as women have entered wage labor in increasing numbers and as marriage rates have declined precipitously, these tensions have emerged in mother-daughter relationships as well. Rela-tions between mothers and daughters (like those between women and their siblings) have always been crucial to women for social and economic reasons (among others). But they have grown in importance over the past century, as sons increasingly departed for work in South Africa, as marriage rates declined in the face of labor migration, and more recently as women themselves have gained increased opportunities for economic independence, migrating for work in ever larger numbers and becoming primary contributors to the domes-tic cash economy (Cole, this volume).

The priorities of global capital have long penetrated Tswana homes. For much of the past century, British colonial taxation policies and growing con-sumer wants pushed Tswana men to sell their labor in South African mines financed by British industrial capital, mines which exported their gold to the global market. Women too began to migrate in search of much-needed wages, but never in as large numbers as men. Deemed unfit for mine work and denied passes to cross into South Africa, where most employment opportunities lay, women in the colonial period faced great impediments to their efforts to secure regular cash.

Beginning in the recession of the mid-1970s, however, as many Tswana gold miners were being fired in the face of mine closures and union-influ-enced hiring schemes that gave preference to South African labor, diamond mines owned and operated by a mix of expatriates and Batswana began open-ing within a newly independent Botswana. Marketed through an international cartel (DeBeers) and purchased for middle-class and wealthy brides-to-be around the globe, diamonds began fueling local economic growth. Though the most fertile new employment sectors—mining, construction, and later the military—continued to be dominated by men, women began finding employ-ment in secondary industry, government, and the service sector.[12] But the historical priorities and policies of colonial-era gold mining set important precedents for the character and wage structure of postcolonial work, despite the relocation of global capital to an independent Botswana. Migrant labor continues to be the norm for those who manage to find work, and wages are set under the assumption that those deemed unfit for wage work—children, the elderly, the disabled: many past and future workers—will remain behind in rural areas, supported by the invisible labor of elderly women.

Though the cost-shifting employment practices that create an implicit reliance on elderly women to reproduce the labor force are of long standing, their results have intensified in recent decades, particularly in their effects on the relationships between mothers and daughters. As suggested above, fathers and sons had struggled since precolonial times for control over cattle, political status, and labor, and colonial-era wage earning refocused these struggles in important ways (Schapera 1940; Carton 2000; Livingston 2005). Mothers-in-law and daughters-in-law experienced a similar refocusing of long-standing tensions around labor, sexuality, and resources in the colonial era, wrought by male labor migration and wage earning. But strained relations between mothers and daughters are a relatively new phenomenon, born of the unprecedented economic and social autonomy possible for single women in the post-colonial economic boom, and the simultaneous pressures to earn cash and support children and mothers. Many sons and brothers also contribute cash (or experience pressure to do so) to support their mothers and sisters (Townsend 1997). As Deborah Durham (this volume) suggests, these tensions are embedded in conflicting notions of self-development that are heightened by recent socioeconomic changes. For daughters, though, the pressure to earn a wage exists in tension with the other domestic and moral pressures that women face as the primary caregivers in Tswana society.

The mineral boom has brought many young women to the nascent cities and large towns of Botswana in search of wage employment or entrepreneurial opportunities. By 1991 migrant women within Botswana outnumbered their male counterparts (Mazonde 1997, 64). Though often employed in lower-paying occupations like domestic service, younger working women, empowered by their much-needed wages, have begun exercising newfound independence in their relationships with their mothers, as well as their boyfriends and husbands (Cole, this volume). Meanwhile, many elderly women in Botswana find themselves in an increasingly tenuous economic position, despite rising average income in the country. Agriculture, older women's economic base, declined substantially during the severe drought of the 1980s, and has failed to fully rebound (Ingstad 1994). These economic transformations all occurred amidst, and contributed to, a radical social transformation rooted in the history of migrant labor: the decline and delay of marriage (Gulbrandsen 1986; Solway 1990; Townsend 1997). The decision by the majority of Tswana women to delay marriage until their mid-thirties or forties or to remain single, a decision that is greatly shaped by a woman's state of economic independence and the support she receives from her parents and siblings, effectively extends mother-daughter interdependencies further into the life course.

The absence of many young women, and the decline of village headmen's and uncles' power to reinforce compliance with older social norms, make the mechanisms that used to ensure wage redistribution to senior women, and other evidence of mutual interdependency, increasingly fragile. In these negotiations over the redistribution of wages, long-standing tensions between "hierarchical privilege and egalitarian achievement" map onto the recent generational disjunctures between economic opportunity and domestic authority (Durham 1999a). Deborah Durham's analysis of the "spirit of asking" (1995, see also her summary in this volume) suggests, in part, why it is difficult for older women to pressure their children to remit the money and material goods they desire. While some older women are able to deploy their bodily impairments or those of their grandchildren to unlock a flow of care, direct requests for monetary help may go unmet. The introduction of old age pensions has provided many juniors with a means to fend off such requests, as the old woman now "has her own money" (Livingston 2003b) and, it may be implied, she will only buy beer with it anyway.[13] Such requests by elderly women also draw on an "expected web of family interdependencies" (Durham 1995) that may be frayed, a possibility which highlights the potentially negative consequences and toxic sentiments (*dikgaba*) that refusal may engender. But the risk of generating such sentiments does not always bring about care. Rather, as Solway and Lambek (2001) suggest, juniors' anxieties over potentially engendering such negative sentiment cause some to preemptively distance themselves from matrilateral female kin.

Furthermore, many young women barely earn enough to cover the basic expenses of town life, and find it difficult to save much from their pay to give to their mothers. Many mothers, who are unfamiliar with the expenses of town, find this hard to understand. At the same time, new and growing markets for imported consumer goods are accelerating the cash-based culture of consumption for those who can afford it. Many of my women friends and acquaintances struggled to moderate their desire to taste Kentucky Fried Chicken, to drink Fanta soda, to use disposable maxi-pads, to carry an imitation designer handbag and cell phone, to sport the latest style of hair extensions, to own their own Korean-made cassette player and Elton John tape, or a television on which they could watch *The Bold and the Beautiful*. The calculus of spending balanced domestic obligations against personal wants. An emerging ethos of self-centered consumerism that younger women exhibited through their commodity purchases, as their male contemporaries had done a generation earlier, has generated friction over the authority, expectations, and responsibilities of motherhood and daughterhood. Elderly women feel this acutely.

Though expectations are not always fulfilled, caring for the children of unmarried daughters offers elderly women an important route to continued economic and social security (Ingstad 1992, 395). Ideally, older women's caregiving facilitates younger women's wage earning and vice versa, while the oldest women, like Neo, are cared for and gradually relieved from daily responsibility for the family. Working mothers, in turn, are expected to provide at least enough grain for their own children to eat and cash for school uniforms, clinic visits, and the like. For example, Nora Kgosietsile cares for her granddaughter, whose unmarried mother works as a schoolteacher in a neighboring village. In return, her daughter visits on all school holidays and weekend breaks, and contributes to the material well-being of the household. Grandmothers provide care and direction which working mothers might not have time to offer, and the village, where cousins, aunts, and uncles may live near or visit the grandparents, is often seen as a better and safer setting for childhood than the city. Children for their part provide company for the elderly and domestic assistance to older women, helping to draw water and carry wood, performing small chores and running errands, and perhaps looking after goats and other animals.

Unfortunately, the ideal does not always match the real, as very young children can provide little domestic help, and many older children are either overwhelmed with schoolwork and other responsibilities or simply seek to shirk domestic obligations. The considerable work that children do perform is also often undermined through a discourse of "play" that adults apply to them (Durham 2004, 2005). But children with profound disabilities, who are often left with their grandmothers because their needs cannot be accommodated by working mothers, particularly highlight the ambiguities of this dynamic. David could not, and it was assumed would never be able to, contribute through chores and errands.[14] For Neo, who had moved beyond responsibility for family needs and decisions, this was not a problem. She had a dutiful daughter (making her a successful mother) and David provided her with love, companionship, humor, and human warmth, a different form of care and one she particularly valued as she grappled with her own gradual marginalization within the family. For Florence, however, David was a child who would never grow up, someone who would only ever "play," an extension of a daughter who took but did not give, and thus would not allow her to age with security and comfort. Furthermore, childhood disabilities like David's diminish other possibilities for placing children with sisters or aunts, often leaving grandmothers as the last refuge for care.

Of course, not all daughters migrate for wage work. Some continue to farm, some work within their village, and others leave home but do not earn. It is not that older women want to prevent their daughters from migrating, though many, of course, miss them terribly and worry about their welfare in their absence. Having a daughter with a steady job is an important form of economic security and prestige for many older women. But failure to find work does not necessarily undermine mother-daughter relations. Mma Moremi lived in a small dilapidated hut with her daughter and five grandchildren, including a disabled granddaughter, and had recently suffered the death of a sixth grandchild when we spoke. Her household was quite impoverished, and she acknowledged how difficult it was to marshal resources to care for children. Mma Moremi considered her daughter's improper sexual behavior (having new partners too soon after the birth of a child) responsible for her granddaughter's disability (which she called *mopakwane*, a term to which I will return later), and she was clearly disappointed in her daughter's failure to "follow the rules" as a proper mother should. But she tempered her moral critique of her daughter with pragmatism. In this very poor female-headed household, food was hard to come by, and boyfriends brought food, food that her daughter shared with her children and mother.

The tensions arise instead around responsibilities in caregiving, the primary axis of intergenerational interdependency that CBR highlights. Caregiving incorporates practical, emotional, and moral concerns into daily practice. Nursing, child minding, performing domestic tasks, attending funerals, visiting relatives and friends, and giving money and material goods are all forms of caregiving imbued with moral valence (Klaits 2001; Durham and Klaits 2002; Lamb 2000; Livingston 2003b). Yet they are also increasingly burdensome responsibilities for women simultaneously coping with an AIDS epidemic, labor migration, a large population of debilitated elderly persons, and the temptations of a global commodity market.

Unable to support the family from her fields, Florence worked as a cook at a local primary school, an arduous and low-paying job. She valued the cash contributions David's aunt made, as well as the domestic, caregiving contributions (carrying wood and water, sweeping, laundry, cooking) that David's older sister performed after school. Both sets of contributions were crucial to maintenance of the family, and both reaffirmed and enhanced Florence's role as mother and head of household. But David, who required care himself and had only love and humor to offer, was emblematic of Florence's failed relationship with a daughter who neither contributed nor cared, a daughter who could not be counted upon to later care for her elderly mother in the way Florence cared for Neo. Neo had her choice of three daughters with whom to live when she became a *motsofe* (elderly person) and relinquished domestic authority in favor of daily care, and she had chosen Florence (cf. Lamb 2000). By contrast, Florence herself, no doubt, saw her own future options as already constrained by the irresponsibility of one of her daughters, a worrisome fact amidst the vagaries of the AIDS epidemic. David's aunt also left her child with her mother, and the little girl was too young to contribute labor to the household. But this was not a source of contention, as evidenced by her abundant clothing, occasional plastic toys, and plump toddler body. Not only did everyone expect this little girl to grow into someone who would perform chores, but also, unlike his own mother, David's aunt contributed these goods, as well as cash, food, and occasional labor, to the household. She regularly visited. She was a dutiful daughter and mother. David's mother, on the other hand, didn't leave the village, but by failing to care for her elders and her own children she left the moral orbit of the family. For Florence, David's body had become a mnemonic reminder of his mother's moral lapses, of her simultaneous failures at motherhood and daughterhood.

Though Florence's attitude toward David was by no means exceptional, it was far from universal. Many grandmothers do embrace their disabled grandchildren and are extremely focused on their needs. Though love and other emotional ties (important aspects of care) drive many of these relationships, as with David and Neo, there are practical concerns here as well. For some grandmothers, the care that they provide, care their working daughter is unable to offer, cements the reciprocal dependencies of female intergenerational life. For example, Mma Phofuetsile and Mma Molefi each cared for a disabled grandchild. As these children's disabilities became apparent, so too did the fact that their mothers could not manage their intensive bodily needs amidst the demands of money earning, and so both, at the grandmothers' suggestion, turned the disabled children over to their care. But each daughter also paid the salary of a maid to help her mother around the house, allowing these grandmothers to choose their own domestic chores, passing the most strenuous and tedious on to the maids.[15] Other grandmothers, with delinquent daughters like David's mother, might still embrace their disabled grandchildren and cast themselves as martyrs in the process, thus accessing a surrogate set of support networks (church, clinic, CBR, neighbors, sisters, etc.) (Livingston 2005; see also Klaits 2001). Yet these auxiliary modes of community and support, while important, could not wholly substitute for a daughter/mother who failed to prioritize reciprocal care (Lamb, this volume).

Elderly Women as Disabled Subjects: Mmamogae and Mary

As I have suggested, daughters are central to elderly women's abilities to cope with the bodily contingencies of aging (Livingston 2003b). Grandmothers and great-grandmothers may feel compelled to forge and maintain intergenerational interdependencies in great part because of their own needs (or expectations of future needs) for care themselves. Sarah Lamb's (2000) work on gendered aging in Bengal highlights the ways in which senescence is an integral part of ordered moral and social aging, something Bengali women are expected to welcome rather than resist. But, as Lamb explains, caregiving is the necessary mechanism through which senescence is made benign and meaningful. The same holds true in Botswana to a great extent. But, amidst the social dislocations of ubiquitous migrancy, uneven capital accumulation, and the changing biological norms of an elderly population, the interlocking experiences of senescence and care entail new uncertainties and shifting priorities.

As I have discussed elsewhere (Livingston 2003a, 2003b), a rising tide of disabling chronic illnesses (e.g., diabetes, aftereffects of stroke, hypertension, cancer) among older people is remaking senescence in southeastern Botswana. For many women this means that senescence now comes on abruptly, and in painful and disabling ways that challenge their abilities to orchestrate a gradual and benign aging process. Adult daughters, who are expected to provide care to their aging mothers, also find that their caregiving responsibilities are accelerating in this changing epidemiological climate. The merging of caregiving stresses with new and disordered aging processes means that older women increasingly strive to reinforce their daughters' sense of responsibility and caregiving ethos as they anticipate requiring that care themselves. Nurturing care by one's daughters in old age is one of the supposed rewards of motherhood that is now in jeopardy for some women, an alarming prospect.

As older women respond to the vagaries of their own aging bodies, CBR provides an added coping resource, since these programs target elderly women as "clients" as well as in their roles as caregivers. But again the results are mixed, and again they refer back to wider efforts at social reproduction. Older women often subordinate their own bodily concerns to their status as mothers. Unleashing the flow of care from daughters that senescence is meant to engender (care which in turn makes senescence benign and meaningful) is central to their own approaches to bodily coping. For many women and their caregivers, this means that regaining various bodily functions and resisting or disrupting the aging process is not necessarily a goal. For others, particularly those who do not understand their impairments as a function of age per se, CBR offers services they value and goals they share.

Mmamogae was a CBR success story. Mmamogae lives on the outskirts of a small village with her only daughter, her son-in-law, and her grandchildren. Her daughter and son-in-law run a mechanic shop on the property. The family gets along quite well, and the daughter and son-in-law would stop their work to come and make themselves available to the CBR team when we arrived. Mmamogae was only fifty-seven years old in 1992 when she had a stroke that left her hemiplegic, but with her speech intact. Many older women feel that their hemiplegia marks a premature onset of senescence. Mmamogae, however, has resisted this understanding, instead continuing to define herself as disabled rather than elderly (cf. Livingston 2003a). She has done a remarkable job in taking on activities of daily living (ADL), the cornerstone of global CBR efforts in Botswana and elsewhere. She takes herself to the toilet in the corner of the compound yard, dresses herself, lifts herself onto her wheelchair. She gets up in the morning, folds her blankets, bathes, and sweeps the compound as is expected of women her age. It took a few years for Mmamogae to develop these skills. Dikeledi described the process with great pride. "I mean when we started with her she couldn't even move onto the wheelchair or from the wheelchair down. But we struggled [through] training, her family members were also struggling, but they had to be patient until they reached that goal. If they had given up then it wouldn't have been."

Here CBR, and global priorities around generating bodily independence, did not interfere with Mmamogae's own priorities around maintaining interdependencies with her daughter (and son-in-law). Instead the family was able to incorporate CBR into the practice of those mutually sustaining relationships. The entire family "struggled together." Rehabilitation became a vehicle for the enactment of family cohesion and cooperation, for the reinscription of kinship onto a mother's body permanently altered by stroke. Mmamogae had indeed produced a dutiful daughter, one whose care publicly reflected the success of Mmamogae's own mothering history, and CBR did not threaten but rather enhanced that fact. Unfortunately, Mmamogae's case was relatively uncommon.

By contrast, Mary Moeti, who was also hemiplegic (and later an amputee), politely and passively resisted all rehabilitation efforts. Mary, who was sixty-seven years old when I met her in 1997, was a former schoolteacher and a staunch Roman Catholic. She had received a mission education in the 1930s and '40s, along with her husband, who had worked as a clerk. They lived together with several young grandchildren and a son who was depressed, unemployed, and (they suspected) a criminal in a cement house, with electricity, a television, and an indoor flush toilet. But despite her exceptional educational background and modern amenities, Mary did not take to CBR. She did not want to learn to feed herself, nor to take herself to the toilet, nor to point to a picture in a communication book to explain what she wanted. Though their compound bore the imprint of a history of better-paid work, and contained gifts from two daughters who married European men and now live abroad, the Moetis subsisted on a tight budget. Nonetheless, the two distant daughters regularly sent money from Europe to pay for a maid. The maid had worked for the family for many years, but with household income drying up (inflation had long ago eroded the value of Rra Moeti's pension), she would have been let go had she not now been needed to care for Mary. This is not to suggest that Mary resisted rehabilitation simply because she didn't want to do her own housework. Rather, her ongoing disabilities marked her as senior and facilitated a flow of care into her home. Having the maid meant that she was loved and respected as an elderly mother should be. Her daughters, unable to tend to her themselves, provided a surrogate daughter to care for their mother. Receiving that daily care—being bathed, carried, cooked for, sung to—meant that she was old and loved, even if the care came via wire transfer.

Subordinating CBR to Social Reproduction

As elderly women orchestrate domestic coping strategies in the event of a grandchild's disability, or in the face of their own senescence, they attempt to parlay their own status as mothers into effective care from their daughters. The globally marketed ideas and practices that CBR workers bring become fodder in domestic debates and mother-daughter struggles over care, responsibility, and motherhood. In the process the purportedly universal aim of achieving bodily independence is subordinated to concerns related to social reproduction.

CBR promotes a set of ideas and norms that reinforce an individualistic "modern" character, norms that are assumed to provide a way out of the socioeconomic and physical perils of disability. In Botswana this means actively promoting rehabilitation agendas and biomedical rationales as modern alternatives to what are seen as destructive "traditional" approaches to disability—the hiding of disabled children at the back of compounds, sequestered from public view, and the promotion of diagnostic regimes that either patholo-gize women's sexual behavior or refer to witchcraft.[16] Within the CBR model, then, it is tempting to cast "modernity" in generational terms and to consider rehabilitation, with its ties to disability rights (modeled on liberal notions of the individual) and biomedicine, as a quintessentially modern phenomenon. In the quest to understand why some elderly women resist or ignore CBR efforts (or other global health programs), many observers in turn rely on the trope, common and recurring in both international development rhetoric and popular Tswana discourse alike, of elderly women as backward, conservative "culture bearers." In this model, versions of which appear in so many health education programs, elderly women, most of whom lack Western education, are unable to comprehend or digest modern ideas, like biomedical concepts, and so they misunderstand the goals of rehabilitation and its processes. They doubt its efficacy.

Some elderly women do question the efficacy of CBR—efficacy in re-habilitation is indeed slippery and often in doubt. Gains are frequently mar-ginal, even for those who faithfully adhere to the program, and progress is painful and protracted over many weeks, months, and even years. Rehabilita-tion is not cure any more than disability is disease. Yet simply assuming that elderly women are too backward to understand rehabilitation fails to explain the myriad of approaches they take to CBR. Some uneducated elderly women do embrace rehabilitation practices, technologies, and attendant biomedical concepts quite readily.[17] Many members of the cerebral palsy mother's group mentioned above, a self-help and support group, were grandmothers. Mary, a member of the progressive, educated elite, resisted rehabilitation, while Mmamogae, who had never been to school, took to it readily. Neo, who was in her mid-eighties, welcomed CBR, while her daughter, who was more than twenty years her junior, rejected it. A focus on rehabilitative efficacy and women's ability to understand modern medical agendas disengages impaired bodies from their social and moral context. Elderly women do care about impairments, but, like David's mother, they often find it difficult to focus on rehabilitative practices if they are not embedded in a field of positive, nurtur-ing social relationships.

Again, the key to understanding what seem like CBR paradoxes lies in women's intergenerational relationships. Some disabled children and adults whose impairments are ameliorated through a combination of therapies or-chestrated through CBR and the corresponding local rehabilitation center gain significant abilities (walking, feeding themselves, toileting themselves, etc.). Efficacy here seems clear, regardless of one's educational background. Yet sometimes return visits to these patients after months or years reveal that capacities gained through rehabilitation, which the able-bodied supposedly value, have been lost again. The same child who walked out of the rehabilita-tion center two years ago (albeit in leg braces with a walking frame) is now again shuffling on her bottom across the compound. Her grandmother may

Figure 6.2. Members of a cerebral palsy mother's group (including a number of grandmothers) celebrating at a Day of the Disabled community meeting. *Photo by Thatcher Ulrich.*

seem less concerned about this than about the whereabouts of the child's mother. Grandmothers often stress the repair of mother-child relationships before they can turn to the repair of bodies.

Elderly women respond to many facets of CBR in their attempts to manage intergenerational dependencies with their daughters. In the interest of space I will only briefly discuss two aspects of the overall global program—the promotion of biomedical explanatory models, and of "activities of daily living" (ADL)—to illustrate how information, care, and capital relate to one another in elderly women's efforts at crafting their daughters into mothers. Cerebral palsy provides a good example of how epistemological differences are resolved in CBR efforts. CBR workers explain cerebral palsy as resulting from fetal oxygen deprivation during labor. This, in turn, affects the child's brain. Tswana medical explanations for conditions that CBR workers diagnose as cerebral palsy, however, usually refer to the illness of *mopakwane*. *Mopakwane* occurs when a parent (though in practice usually women are blamed) breaks a rule prohibiting postpartum sexual relations with anyone but the child's other parent. It is based on a biological logic that links parents and children through *madi* (blood, semen, money) and *mashi* (milk), and which recognizes that impurities in the blood can build up in the heart, causing various forms of debility and disease. A diagnosis of *mopakwane* implies that a woman is a bad mother, that she sacrificed her own child's well-being to her sexual desires. Some grandmothers (and mothers) find CBR greatly appealing because it provides a language with which to rebut the stigmatizing moral accusations of a mother's sexual improprieties. By invoking "cerebral palsy," grandmothers stand up for their daughters against others who would accuse them of causing *mopakwane*, reasserting that their daughters are, in fact, good mothers. Mma Molefi (whose daughter, as noted above, provides her with a maid to help in caring for her disabled granddaughter) embraced the cerebral palsy diagnosis, and the rehabilitation program that presented it, as she shielded her daughter from the gossip of neighbors.

To other grandmothers the reasoning behind a diagnosis of cerebral palsy is clearly wrongheaded, yet they continue to utilize and enjoy other CBR services. Mma Phofuetsile, who also cares for her disabled granddaughter with the help of a maid, did not agree that the child had cerebral palsy, and instead recognized her daughter as having clearly caused her granddaughter's *mopakwane*. She used this moral leverage to ensure wage remittances and the like. In the process Mma Phofuetsile also referred to the other central paradigm through which many childhood disabilities are understood: Christianity. Her granddaughter was a "gift from God" to the old woman, which meant a direct public recognition of her own motherly attributes: moral superiority, a patient heart, and kindness (Livingston 2005; see also Ingstad 1992). By welcoming visits from the CBR workers (who provided a walking frame for her grand-daughter as well as other services), despite her disagreement with the program's fundamental reasoning, Mma Phofuetsile continually demonstrated her commitment to the child. Doing so contrasted her with her daughter, who was in turn pressured to provide monetary care and to visit in order to gain moral footing with her mother, by proving herself to now be a responsible daughter and mother.

Epistemological grounds are not the only ones on which global frame-works may—or may not—be found appealing. Responses to training in ADL vary in ways that again depend on intergenerational relationships. In the industrialized West, training in ADL is part of a larger set of efforts to stave off the threat of segregated institutionalization and to position people to better access economic and social opportunities. In Botswana, which for the most part lacks such institutions and where economic opportunities are already greatly constrained by the priorities of a narrow flow of global capital, independence in ADL takes on a different role for many (Priestly 2001, 10). Taking elderly women as disabled subjects provides the clearest examples of the ambiguous ways in which elderly women approach the issue of functional independence.[18]

Many elderly women like Mary, who appreciated the care that Dikeledi provided by visiting, had no intention of working on their ADL. Elderly women might want to let themselves age—to become blind, to walk with a stick, to become bedridden. A slower, shorter range of bodily movements itself marked the moral authority of seniority and self-restraint (Durham 1999a). Such bodily manifestations of aging (which are accelerated in the case of stroke, amputation, cataracts, etc.) ideally facilitate a flow of care from juniors to seniors, most critically from daughters to mothers, as bodily needs mark decreased responsibilities and are met with various forms of assistance (cf. Lamb 2000). As Benedicte Ingstad (1994) has documented, however, again the reality is not always so harmonious, and many frail elderly lack necessary care and even continue to bear responsibility for tending to the needs of others. Nonetheless, and often lacking other options, some women do prefer to succumb to senescence rather than struggle to maintain or regain bodily abilities, in the hopes that doing so will bring care.

Daughters and other junior relatives can also resist CBR efforts at ADL training for aged mothers, to retain their own moral footing as people who provide proper care. Ingstad and Bruun explain, "A family that lets its elderly person do too much on their own may easily be seen as one that does not give proper care. Thus in a previous study of disabled people in Botswana we found one daughter-in-law who simply refused to teach the old blind lady to move around alone with the help of a stick outside the compound, because 'what would people say if I let her go out alone'" (Ingstad and Bruun 1994, 71). Likewise, some elderly women refuse to train their disabled children and grandchildren in ADL, as they feel that this violates their moral obligation to care for them. This feeling is exacerbated by the fact that many rehabilitation activities are quite painful for the patient, and many women feel strongly that it is their moral duty as mothers to ease, not inflict, physical suffering.

In the end, it is only fragments and shards of the global—a bricolage of sorts—that permeate and succeed in the local of grandmothers here, not the multiple Western-derived concepts that underpin CBR—individualism, independence, and human rights—and that circulate as universal aims. Patrick Devliger asks,

> What is global knowledge of disability? . . . Global knowledge is knowledge that easily survives in conferences, policies, and legislation. It becomes local if it survives the stage of reflection and conceptualization and permeates culture and history. Local knowledge of disability is cast in the daily relationships between disabled and able-bodied individuals. It is found in the particulars of languages and cultural capital; in the history of the emergence and disappearance of disabilities; in the social, political, racial, sexual, and ecological environments of individuals; and in the very history of services and supports for disabled people as reflected by the moral and political relationships between a society and its members with disabilities. Local knowledge is not static because cultures and societies are not static; culture is built and built upon. (Devliger 1999, 170)

Rewriting Kinship

Key shifts in women's economic and social opportunities have generated complex intergenerational struggles among women over interpenetrating domains of bodily, social, and moral life. These domains converge in instances of disability. Older women and their daughters, in turn, respond to the complex dilemmas that bodily impairment engenders by rewriting kinship. They entangle CBR in these kinship revisions. Comaroff and Roberts (1981) have described how plastic kinship is in Botswana, open to ongoing negotiations by men that continually recast relationships. In recent decades, movements of global capital, ideas, and practices in Botswana have placed women, too, at the center of kinship negotiations. But age and gender converge here in fragile ways, as the elderly are people whose social connectivity is in the process of unraveling if it is changing at all (Durham 2005). Surrogate and auxiliary caregivers (CBR workers and maids), disordered aging processes (children who cannot grow up and elderly who grow old too suddenly), missing daughters, an absence of daughters-in-law, epistemological challenges, all reveal the dynamic and highly tenuous nature of female kinship as practiced in contemporary Botswana.

Rapp and Ginsburg (2001) suggest that efforts around disability highlight these types of changes, as disability itself necessitates an active sorting out of roles and resources:

> The parent-child relationship is a nexus at which dramatic alternatives are articulated: dependency versus autonomy; intimacy versus authority; the acceptance of caretaking versus its rejection; normative cultural scripts versus alternative, more inclusive "rewritings." . . . The birth of a disabled child who is, in one sense, profoundly different from other family members can pose an immediate crisis to the nuclear and extended family. In addition to providing medical support for the affected child, families face the task of incorporating unexpected differences into a comprehensible narrative of kinship. The birth of anomalous children is an occasion for meaning-making, whether through the acceptance of "God's special angels" or the infanticide of offspring deemed unacceptable. (Rapp and Ginsburg 2001, 536)

Rapp and Ginsburg are interested here in contemporary American society, including how material pressures brought by increased household dependency on maternal employment prompt anticipatory thinking and action around the potential for disability in an "already tight domestic economy." Similar material pressures and economic opportunities are brought to bear in Botswana. In the U.S., new media, biotechnologies, and disability rights movements have created alternative forms of community, identity, and support for disabled persons and their families.

In Botswana, most of these alternative resources are lacking or, as we see in the case of CBR, contested. Not only is the domestic economy more and more "tight," but the ability of a family to marshal care increasingly rests on the often frail shoulders of grandmothers. Rapp and Ginsburg's parent-child nexus must be stretched in Botswana to a grandmother-mother-child relationship, in which the "dramatic alternatives" they present accumulate amidst an abundance of bodily difference and peril. The complex interplays and interdependencies among multiple generations of women necessary to manage care, and to produce and enact kinship narratives that facilitate the reproduction of responsible motherhood as family members age (or don't), are the central locus of activity. Disabilities, of both children and older women, become the contested terrain on which intergenerational relationships are renegotiated in the context of disruptions caused by a combination of shifts in global capital and new types of knowledge and practice around disability. Meaning making around disability inflects this process, and CBR provides a new set of language and tools that elderly women may engage or resist in pursuit of domestic well-being. They focus this pursuit, as we have seen, in great part on creating mothers out of daughters.

NOTES

1. Pseudonyms are used for informants throughout.

2. For a longer and more detailed description of CBR, one to which my own brief sketch is indebted, see Ingstad 1992.

3. I learned this diagnosis from reading David's client file, which the rehabilitation program maintains.

4. Some children may often get short shrift at family meals, but children who must be spoon-fed are at added risk. Unless the family is vigilant about ensuring the child is regularly fed, often with special soft foods (a time-consuming process), it can be difficult to ensure proper nutrition. I saw several spoon-fed children who, like David, were markedly skinnier than the other children in the family, a fact which rehabilitation workers and neighbors might comment on or take to suggest neglect.

5. As Durham (this volume) suggests, this ideal of reciprocity is not as concrete or overt a logic as that described by Magazine and Ramírez Sánchez (this volume).

6. This is only a very general description of epidemiological trends, which are hard to document (for more, see Livingston 2003b). But note that there is much regional variation, and the scenario described is most characteristic of the southern and eastern regions of the country.

7. We should read this statistic in the most general of terms, since definitions of disability are slippery (Kohrman 2003).

8. These households are disproportionately rural. In 1998, an American researcher who conducted a series of pilot studies found 14 to 17 percent of rural households housing at least one disabled resident (Stephanie Cohen, personal communication).

9. In the late 1990s thirty-plus villages in Botswana were served by CBR programs. These included several large urban villages like Mogoditshane and Thamaga, with tens of thousands of residents, and many medium-sized and small villages. The frequency

and consistency of service depended in large part on the economic and bureaucratic stability of each of the handful of NGOs providing CBR at the time.

10. Similarly, many disabled adult "clients" of CBR programs hope for employment and other forms of social and political "self-actualization."

11. This is not unlike how elderly Indians approach new social services and eldercare institutions in India and the U.S., according to Lamb, this volume.

12. As Anne Griffiths (1997) suggests, working women on professional tracks, as teachers, nurses, bureaucrats, and businesswomen, enjoy a different degree of autonomy and social-political status relative to their families and communities than do women employed in low-paid and often insecure wage work.

13. Many older churchwomen are teetotalers, and so this rhetorical move would not apply to them.

14. Many children with physical or mental impairments can contribute substantial labor to their households, but many also cannot. Furthermore, for many children in developing countries, in contrast to their Western counterparts who have greater and more regular access to services from the onset of their impairments, the explicit lack of stimulation, analgesics, massage, and exercise they receive contributes to a long-term process of intensification of their impairments. For example, if joints are not moved regularly, they become less supple and over time develop fixed contractures that prevent further movement.

15. Maids, particularly those who are employed in rural villages, receive very meager pay in addition to food and shelter. Nonetheless, many daughters can ill afford to hire even such a poorly paid surrogate. In such cases, even small gifts of food and visits help demonstrate a commitment to mothering.

16. Hiding disabled children was a relatively recent development, brought on by the pressures of labor migration in the late 1940s, and was practiced only briefly and spottily. Yet it is regularly held up as the classic example of the backwardness of Tswana approaches to disability. For the history of the practice, see Livingston 2005; for an analysis of contemporary CBR rhetoric concerning the practice, see Ingstad 1992.

17. This is not surprising, as Batswana have been quite receptive to multiple healing systems: Tswana medicine, healing prophesy, biomedicine, Chinese medicine, etc.

18. Many disabled persons in Botswana do embrace training in ADL and strive to achieve greater levels of functional autonomy. This is especially the case for men and women in their youth and middle age, many of whom desire to enter or remain in wage work. My point here is not to deny the opportunities that CBR can and should offer, but rather to better explain why these opportunities are not universally embraced.

WORKS CITED

Bledsoe, Caroline. 2002. *Contingent Lives: Fertility, Time, and Aging in West Africa.* Chicago: University of Chicago Press.

Carton, Benedict. 2000. *Blood from Your Children: The Colonial Origins of Generational Conflict in South Africa.* Charlottesville: University of Virginia Press.

Central Statistics Office, Government of Botswana. 1996. *Living Conditions in Botswana: 1986–1994: Socio-economic Indicators Based on the 1985/6 HIES, 1991 Census and 1993/4 HIES.* Gaborone: Government Printer.

Comaroff, John L., and Simon Roberts. 1981. *Rules and Processes: The Cultural Logic of Dispute in an African Context.* Chicago: University of Chicago Press.

Coombes, Yolanda, Pilate Khulumani, and Enock Ngome. 1994. "Profile of the Elderly in Botswana." In Frank Bruun, Mbulawa Mugabe, and Yolanda Coombes, eds., *The Situation of the Elderly in Botswana: Proceedings from an International Workshop*, 21–27. Gaborone, Botswana: University of Botswana, National Institute of Development Research and Documentation.

Das, Veena, and Renu Addlakha. 2001. "Disability and Domestic Citizenship: Voice, Gender, and the Making of the Subject." *Public Culture* 13 (3): 511–531.

Devliger, Patrick. 1999. "Local Knowledge and International Collaboration in Disability Programs." In Brigitte Holzer, Arthur Vreede, and Gabriele Weigt, eds., *Disability in Different Cultures: Reflections on Local Concepts*, 169–177. New Brunswick: Transaction Publishers.

Durham, Deborah. 1995. "Soliciting Gifts and Negotiating Agency: The Spirit of Asking in Botswana." *Journal of the Royal Anthropological Institute* 1 (1): 111–128.

———. 1999a. "Civil Lives: Leadership and Accomplishment in Botswana." In John L. Comaroff and Jean Comaroff, eds., *Civil Society and the Political Imagination in Africa*, 192–218. Chicago: University of Chicago Press.

———. 1999b. "The Predicament of Dress: Polyvalency and the Ironies of Cultural Identity." *American Ethnologist* 26 (2): 389–411.

———. 2004. "Disappearing Youth: Youth as a Social Shifter in Botswana." *American Ethnologist* 31 (4): 589–605.

———. 2005. "Did You Bathe This Morning? Baths and Morality in Botswana." In Adeline Masquelier, ed., *Dirt, Undress, and Difference: Critical Perspectives on the Body's Surface*, 190–212. Bloomington: Indiana University Press.

Durham, Deborah, and Frederick Klaits. 2002. "Funerals and the Public Space of Mutuality in Botswana." *Journal of Southern African Studies* 28 (4): 777–795.

Griffiths, Anne. 1997. *In the Shadow of Marriage: Gender and Justice in an African Community.* Chicago: University of Chicago Press.

Gulbrandsen, Ornulf. 1986. "To Marry—or Not to Marry: Marital Strategies and Sexual Relations in a Tswana Society." *Ethnos* 51 (1–2): 7–28.

Ingstad, Benedicte. 1992. "The Myth of the Hidden Disabled: A Study of Community-Based Rehabilitation in Botswana." Working Paper No. 1, Section for Medical Anthropology, Institute of Community Medicine, University of Oslo.

———. 1994. "The Grandmother and Household Viability in Botswana." In Aderanti Adepoju and Christine Oppong, eds., *Gender, Work, and Population in Sub-Saharan Africa*, 209–225. Portsmouth: Heinemann, for the International Labor Office, Geneva.

Ingstad, Benedicte, and Frank Bruun. 1994. "Elderly People as Care Providers and Care Receivers." In Frank Bruun, Mbulawa Mugabe, and Yolanda Coombes, eds., *The Situation of the Elderly in Botswana: Proceedings from an International Workshop*, 69–78. Gaborone, Botswana: University of Botswana, National Institute of Development Research and Documentation.

Klaits, Frederick. 2001. "Housing the Spirit, Hearing the Voice: Care and Kinship in an Apostolic Church during Botswana's Time of AIDS." Ph.D. diss., Johns Hopkins University.

Kohrman, Matthew. 1999. "Motorcycles for the Disabled: Mobility, Modernity, and the Transformation of Experience in Urban China." *Culture, Medicine, and Psychiatry* 23 (1): 133–155.

——. 2003. "Why Am I Not Disabled? Making State Subjects, Making Statistics in Post-Mao China." *Medical Anthropology Quarterly* 17 (1): 5–24.

Lamb, Sarah. 2000. *White Saris and Sweet Mangoes: Aging, Gender, and Body in North India.* Berkeley: University of California Press.

Livingston, Julie. 2003a. "Pregnant Children and Half-Dead Adults: Modern Living and the Quickening Life Cycle in Botswana." *Bulletin of the History of Medicine* 77 (1): 133–162.

——. 2003b. "Reconfiguring Old Age: Elderly Women and Concerns over Care in Southeastern Botswana." *Medical Anthropology* 22 (3): 205–231.

——. 2005. *Debility and the Moral Imagination in Botswana.* Bloomington: Indiana University Press.

Mazonde, Isaac. 1997. "Poverty in Botswana and Its Impact on the Quality of Life." In Doreen Nteta and Janet Hermans, eds., *Poverty and Plenty: The Botswana Experience,* 61–76. Gaborone: The Botswana Society.

Nordholm, Lena, and Birgitta Lundgren-Lindquist. 1999. "Community-Based Rehabilitation in Moshupa Village, Botswana." *Disability and Rehabilitation* 21 (10–11): 515–521.

Pigg, Stacy. 2001. "Globalizing the Facts of Life." Paper presented at "Belief Systems and the Place of Desire," third conference of the International Association for the Study of Sex, Culture and Society, Melbourne, October 1–3.

Priestley, Mark. 2001. "Introduction: The Global Context of Disability." In Mark Priestley, ed., *Disability and the Life Course: Global Perspectives,* 3–14. Cambridge: Cambridge University Press.

Rapp, Rayna, and Faye Ginsburg. 2001. "Enabling Disability: Rewriting Kinship, Reimagining Citizenship." *Public Culture* 13 (3): 533–556.

Schapera, Isaac. 1940. *Married Life in an African Tribe.* London: Faber and Faber.

Solway, Jacqueline. 1990. "Affines and Spouses, Friends and Lovers: The Passing of Polygyny in Botswana." *Journal of Anthropological Research* 46 (1): 41–66.

Solway, Jacqueline, and Michael Lambek. 2001. "Just Anger: Scenarios of Indignation in Botswana and Madagascar." *Ethnos* 66 (1): 49–72.

Townsend, Nicholas. 1997. "Men, Migration, and Households in Botswana: An Exploration of Connections over Time and Space." *Journal of Southern African Studies* 23 (3): 405–420.

UNAIDS. 2002. "Botswana: Epidemiological Fact Sheet on HIV/AIDS and Sexually Transmitted Infections." http://www.unaids.org.

7

The Old World and Its New Economy

Notes on the "Third Age" in Western Europe Today

JESSICA GREENBERG AND ANDREA MUEHLEBACH

The celebration and circulation of the concept of the third age characterizes public discourses all over Europe today and signals an attempt to reconceptualize the ten to twenty usually healthy years following working adulthood. In Western Europe, the concept of the third age first appeared in the 1970s, as activists on aging attempted to create a new language for the life cycle; the term "third age" designated a crowning point filled with energy and independence, and "fourth age" a subsequent period of chronic illness and dependency (Laslett 1991, 2–3). Today, this particular vision of the life cycle is mobilized not just by older activists, but by policy makers and European Union (EU) bureaucrats, politicians from all spectrums, and the popular and scholarly press. Why does it feature so prominently in public debates over the future of Western Europe, its population, and its welfare? What has the third age come to mean in the current political and global economic context? How does the emergence of this new age category in the life cycle affect intergenerational relations? Instead of invoking universalizing, even celebratory explanatory models of "the postmodern life cycle" (Moody 1993), we address these questions through an analysis of historically and regionally specific social and economic factors. In particular, we discuss the way in which Western European policy makers, scientists, journalists, and elderly activists are rethinking public welfare policies and the intergenerational relationships they depend on and produce. We relate these issues to shifting structures and ideologies of work, regional economic restructuring in light of global pressures, and changing population age structures.

Gerontologists and demographers have forecasted the collective aging and decline of Western European societies for three decades (Harper 2000), but it is only in the last ten years that the region has seen an explosion of EU policy documents and anxiety-laden national media texts on this issue. Demographic shifts, as the journalist Thomas Fuller wrote recently in the *International Herald Tribune* (2002), represent "perhaps the biggest challenge to the welfare state since Bismarck invented the pension system in the 1890s." Indeed, there exists a growing consensus that these shifts threaten not only the physical reproduction of a "dying" Western European population, but the region's distinct welfare system[1] and the workforce upon which future economic strategies rely.

In the face of this impending crisis, current Western European governments have not opted for large-scale pronatalist campaigns aiming to manage and control women's reproductive labor, as they and governments elsewhere have historically done (Gal and Kligman 2000; Quine 1996; Ginsburg and Rapp 1995). Nor have they opted for so-called "replacement migration," which, as the United Nations Population Division provocatively suggested (2000), would include a systematic attempt to attract skilled and unskilled migrants to replace dwindling national labor capacities.[2] Instead, governments and public opinion makers are revaluing and reimagining internal populations—in particular, the third age—as a key solution to what Pope John Paul II has called Europe's "demographic winter" (Borneman and Fowler 1997, 507).

This chapter documents how old age is (re)defined as older people are called upon to provide labor for these societies in crisis. At the same time, we consider the implications of this redefinition for relationships between generations. Our analysis of generations hinges on our understanding of the welfare state as a specific modern social formation that brought generations into a particular type of state-mediated relationship to each other. We therefore foreground the welfare state's intergenerational redistributive system, in the form of a "welfare contract," rather than its interclass character (Phillipson 1998; Thomson 1996; Walker 2002). Scholars have interpreted this contract between generations as based on reciprocity—the young and middle-aged support the elderly in return for the latter's contribution to work and welfare earlier in their life, and expect to receive similar assistance themselves when they grow old (Phillipson 1998, 117). They have also characterized it as a complex relationship of duty—of the state to its citizens (Marshall 1981), of citizens to the national collectivity through a system of pensions and other methods of redistributing wealth (Walker 2002, 300; Roche 1992, 30), and of the elderly to younger workers, since the elderly were expected to bear the brunt of high unemployment and retire early when work was scarce (Laczko and Phillipson 1991; Phillipson 1998, 92; Graebner 1980). Many scholars place special emphasis on the solidarity and citizenship rights encoded in the modern European welfare state project. For Walker, the ethical principle of intergenerational solidarity was not only embodied in social policy, but was also regarded as sound economics under the guidance of Keynesian theory and practice (Walker 2002, 300). Phillipson points to the assumption, embedded in the idea of the welfare state, that problems of aging should be solved by generations working together through a structure of interdependency mediated by the state (Phillipson 1998, 86). Indeed, some of the great architects of welfare explicitly based their vision and defense of the always embattled idea of the welfare state on the Durkheimian notion of organic solidarity—a solidarity that was the necessary result of society's becoming increasingly differentiated, specialized, and therefore more socially dependent (Titmuss 1958, 44). This was not an idea that ever went uncontested, and it often existed more de jure than de facto. But it was nevertheless a dominant paradigm in the building of the modern welfare state (Roche 1992, 13).

Today, the idea of the intergenerational contract is under fire, as is the idea of the mediating state. Our goal in this chapter is to outline the ideological and discursive work that goes into the replacement of the ideas of collective solidarity and duty between generations with ideas of equal rights and nondiscrimination in the marketplace. We also show how the concepts of solidarity and duty currently only emerge in highly circumscribed contexts (usually in relation to the "non-self-sufficiency" and neediness of the fourth age) and for fundamentally transformed reasons. We thus focus not on intergenerational solidarity as it plays itself out privately within the family (see Lamb, this volume; Magazine and Ramírez Sánchez, this volume), but on how this highly abstracted, state-mediated relationship between the young and old is discursively reimagined in the public sphere of a changing European Union.

To build our argument, we draw on a series of diverse but interlocking texts reflecting changing attitudes toward, and programs and policy initiatives concerning, the third age. Specifically, we analyze three key EU documents and German, British, Italian, and Swiss media texts through which old age is being redefined. Each of these texts emerged in the context of a growing concern over the early retirement policies of European welfare states in the 1990s, and they make up part of a contested field within which age and aging have become a site of intervention and concern. Together they produce a persuasive and consistent vision of both the nature and desirability of third-age labor and the need to reformulate intergenerational relations. By analyzing this series of documents we trace the emergence of a mutually reinforcing, normative set of arguments that are creating the conditions of possibility for (a) the questioning of the welfare state idea and the model of the life cycle it implies, (b) a shift from ideals of intergenerational solidarity and duty toward equity and nondiscrimination among all citizens as participants in the labor market, and (c) an emerging ideology of age-based skills and the complementarity of generations that aims to alleviate intergenerational tensions as the elderly are drawn back into the workforce and compete with younger workers.

Economy, Demography, Immigration, and Old Age: Some Context

Western European economic and social policy making is currently characterized by dramatic struggles over the future of the welfare state in the face of changing economic and political conditions, and a pervasive sense that markets rather than state institutions may be the best tools with which to manage the political, economic, and demographic future of the region. Many scholars have associated this tendency toward market solutions with contemporary neoliberal ideology, which relocates responsibilities for welfare and security in the flexible and retrainable private individual rather than in the state (cf. Comaroff and Comaroff 2000; Habermas 1999; Barry, Osborne, and Rose 1996). In the specific case of Western Europe, the neoliberal move from welfare and its core ideas of duty and solidarity toward individual responsibility and equal opportunity in the labor market simultaneously translates demographic crisis into social opportunity. EU officials have characterized the current moment as a massive shift in global economic organization, production, and technological and scientific innovation (Commission 1995). They have responded by developing a strategy for international economic competitiveness that meets changing needs with globally marketable local resources, labor markets, and commodities. This strategy is based on scientific and technical innovation, knowledge and education, and the growth and flexibility of the labor force. At the intersection of knowledge-based work and flexible labor stands the so-called knowledge economy. As we will show below, EU officials think of this economy as adaptable to new global conditions even as it relies on the skills, capacities, and knowledge of an aging European workforce.

At the same time, demographers draw a bleak picture of the labor reserves deemed necessary for these strategies, especially in light of demographic projections for economic competitors, such as the United States.[3] Populations in Western Europe are declining and rapidly aging, because fertility and mortality rates are lower than they have ever been. Demographers have warned that the region's population structure will change dramatically within the next two generations if fertility, mortality, and migration rates do not change. The United Nations Population Division (UNPD) estimates that 35 percent of the population in countries like Italy will be over the age of sixty-five by the year 2050. In Germany, the percentage is projected to be 28, and in the United Kingdom 25 (UNPD 2000). With subreplacement fertility the norm in most Western European countries today,[4] most analysts agree that the relationship between the projected increase of the elderly and the continuing decrease of working-age people is a particular cause for concern.[5] National age structures are projected to include relatively greater proportions of older than younger age groups, thereby rapidly turning the population pyramid on its head. At stake is a specific population age structure that helped make possible a national pension system within which a large number of working-age citizens paid for the pensions of a smaller number of retired citizens.

"Replacement migration," as a provocative UN policy paper recently called the replacement of dwindling European populations by migrants, will almost certainly not be a politically viable option, especially in light of the rise of "Fortress Europe," which has witnessed increasing anti-immigrant sentiments and regulation of immigrant flows (Geddes 2000). Indeed, the immigration and labor policies of the region often stand in direct contradiction to each other: the former increasingly xenophobic, the latter increasingly demanding foreign labor. With the rise of the region's New Right in the last decade, including Jörg Haider's Freedom Party in Austria, Italian prime minister Silvio Berlusconi's rightist coalition, Belgium's Vlaams Blok, France's Front National, Switzerland's Schweizerische Volkspartei, and rightist governments in traditionally liberal societies such as Denmark and the Netherlands, it is unlikely that Western European governments will encourage large-scale increases in immigration to replace the dwindling labor force at home.

And so Western European nations have turned to their internal populations. All over Europe, people are asking why a diminishing number of younger citizens should have to shoulder the burden of paying for a growing number of healthy, active pensioners, particularly when such security may not be guaranteed them in their own old age. And conversely, people ask, don't the increasingly healthy elderly have the duty to continue working in order to supplement a dwindling, tax-burdened younger workforce? Why should Europe not draw on and profit from its wealth of active elderly?

Public debate on this issue increasingly centers on questions of how and why the third age should figure as a new, socially acceptable, and viable labor resource. While plans to raise mandatory retirement ages are currently widely debated and protested in all of Western Europe, both policy makers and the popular press are proposing that deferred retirement and "active aging" are both feasible and socially acceptable.[6] New meanings of age and aging center on critiques of the "modern life course" that was institutionalized through the modern welfare state system (Cole 1992, 3–4). This model of the life cycle has been heavily criticized by parts of the European press, the scholarly literature, policy makers, scientists, and elderly activists, many of whom argue that it has kept an aging but increasingly healthy population from realizing its full potential. We review these critiques below, and outline how arguments about the increased health, longevity, and diversity of older populations make links previously taken for granted between biological age and specific capacities—or incapacities—obsolete. Western European media are full of attempts to reconceptualize life cycles outside a trajectory of inevitable physical decline that comes with age. Instead, the new life cycle is defined through visions of multiple phases of renewed activity and rebirth, a "postmodern phenomenon" some scholars have welcomed and celebrated (Moody 1993; Laslett 1991).

The three EU documents we examine below are a survey commissioned by the European Community to assess attitudes about aging; the white paper "Teaching and Learning: Towards the Learning Society," which was meant to stimulate member-state policy initiatives and influence the development of EU-wide educational programs; and an EU communication, "Towards a Europe for All Ages," which was released for the UN International Year of Older Persons and was intended to set the tone for further policy initiatives by EU member states. None of these documents had the force of law. However, each represented a high-level intervention that defined the problem of aging in Europe in specific ways and set parameters for policy solutions. When read together, these documents cohere to produce a framework for understanding aging and retirement, both of which are being transformed in the context of new economic strategies, changing visions of the relationship between citizens and the state, and a new emphasis on flexible, knowledge-based work. All are part of a hybrid set of actors, institutions, and policies that make up what Cris Shore has called "agents of European consciousness" as they help to persuade a broader public of the ideas of particularly European culture and identity and the relationships they ought to entail (Shore 2000).

The core ideas encoded in these documents mediate and naturalize a particular vision of aging, new forms of labor, and intergenerational relations. They also circulate and are reformulated through a variety of other sites, most notably the popular and scholarly press within EU member countries, which interpret and apply policy frameworks to their particular contexts of aging populations and economic decline. We are not proposing that policy makers intentionally disseminated certain ideas and concepts (although some media coverage may have done so). Rather, the media texts we analyze here are representative of the "social work" that goes into redefining aging. These are public sites through which new ideas are mediated, challenged, and taken up by a variety of actors, including elderly activists who look back on at least three decades of struggles against "ageism." We are particularly interested in those texts that naturalize what the policy documents actively worked to construct as the problem: an aging population in the context of a troubled welfare state. Many of the authors we discuss interpret current shifts in regional economic and labor policy and the concomitant reimagining of welfare regimes as inevitable reactions to "natural" developments on the ground. In other words, they represent contemporary restructuring as necessarily emerging from changing biological and technological conditions, such as prolongation of health, improved medical science, and the increased flexibility of the new old.

Rethinking the Intergenerational Contract

Given rising concerns about aging populations, a shrinking workforce, and the instability of pension systems, European Community policy makers began to question the early retirement policies of European welfare states in the early 1990s. In 1993, they commissioned a survey called "Age and Attitudes" to assess perceptions of aging in the member countries.[7] The survey targeted both the "general public" and older people, which the report defined as the third age (fifty to seventy-four years old) and the fourth age (seventy-five and older). It covered a range of topics: the viability of pension systems, the willingness of young people to support the elderly through those systems, the social inclusion and exclusion of aging men and women and their financial security, older people's social and political participation, and issues related to work and retirement. The survey report concluded that the early retirement and pension schemes of the European welfare state were based on outmoded perceptions of older populations as passive.

> Alongside of the ageing of the population we are witnessing a profound transformation in the experience and meaning of old age in late twentieth century society. Retirement is no longer the straightforward entry-point to old age that it once was and, therefore, it is increasingly anachronistic as a definition of older people. More and more people throughout the Community are leaving the labour force in different ways: early retirement, partial retirement, redundancy, unemployment, disability and so on. At the same time, with increased longevity, older people are living longer and healthier old ages and, as a result, the threshold of frailty is being pushed back. These changes in age structure, health and patterns of employment are transforming the nature of old age. They are, thereby, posing sharp questions about both the traditional passive roles expected of older people and the extent to which policy makers and major economic and political institutions have adjusted to socio-demographic change. (Commission 1993, 3)

In a section entitled "The Older European Citizen," the report juxtaposed an image of active older men and women with the image of passive retirement. The authors cited survey data from older respondents who overwhelmingly chose to be called "older people" and "senior citizens" rather than by such terms as "elderly," "retired," "golden age," or "pensioners." The survey analysts argued that the choice of "senior citizens" in particular demonstrated the changing nature of old age in Europe because "it carries connotations of individuals as civic actors with both rights and duties and, therefore, emphasises the integration of older people rather than their separate group status" (Commission 1993, 6). The analogy established between work and activity and between retirement and passivity is given new political import when "activity" is aligned with a more desirable model of civic action, rights, and integration of the elderly. By implication, the welfare state system is aligned with retirement and passivity. In addition, the authors included a critique of early retirement in the report's analysis of pensions.

> The changing character of old age . . . is partly reflected in the transition from fixed age retirement to more flexible forms of labour force exit. Unfortunately, for many older workers this "flexibility" has been down the age range only and early exit has often been largely beyond their control. Public policy measures have been used recently in several EC countries to encour-

age older workers to leave the labour market and make way for younger ones. Now, with the rising cost of pensions and, in some countries, predicted shortages of young labour market entrants, attention is being turned towards the potential for postponing retirement. (Commission 1993, 24)

The report argues, then, that older men's and women's desire to continue working challenges the legitimacy of a system of institutionalized life stages which moved older people out of the workforce to make way for younger generations. Despite the fact that the report states that "the social contract is in good shape" because people continue to feel a duty to ensure that older people have a decent standard of living, the report foregrounded concerns about younger workers' "willingness to continue to [pay taxes to fund pensions, on which] hangs the social contract that underpins all pensions and social protection systems in the EC" (Commission 1993, 15). But even while the sense of duty toward the elderly may be in "good shape," the report concludes that retirement is neither beneficial nor desirable for older men and women.

The Third Age as Future

These high-level policy debates about aging in Europe did not take long to reverberate with journalists, analysts, and elderly activists, who soon concluded that older people not only want to work longer but are also biologically capable of doing so. Some took this point further by arguing that the extension of the retirement age would not only make personal, biological, and economic sense for elderly Europeans, but was also a moral imperative. Western Europe's media announced the beginning of a new era in which biological age and productive activity were becoming unhinged, making a naturalized progression from work to retirement less credible. This undermined the distribution of entitlements and relations of duty based on this progression. As journalist Ross Tieman wrote in Sabena Airlines' in-flight magazine, quoting a report by the U.K. Chartered Institute of Personnel and Development, connections between age and capacity are nothing more than "lazy assumptions about what people are capable of based on their date of birth" and in fact lead to a loss of "valuable skills and experience" (Tieman 2001, 14). Similarly, the leftist Italian daily *la Repubblica*, advancing an anti-discrimination position, claimed that any substantive distinction based upon age is impossible. In fact, *la Repubblica* went on to claim that old age, like adolescence, is nothing but a "virtual reality—the former never really begins, while the latter never really ends" (2001). The fact that leftist media, historically supportive of the right to retirement, are also celebrating virtual aging suggests that the connections between this celebratory discourse and attempts to dismantle retirement and pension benefits are not always recognized, even by those social actors who align themselves with leftist commitments to retirement and pension benefits.

The denaturalization of the connection between age and capacity has converged with attempts to imagine life trajectories as cycles of constant remodeling and rebirth. Both newspaper texts and elderly activist organizations have in the last few years increasingly reinterpreted "retirement" as "rebirth" (EUROPAMICA 2000) and as a new productive phase of life. New beginnings, flexibility, rebirth, and "second and third careers," rather than simple trajectories ending in retirement, have come to structure an individual's life cycle. Revitalization is increasingly understood in the context of the generational cycle of births and deaths, but in the light of constant and flexible self-invention of aging collectivities that are fitter than ever before, and naturally desirous of work and other types of productive activity. The consistent juxtaposition of work (seen as rebirth) with retirement (seen as passivity) suggests that the flexibility and productivity of the elderly is a moral good at a moment when national economies, societies, and the welfare of nations are in crisis.

The discourse depicting the old as the future is marked by an interesting moral ambivalence. The reinvention of oneself as an older person is represented both as an individual choice based on personal motivation, and as a duty to the collective or national interest. Talk about the increased fitness of third agers oscillates between three modes: it is the new natural state of an aging Western Europe whose medical advances have triumphed over early death, it is a choice of life style all have access to if they wish it, and it is one's duty to the collectivity and particularly the younger workers, whose pension system and medical insurance are constantly represented as hopelessly overburdened. Two German journalists expressed this ambiguity when they wrote,

> Old age is what you make of it. Science has underscored this message by, for example, announcing that grey cells also reproduce themselves in old age, but only if the brain is kept fit. The threat of senility can be countered. Important muscles can, within one or two years, be trained to reach the capacity of those of middle-aged people. In sum, a high quality of life during one's "third age" is not only a gift. It is also one's duty—a duty that consists of exercise, healthy foods, education, and enriching social networks. Those who have neither money nor the motivation to work on themselves, fail. (Heuser and Niejahr 2000)

Welfare and Generations

More and more, the media, the private sector, and third agers claiming their right to work distinguish between a past of irrational and unnatural welfare state policies and management, and a present of rational, natural shifts in Western European labor policy. Their argument entails a critique of current labor policies, of ideologies of corporate restructuring, and, as journalist Sarah Hall reports, of a "culture of early retirement" which has seen an increasing number of elderly people either pushed out of work or (apparently) leaving voluntarily (Hall 2001). As Helmut Schmidt wrote in *Die Zeit*, the "collective foolishness" that had seen older workers (and thus their experience and knowledge) go to waste for the last several decades was shared and reproduced by all—lawmakers, labor ministries, business consultants, company heads, and unions (Schmidt 2001, 19). A large part of the media critique is directed toward the belief that took hold as the world's workforce grew in size during the baby boom of the 1950s and '60s—that older workers should make way for the young and the unemployed. Ross Tieman wrote that early retirement became "part of the natural order of things," even though it is "an historical aberration that fortunately won't last" (Tieman 2001, 14). Against this privileging of the young, including the fetishization of the youthful entrepreneur in the dotcom and technology boom in the late 1990s, Helmut Schmidt heralded the coming of a "paradigm shift" in the German economy. The "absurd fashions" of revering the young and of constantly rejuvenating the labor forces are on their way out, he proclaimed, mainly because of projected demographic shifts. In fact, he concluded, more and more companies have grasped the fact that "the future belongs to the old" (Schmidt 2001, 19).

Age, within this framework, has become a "virtual reality," and the modern, age-based life cycle an inflexible aberration. Concomitantly, the stage of the life cycle that was meant to guarantee a pension while at the same time open up jobs for the young has been questioned, as are the state institutions that supported it. Consequently, the relationship between generations is shifting in a number of ways. The young, on the one hand, are increasingly considered to be loath to enact "solidarity" via heavy tax burdens. As Phillipson says (1998, 44), society today sees workers not as future pensioners, but as pitted against current pensioners. A basic, structurally necessary relationship of imagined intergenerational continuity and support is, in other words, in decline. At the same time, the healthy third age provides both the basic "human material" for a reformulation of the modernist intergenerational contract and the life cycle that contract implied. Instead of an intergenerational relationship structured by solidarity, duty (of the young toward the elderly, and of the latter to move out of the workforce), and rights (of the elderly to a pension after a life of work), Europe is left with a residual, quasi-charitable solidarity directed almost exclusively toward the needy, frail, dependent, and vulnerable —the fourth age.[8] In Italy, for example, the question of whom the welfare state should target and where it should intervene frequently focuses on what are called the "non-self-sufficient"—the fourth agers—which is a stark reminder that only those who cannot help themselves are worthy of solidarity, not citizens as such.

From Solidarity to Equity

Deferring retirement for elderly men and women is integral to making the EU workforce more flexible. The advent of the European Union as a political and economic bloc in the 1990s coincided with a prolonged economic downturn that played a prominent role in EU policy makers' decision to reshape Europe's place and future in world markets. The European Commission's 1995 white paper "Teaching and Learning: Towards the Learning Society" was directed toward making Europe an economically competitive knowledge-based economy in the context of globalization. As a policy document proposing a new economic strategy, the white paper promotes education and training programs to support employment and economic growth by creating a flexible workforce able to interpret information and capitalize on scientific and technological innovation. The white paper integrally links knowledge and flexibility to both economic and social opportunities for European citizens.

The white paper also suggests that the development of a knowledge economy is a natural step for the EU because of Europe's history of scientific progress. The paper admonishes the European "public" for its fear of scientific and technological progress, a fear, the paper argues, that parallels the anxiety felt during the great revolution in knowledge that characterized the transition from the Middle Ages to the Renaissance. The comparison implies that Europe is again at a historical crossroads at which it is necessary to accept progress and the spread of an "innovative culture" (Commission 1995, 8). This valorization of Europe's legacy of scientific progress coincides with increasing pressure to make the EU attractive to investors and employers. One way to promote Europe, as the white paper makes clear, is to stress that the knowledge and skills there are distinctively European, and not matched elsewhere. Another is to ground the European knowledge economy in a "learning society," in which labor is adaptable to changing demands. The presence in the white paper of these two constructions of knowledge under conditions of globalization—specificity (bound by local or European forms of knowing and a legacy of knowledge production) and flexibility (characterized by a capacity to learn new skills and thus to shift according to the needs of a global market)—points to how new labor resources are produced and revalued under changing economic conditions. What is interesting about the white paper is that this new economic-cultural strategy is not simply a reaction to economic pressures. It is the basis for an entirely new vision of citizenship and a new relationship between individuals and society. Most significantly, the white paper locates the equal rights of citizens within the labor market and not in the welfare state, a premise that is echoed and expanded by third age rights activists.

The society of the future, the European Commission writes, will be made up of "an increasing variety of physical objects, social situations and geographical and cultural contexts . . . [as well as] a mass of fragmentary and incomplete information open to varying interpretations and partial analysis" (Commission 1995, 9). Reading, controlling, and analyzing the world will become increasingly problematic. The white paper outlines a set of techniques for dealing with such problems and promotes a vision of the kind of subject that will be able to manage this shifting context—educated, flexible, independent, knowledgeable, self-realizing, economically competitive, and socially integrated. The paper, in effect, proposes a knowledge-based vision of sociality.

> The individual's place in relation to their fellow citizens will increasingly be determined by their capacity to learn and master fundamental knowledge. . . . The position of everyone in relation to their fellow citizens in the context of knowledge and skills therefore will be decisive. This relative position which could be called the "learning relationship" will become an increasingly dominant feature in the structure of our societies. (Commission 1995, 2)

Good citizenship is determined by equal access to knowledge. The white paper explicitly links individual knowledge to the future of European education, culture, democracy, and economy. It notes, for example, that "democracy functions by majority decisions on major issues which, because of their complexity, require an increasing amount of background knowledge" (Commission 1995, 10). The capacity to be a discerning citizen also underlies that of making informed decisions as a consumer, as well as that of being an innovator at the heart of a productive economy (Commission 1995, 11). The informed choices and interpretation that underlie good citizenship thus feed back into being good workers, good consumers, and self-sustaining individuals. Democracy, business, and the state in the information society are understood to be mutually reinforcing. They all rely on a certain kind of educated citizen whose capacity for scientifically informed, rational debate and decision making ensures his or her future welfare, employability, democratic participation, and Europeanness, and ultimately the economic competitiveness of the Union.

But "there is . . . a risk of a rift in society," the Commission writes, "between those that can interpret; those who can only use; and those who are pushed out of mainstream society and rely upon social support: in other words, between those who know and those who do not know" (Commission 1995, 9). The white paper's response to the possible social exclusion of marginal groups is to allow marginalized people to move into the workforce of a knowledge economy by giving them access to knowledge. This focus on employment as the key right and function of citizens displaces state and social responsibility onto individuals. Furthermore, the white paper emphasizes that while current forms of social upheaval have a global context, they require particularly European responses in order to preserve the technological, social, and scientific gains of the "European social model" (Commission 1995, 7). This is the only moment in which the white paper even obliquely refers to European welfare state structures. The absence of the welfare state as a significant factor in either educational policy or economic restructuring is symptomatic of the basic assumption structuring the paper—that social well-being, unlike traditional ideas of social support, is located within the labor market. Within this EU policy vision, then, people are expected to access well-being through employment (cf. Levitas 1996). In this sense, the new European subject's ability to know eliminates the need for the social welfare state itself.

Flexibility as a Human Right

There is an equally powerful discourse at play in this debate, voiced by very different actors and based not on the language of labor policy but on the celebratory language of universal human rights. This is the language of activist elderly themselves, who rally around the cause of anti-ageism—a cause that plays an important role in the move we chart from ideologies of intergenerational solidarity and duty to a rights-based discourse of equity and nondiscrimination within the labor market.

Ninety-year-old Lady Margaret Simey, the Baroness Castle of Blackburn and long-time feminist activist, complained bitterly in a recent interview about "having been retired." That was the day that "life as an ordinary citizen came to an abrupt end." In fact, she went on, "the whole welfare system seems hellbent on keeping me in what they think is my proper place. . . . Ageism is a European phenomenon, a comparatively recent byproduct of European industrial society. In that context, as nonworkers, older people are a drag on the market, of no value, a cost and a problem. Is there no alternative?" (*The Guardian*, September 27, 2000). In the same year, an Italian third ager, speaking at a meeting of the Italian Labor Union (UGL), stated that he planned to rally against "retirement as an authoritative act by the state," and for "flexible retirement" as an act of choice (Di Giuseppe 2000).

Despite class and educational differences, both activists' statements converge to paint a picture of a welfare and pension ideology that, in their eyes, has nothing to do with intergenerational solidarity or social welfare, and everything to do with ageism, discrimination, and exclusion. These older activists argue that retirement is not always something people want, but may be something they are forced to accept. Similarly, EUROPAMICA, an Italian organization committed to furthering dialogue among European citizens, responded to the 1999 EC communication "Towards a Europe for All Ages" with an open letter on its web page which pointed to the ageism older workers are consistently confronted with (EUROPAMICA 2000). Instead of compulsory retirement, the organization writes, "there is a need for professional retraining and reorientation, and for a flexible organization of work that does justice to the value of older workers." A Western European organization for the elderly, EURAG, went even further to speak not of the need, but of the human right to professional retraining and life-long learning (Stadelhofer 2001). Education, knowledge, and, above all, the choice to retire when one feels ready, EURAG went on to say, are the basis for nondiscrimination and participation in the knowledge society.

Arguments about flexible retirement, then, frequently coincide with the language of universal human rights, implying that pension reform is one of the last frontiers in the struggle against all types of discrimination. Media use of the language of human rights frequently slips between the rights of elderly to work longer and the rights of all generations to equal opportunities and access to resources (in some cases time, in others, work). Either way, rights for all generations lie in their access to the labor market. Sociology professor Peter Gross took this position recently in the conservative Swiss newspaper *Neue Zürcher Zeitung*, for example, when he wrote that the current retirement system is built on "crass inequalities in the availability and societal distribution of time." To Gross, pensioners possess a "wealth of time," while the working population is burdened by its lack (2001, 55). His article ends with an appeal for a new politics of time, in which available time is distributed equitably and equally between generations. Similarly, Italian star demographer Massimo Livi Bacci has argued that large-scale societal changes need to be made in order to guarantee "intergenerational equity" (Livi Bacci 2002).

This universalist human rights language, while distinct from the language of labor policy, maps neatly onto the emergent general consensus that, as the Confederation of British Industry recently noted, "flexibility—not a 'one size fits all' solution—[has] to be the 'name of the game' " (Hall 2001). "The Tories," the journalist Sarah Hall wrote, "said flexible retirement chimed with the responsible society they wished to create." In fact, as we write this, a British government working group is hammering out the details of a law which would ban compulsory retirement at any age by the year 2006. This is the very same year in which the European Commission intends to outlaw ageism throughout the European Community (Tieman 2001, 14). Policy and pension reform are being articulated and naturalized through the language of human rights, a language integral to this global neoliberal moment in that it intrinsically promotes the rights of individuals to the detriment of more collectivist visions of rights and duties (Comaroff and Comaroff 2000). Western Europe, like other places, is seeing the emergence of visions of human rights based on individual economic independence, with the result that modern meanings of age, which was previously defined by relations of social interdependence, are fundamentally challenged (see Durham, this volume). The circulation of a particular, powerful set of ideal forms of citizenship and labor linked with notions of individual responsibility and physical wellness presents a challenge to social economies of care and intergenerational responsibility through which age categories have been previously defined (see Livingston, this volume). Flexible retirement, in turn, is conceptualized not only as that which naturally emerges from shifts in the region's population base, or as something that the management of the Western European labor force calls for. In this framework, third agers' independence from any state system of social welfare becomes a universal human right.

A Europe of All Ages

In 1999, the European Commission's communication "Towards a Europe for All Ages: Promoting Prosperity and Intergenerational Solidarity" brought together earlier concerns with aging and retirement and the economic and social vision of life-long learning sparked by the white paper. The European Commission adopted this communication in May 1999 as its official contribution to the 1999 UN International Year of Older Persons. In effect, the communication set the parameters for how the European Commission defined the particular problems presented by aging populations, intergenerational relations, and retirement, and their solutions. It was a policy attempt to promote flexible labor among aging populations in order to develop life-long learning and the learning society. Earlier calls for men and women to push back their retirement age became attached to specific work opportunities through which the third age could realize its social potential.

The 1999 communication's primary concern is the link between increasing economic growth and the need to draw on existing labor-force reserves. The report notes that "if economic growth is to be sustained in the face of a significant drop in the size of the population of working age, the activation of existing labour force reserves will be required" (1999, 7). Furthermore, the communication argues that policies regarding aging should not stymie healthy and active older people who want to work and engage in life-long learning. Early retirement wastes valuable labor resources of education, skills, and ability.

> Surveys demonstrate that about 40% of early retirees regard their labour market exit as primarily involuntary and would have liked to continue working in some capacity. Does it really make sense for individuals to retire 5–10 years earlier than their parents did, when they are in far better health . . . ? Might the choice not be different if older workers had the opportunity to enhance their work skills and acquire new ones? . . . The baby boom generation is probably the most resourceful, best-educated and healthiest generation to date. . . . To squander their contribution through the continuation of current labour market practices would be very wasteful. (Commission 1999, 12)

The knowledge and resources embodied in older people are here represented as important economic values best realized and preserved in the labor market. The language of choice is a vital aspect of how age is redefined. According to the report, the benefits of exercising such choice will include "better status and better quality of life" for older people (Commission 1999, 14). Countering the fears and costs of dependence which early retirement and aging signal, the communication argues that older people should gain self-reliance and personal satisfaction by working later in life:

> Preparing for longer, more active and better lives, working longer, retiring more gradually and seizing opportunities for active contributions after retirement are the best ways to secure the maximum degree of self-reliance and self-determination throughout old age. (Commission 1999, 22)

According to this policy document, older men's and women's final life stages can be the most vital of their life, enriched by part-time jobs in the flexible labor force. These kinds of jobs, the report argues, would also provide opportunities for economic expansion and employment growth for Europe more generally.

> It is also worth recalling that those sectors which offer good opportunities for employment growth may also be most suitable for the use of new flexible working arrangements. Work in the services sector, in community and third sector enterprises is often offered in part-time and short-term form. Thus it may often meet the requirements for promoting active ageing and gradual retirement. (Commission 1999, 10)

Older people are represented as the perfect resource with which to meet Europe's need for economic growth, and as fitting neatly into its new economic strategy precisely because the area in which this growth is most likely—flexible, part-time labor—represents a smooth transition between work and retirement. Such labor also does justice to the increased health of older people. In turn, the move to part-time labor opportunities complements and justifies the delayed and decreased distribution of state pensions. In this sense, the redefinition of aging lays the groundwork for a critique of welfare state institutions, a reframing of state responsibility for social support, and increased acceptability of new forms of labor among elderly populations. Facing unemployment, social and economic marginalization, and failing state support, the elderly are specifically transformed into valuable players in the new economy.

But what do young workers think of the attempt to draw third agers into active productivity, especially in light of the fact that younger people often enter the labor market through precisely the flexible, part-time jobs that third agers are supposedly made for? After all, the magical resolution of intergenerational tensions via the insertion of active elderly into the workforce might in fact be undermined by a new set of tensions emerging as older and younger workers—now "equalized" in their right to work—compete for similar jobs in the flexible knowledge economy. Many scholars as well as policy makers seem to address such anxieties by promoting ever finer gradations of skills attached to age, a difference in market value which supposedly precludes competition for the exact same jobs. Despite claims that age is "virtual" and should no longer count in the labor market, the specter of competition and strife between generations has led to the paradoxical emergence of a parallel and connected discourse on precisely the value of age. Generations, as a result, are imagined as participating in the creation of a world of complementarity rather than competition, and sharing and cooperation rather than elimination.

Complementarity as Solidarity:
New European Subjects/New European Skills

Echoing policies such as those outlined above, media discourses have privileged the third age as a locus of knowledge, wisdom, experience, and emotional intelligence, and as a site where visions of a Western European future play themselves out. Journalists report and often mirror the private sector's new romance with the wisdom of the old and are calling for investment in and the training of "gray cells" (Tieman 2001; Thoms 2001; Simmons 2000) and for a "new set of employment gospels" that are now based on a "balanced work-force" in which distinct types of knowledge are shared (Tieman 2001, 14). Ironically, it is in the new imagined ethos of knowledge sharing in the work-place that a new species of organic solidarity has come to be envisioned. Many experts suggest that the old complement the young, and argue that work capacities do not necessarily diminish with age, but shift to encompass factors such as experience, people skills, and maturity (Gehrmann 2001). Gerontolo-gist Paul Baltes, of the Max Planck Institute in Berlin, was emblematic of this trend when he wrote in *Die Zeit* that the capacities and knowledge of older people could never be represented by a single teleology of slow and inevitable decline. Instead,

> there are fields of achievement and knowledge where older people count themselves amongst the best. The more experience and mental strength a complex human problem entails, the more older people can shine. Youth-ful speed in mental and physical capacity can under these circumstances be a burden. Just think of the wisdom and the slowly generated expert knowl-edge of musical conductors. All expert knowledge needs time and system-atic practice: about 10,000 hours or 10 years on average. (Baltes 2002, 13)

Another journalist stated,

> Job-related skills need not decline with age. Until the age of 65, discrepan-cies in skills amongst same-aged workers are usually larger than those be-tween the old and the young. Those tired at the age of 65 are usually not tired because of their age, but because of a work-biography that has wrecked them. Slowly but surely, those baby-boomers who spent their lives jogging and in fitness studios are coming of age—we can thus in the near future count on more rather than less capacity amongst the old. Of course, some skills decline with age—those of quick perception, bodily strength, and rapid psychomotoric skills. But old people compensate with their experi-ence. Younger secretaries, for example, manage more strokes per minute on the PC than older secretaries. Nevertheless, older secretaries are usually quicker at producing a manuscript of the same length because they have learned to read and grasp it more quickly in its entirety. (Thoms 2001)

These types of knowledge and experience, experts agree, should not be wasted, especially because they cannot be found in younger workers. Because older people and their knowledge cannot be replaced, they must instead be harnessed by society in a holistic attempt to combine, balance, and comple-ment the skills of younger generations. The multifaceted problems of the globalized world of highly specialized information can only be resolved by using the full range of differentiated intergenerational knowledge. It is at

Figure 7.1. In this cartoon, published in the Italian third age magazine *50&Più* (*50 Plus*), a young mountaineer exclaims, "I have the strength to climb mountains!" The old mountaineer responds, "And I, in contrast, know how to do it." Youth and old age are represented as having different but complementary capacities—energy versus knowledge, physical strength versus experience. *Cartoon by Vincenzo Zap, used by permission.*

moments such as these that generations come to signify and even naturalize new oppositions (see also Lamb, this volume).

Baltes ends his article with the following:

> The optimization of the general welfare of society relies on the orchestration of the different bodies of knowledge and experience epitomized by different ages and generations. . . . The source of all general political rationality . . . is the full cooperation and effort of all life phases and generations.

Baltes envisions a general political rationality that hinges on the reimagining of existing European populations as an integrated, organic whole structured around a newly defined division of labor. This is to be achieved via the proliferation of generationally defined and gradated skills and capacities that complement each other in the new knowledge economy. It is in this context that an ethos of intergenerational solidarity suddenly rears its head again, though in completely transmuted form. Solidarity lies inside of the market, in the form of an ethos of "knowledge sharing" and "complementarity" between differently skilled age groups. What is imagined is an organic whole with the particular contributions of generationally defined experience, but without the deficits and limitations of physically aging citizens or the cruel competition characteristic of the market. This is, in other words, the vision of a benign division of labor that harmonizes so well because skills are perfectly differentiated and therefore not in competition with each other. In the imaginary which surrounds and produces the third age, it is only the fantasies of integrated wholeness that enable Western Europe to imagine itself as averting the failure to reproduce itself, its workforce, its economy, and its welfare.

Conclusion

Western Europe today is home to the emergence of a specific interconnection between large-scale economic and political shifts and the private bodies of an aging population. This is a moment when not only individual life cycles, but collective cycles of leisure and labor, work and retirement, duties and entitlements, and health and illness are being rethought. Old age, in the visions outlined, may be an economic advantage. Much like China's "quality" children (see Woronov, this volume), members of the aging body politic are expected to insert their specifically marketable bodies-as-goods into the global marketplace. They are to do so even though this move inevitably results in increased competition, especially with younger workers who often rely on flexible, part-time work to enter this marketplace.

The concomitant reformulation of life cycles and the conceptualization of national collectivities as organic units made up of separate but intimately intertwined complementary generations provide the rationale for fundamental changes in the ways in which welfare states govern and care for their populations. These reconfigurations seem not only appropriate and even natural responses to on-the-ground developments, but morally superior because they are explicitly linked to universal human rights discourses and the politics of anti-ageism. The deferral of retirement via active aging and active citizenship bypasses what are characterized as old-fashioned, stifling welfare state structures and outmoded relationships among different generational groups. These reformulations pave the way for the management of welfare and labor forces according to new, naturalized individual and collective life cycles. Crucial to this process are experts—sociologists, doctors, and demographers, as well as elderly activists—who have declared that health and ability are not determined by date of birth. Rather, age is a function of the work that is geared toward the individual body, and of the social respect that this new elderly body, including its long undervalued skills, deserves.

We end this chapter on a cautionary note. The last two years have seen tens of thousands of people protesting pension reforms on the streets in countries like France, Italy, and Germany. The protests point to the fact that the emerging societal imaginary outlined above does not quite fit into the realities and expectations for security of large parts of the European population, in particular middle-aged workers. The fact of the matter is that the current politics of aging and pension reform deeply contradict the hiring and firing practices in the contemporary European marketplace. Older workers still risk being fired because of their age. With changing pension regulations and the

Europe-wide raising of retirement ages, many middle-aged workers today find themselves risking poverty because they are deemed too old to work, and yet too young to receive state pensions. In other words, they risk poverty and exclusion precisely at the moment in the life cycle where policy and media texts predict that they should be at their most productive. With the exception of, perhaps, a small elite of cosmopolitan managers who directly fit the ideologies of wisdom, flexible work schedules, and "active aging," Europe might very well see the emergence of sectors of the third age that are unemployed (or underemployed) and deeply marginalized.

NOTES

1. Of course, the diversity of welfare types has been long documented and much debated among scholars of the welfare state (see, for example, Esping-Andersen 1990; Ferrara 1998; Lister 1995; and Orloff 1993). For the purposes of this paper, however, we assume certain basic commonalities between these different types—commonalities that rest on a highly abstract idea of intergenerational contract that, like the idea of a contract between classes, was a fundamental prerequisite to the modern European welfare state.

2. The exception is Germany, which in the mid-1990s made an unprecedented offer of twenty thousand "green cards" (residency permits) to information technology specialists from South Asia. At that time, German companies needed access to overseas labor to make up for the domestic shortfall. The term "green card" is misleading, however, because these specialists were not guaranteed the right to stay on after many of them lost their jobs in the dotcom bust. In fact, many lost their right of abode before they were able to find new jobs, and have since left for their home countries (Schulz 2002).

3. The United Nations Population Division says,

> the European Union and the United States—the world's two largest economic blocks, often in competition with each other—are projected to follow starkly contrasting demographic paths in the coming decades; while the population of the United States would increase by 82 million between 1995 and 2050, that of the European Union would decline by 41 million. . . . As a result, the population of the United States, which in 1995 was 105 million smaller than that of the European Union, will become larger by 18 million by 2050. The same trends will characterize their working-age populations: while the number of people aged 15–65 years will decline by 61 million in the European Union, in the United States it will increase by 39 million. By 2050, the working-age population of the United States will outnumber that of the European Union by 26 million, while in 1995 it was outnumbered by 75 million. Therefore, although the elderly population would increase more and faster in the United States than in the European Union, the potential support ratio will continue to be less favorable in the European Union compared to the United States—in 2050 it would stand at 2.0 persons of working age per elderly person in the case of the European Union, against 2.8 in the United States. (UNPD 2000, 22)

See also a recent front-page article in the *Economist* (2002) titled "A Tale of Two Bellies."

4. Current UNPD projections are based on the assumption that fertility rates in Western Europe will rise only slightly until the year 2050, and then remain constant at a subreplacement target level of 1.7 to 1.9 children per woman. To ensure the replacement of a population, demographers have calculated, women must bear an average of 2.1 children. The current Western European rate is 1.4.

5. The UNPD estimates that the number of working-age people per older person in France and Germany is likely to be halved within less than two generations. In Italy, the proportion will most likely be reduced by more than two-thirds. These are fundamental changes in what demographers call the "dependency ratio"—the ratio of the old to younger, working-age populations. In 1995, the ratio of workers to each EU pensioner was 4.3 to one. The UNPD projects that in Italy in the year 2050, the ratio will most probably drop to as low as 1.52 to one (UNPD 2000, 7).

6. Retirement ages, in theory, currently vary from sixty in France to sixty-five in Germany, Spain, Holland, and Great Britain. In practice, people usually retire at age sixty or younger.

7. While many have pointed to the complexities of defining a state (for an overview cf. Nagengast 1994; Trouillot 2001), the definition of a supra-state body such as the EU poses just as many methodological and theoretical questions. The European Union could also be defined as a set of concrete institutions, bureaucratic procedures, micro-practices, a ruling idea, and a set of effects. Furthermore, speaking about agents or authors when dealing with policy documents is problematic, in part because the policy document is itself a genre that elides authorship in the name of being representative. When thinking about authorship of the documents analyzed below, we take to heart Cris Shore's definition of "agents of European consciousness" in his ethnography of the EU:

> By this term I do not mean simply those institutions and actors at the center stage of European Union affairs, nor am I concerned with individual consciousness in the psychological sense. Rather, I refer to those forces and objects through which knowledge of the European Union is embodied and communicated as a socio-cultural phenomenon: in other words, *all* those actors, actions, artifacts, bodies, institutions, policies and representatives which, singularly or collectively, help to engender awareness and promote acceptance of the "European idea." (Shore 2000, 26, emphasis in the original)

8. The impression one gets from reading these media texts is that only at the outer edges of the life cycle—that is, in the very old fourth age and childhood—is biological age still understood to necessitate a particular responsibility on the part of society toward people in those life stages, whose status and positions in life are determined by their vulnerabilities.

WORKS CITED

Baltes, Paul. 2002. "Altern hat Zukunft" [Aging Has a Future]. *Die Zeit* 2002 (14): 13. http://www.zeit.de/archiv/2002/14/index.

Barry, Andrew, Thomas Osborne, and Nikolas Rose, eds. 1996. *Foucault and Political Reason: Liberalism, Neo-liberalism, and Rationalities of Government.* Chicago: University of Chicago Press.

Borneman, John, and Nick Fowler. 1997. "Europeanization." *Annual Review of Anthropology* 26: 487–514.

Cole, Thomas. 1992. *The Journey of Life: A Cultural History of Aging in America.* Cambridge: Cambridge University Press.

Comaroff, Jean, and John Comaroff, eds. 2000. "Millennial Capitalism: First Thoughts on a Second Coming." In "Millennial Capitalism and the Culture of Neoliberalism," special issue, *Public Culture* 12 (2): 291–343.

Commission of the European Communities. 1993. *Age and Attitudes: Main Results from a Eurobarometer Survey.* Special report 69. http://europa.eu.int/comm/public_opinion/archives/ebs/ebs_069_en.pdf.

——. 1995. "Teaching and Learning: Towards the Learning Society." http://europa.eu.int/comm/education/doc/official/keydoc/lb-en.pdf. Luxembourg: Office for Official Publications of the European Communities.

——. 1999. "Towards a Europe for All Ages: Promoting Prosperity and Intergenerational Solidarity." http://europa.eu.int/comm/employment_social/soc-prot/ageing/com99-221/com221_en.pdf.

Di Giuseppe, Franco. 2001. Speech delivered to the Unione Generale del Lavoro/Pensionati [General Labor Union/Section Pensioners], Rome, June 6.

Economist. 2002. "A Tale of Two Bellies." August 24–30.

Esping-Andersen, Gøsta. 1990. *The Three Worlds of Welfare Capitalism.* Princeton, N.J.: Princeton University Press.

EUROPAMICA. 2000. *Un'Europa per tutte le età* [A Europe for All Ages]. Response to the Commission of the European Communities report "Towards a Europe for All Ages." December 15. http://www.europamica.it/database/europamica/europamica.nsf/pagine/25FD89AA40ED376DC12569DF002EFF9F?OpenDocument.

Ferrara, Maurizio. 1998. "The Four 'Social Europes': Between Universalisms and Selectivity." In Martin Rhodes and Yves Mény, eds., *The Future of European Welfare: A New Social Contract?* Pp. 79–96. London: Macmillan.

Fuller, Thomas. 2002. "Low Birthrates Pose Challenge for Europe." *International Herald Tribune,* December 12.

Gal, Susan, and Gail Kligman. 2000. *The Politics of Gender after Socialism: A Comparative Historical Essay.* Princeton, N.J.: Princeton University Press.

Geddes, Andrew. 2000. *Immigration and European Integration: Towards Fortress Europe?* European Policy and Research Unit Series. Manchester: Manchester University Press.

Gehrmann, Wolfgang. 2001. "Die Alten kehren zurück" [The Return of the Old]. *Die Zeit* 2001 (16): 19–20. http://www.zeit.de/archiv/2001/16/index.

Ginsburg, Faye D., and Rayna Rapp, eds. 1995. *Conceiving the New World Order: The Global Politics of Reproduction.* Berkeley: University of California Press.

Graebner, William. 1980. *A History of Retirement.* New Haven, Conn.: Yale University Press.

Gross, Peter. 2001. "Grauer, aber bunter—kein Widerspruch. Das neue Altern und die Grenzen des Rechnens." [Grayer, and More Colorful—No Contradiction. The New Aging and the Limits of Calculation.] *Neue Zürcher Zeitung,* international edition, November 11: 55.

Habermas, Juergen. 1999. "The European Nation-State and the Pressures of Globalization." *New Left Review* 235: 46–59.

Jessica Greenberg and Andrea Muehlebach

Hall, Sarah. 2001. "Ministers to Scrap Retirement Age." *Guardian* (Manchester), February 14. http://www.guardian.co.uk/guardianpolitics/story/0,,437713,00.html.

Harper, Sarah. 2000. "Ageing 2000—Questions for the 21st Century." *Ageing and Society* 20: 111–122.

Heuser, Uwe Jean, and Elisabeth Niejahr. 2000. "Alter hat Zukunft." [(Old) Age Has a Future.] *Die Zeit* 2000 (28). http://www.zeit.de/archiv/2000/28/index.

Laczko, Frank, and Chris Phillipson. 1991. *Changing Work and Retirement.* Milton Keynes: Open University Press.

Laslett, Peter. 1991. *A Fresh Map of Life: The Emergence of the Third Age.* Cambridge, Mass.: Harvard University Press.

Levitas, Ruth. 1996. "The Concept of Social Exclusion and the New Durkheimian Hegemony." *Critical Social Policy* 16: 5–20.

Lister, Ruth. 1995. "Dilemmas in Engendering Citizenship." *Economy and Society* 24 (1): 1–40.

Livi Bacci, Massimo. 2002. *Intervista sulla demographia* [Interview on Demography]. Milano: Etas.

Marshall, T. H. 1981. *The Right to Social Welfare and Other Essays.* London: Heinemann.

Moody, Harry. 1993. "Overview: What Is Critical Gerontology and Why Is It Important?" In Thomas Cole, Andrew Achenbaum, Patricia Jakobi, and Robert Kastenbaum, eds., *Voices and Visions of Aging: Toward a Critical Gerontology.* Pp. xv–xli. New York: Springer Publishing Company.

Nagengast, Carol. 1994. "Violence, Terror, and the Crisis of the State." *Annual Review of Anthropology* 23: 109–136.

Orloff, Ann. 1993. "Gender and the Social Rights of Citizenship: The Comparative Analysis of Gender Relations and Welfare States." *American Sociological Review* 58: 303–328.

Phillipson, Chris. 1998. *Reconstructing Old Age: New Agendas in Social Theory and Practice.* London: Thousand Oaks.

Quine, Marie Sophia. 1996. *Population Politics in Twentieth-Century Europe: Fascist Dictatorships and Liberal Democracies.* London: Routledge.

La Repubblica. 2001. "L'Italia va all'appello ma quanto è cambiata" [Italy Goes to the Census—and How Much It Has Changed]. October 11: 33.

Roche, Maurice. 1992. *Rethinking Citizenship: Welfare, Ideology, and Change in Modern Society.* Cambridge: Polity Press.

Schmidt, Helmut. 2001. "Alle müssen länger arbeiten" [Everyone Needs to Work Longer]. *Die Zeit* 2001 (2): 6. http://www.zeit.de/archiv/2001/02/index.

Schulz, Thomas. 2002. "Lasst uns hier abhauen" [Let's Get Out of Here]. *Der Spiegel,* September 2: 138–142.

Shore, Cris. 2000. *Building Europe: The Cultural Politics of European Integration.* London: Routledge.

Simmons, Michael. 2000. "Golden Oldies." *Guardian* (Manchester), September 27. http://www.guardian.co.uk/guardiansociety/story/0,,373528,00.html.

Stadelhofer, Carmen. 2001. "Zugang älterer Menschen zur Bildung. Lifelong Learning als Wissenserwerb und Voraussetzung in eEurope" [Elderly People's Access to Education: Lifelong Learning as Knowledge Acquisition and Prerequisite in eEurope]. Report on an international EURAG colloquium. In *EURAG Schriftreihe,* Vienna, February 9, pp. 58–61.

Thoms, Eva-Maria. 2001. "Graue Zellen kneten." [Kneading Grey Cells.] *Die Zeit* 2001 (11): 29. http://www.zeit.de/archiv/2001/11/index.

Thomson, David. 1996. *Selfish Generations? How Welfare States Grow Old.* Cambridge: White Horse Press.

Tieman, Ross. 2001. "The Age-Old Debate." *Passport: Sabena Inflight Magazine,* May: 14.

Titmuss, Richard Morris. 1958. *Essays on "The Welfare State."* London: Allen and Unwin.

Trouillot, Michel-Rolph. 2001. "The Anthropology of the State in the Age of Globalization." *Current Anthropology* 42 (1): 125–138.

United Nations Population Division (UNPD). Department of Economic and Social Affairs. United Nations Secretariat. 2000. *Replacement Migration: Is It a Solution to Declining and Ageing Populations?* March. ESA/P/WP.160. http://www.un.org/esa/population/publications/migration/migration.htm.

Walker, A. 2002. "The Politics of Intergenerational Relations." *Zeitschrift für Gerontologie und Geriatrie* 35 (4): 297–303.

CONTRIBUTORS

JENNIFER COLE, an anthropologist, is Associate Professor in the Department of Comparative Human Development at the University of Chicago and author of *Forget Colonialism? Sacrifice and the Art of Memory in Madagascar.*

DEBORAH DURHAM is Associate Professor of Anthropology at Sweet Briar College. Her research on cultural identity, citizenship, and youth, both in Botswana and more generally, has appeared in the *Journal of the Royal Anthropological Institute, American Ethnologist, Ethnos,* and other journals.

JESSICA GREENBERG is a Ph.D. candidate in the Department of Anthropology at the University of Chicago.

SARAH LAMB is Associate Professor of Anthropology at Brandeis University. She is author of *White Saris and Sweet Mangoes: Aging, Gender, and Body in North India* and coeditor (with Diane P. Mines) of *Everyday Life in South Asia* (Indiana University Press, 2002).

JULIE LIVINGSTON is Assistant Professor of History at Rutgers University and author of *Debility and the Moral Imagination in Botswana* (Indiana University Press, 2005).

ROGER MAGAZINE is Professor and Researcher in the Graduate Program in Social Anthropology at the Universidad Iberoamericana in Mexico City, Mexico. He has published articles on Mexico City's soccer fans and street children in *Social Anthropology,* the *Journal of Latin American Anthropology,* and *Men & Masculinities.*

ANDREA MUEHLEBACH is a Ph.D. candidate in the Department of Anthropology at the University of Chicago.

MARTHA ARELI RAMÍREZ SÁNCHEZ is Adjunct Professor in the Department of Social and Political Sciences at the Universidad Iberoamericana.

T. E. WORONOV is Assistant Research Anthropologist at the Bureau of Applied Research in Anthropology, University of Arizona.

INDEX

Index

Index

Index

Index

Index

xenophobia, 194
Xinhua store, 29
xocoyote, 60

youth and youth culture: and age complementarity, 205–208; and consumerism, 82; defining, 126n12; and economics, 81; education, 122–23; and empowerment, 105–108, 108–109, 109–12, 120–22, 122–23; and mythical heroes, 22n5; and sexuality, 77–80, 83–84, 86–91, 94–96, 99n12; and social connections, 118–19; social regeneration, 18; urban youth culture, 84–85

Zambia, 108
Zhu Rongji, 33
Zulu culture, 112

TRACKING GLOBALIZATION

Illicit Flows and Criminal Things: States, Borders, and the
Other Side of Globalization
Edited by Willem van Schendel and Itty Abraham

Globalizing Tobacco Control: Anti-smoking Campaigns in California,
France, and Japan
Roddey Reid

Generations and Globalization: Youth, Age, and Family in
the New World Economy
Edited by Jennifer Cole and Deborah Durham